Creative Writing
New Humanities

'It is rare to have a text that not only meets a very real need academically, but one that is written with heartening persuasion and clarity. This is clearly excellent scholarship.'

David Morley, Director – University of Warwick
Writing Programme

'Distinguished by its attention to the interplay between Creative Writing and other disciplines, Dawson's study should both enlarge and enliven the disciplinary conversation.'

Jim Simmerman, Northern Arizona University

'The approach to the subject is lively and impeccably researched as well as highly engaging . . . I think this book is essential and timely reading.'

Julia Bell, Birkbeck, University of London

Discussions about Creative Writing have tended to revolve around the perennial questions 'can writing be taught?' and 'should it be taught?'

In this ambitious new book, Paul Dawson carries the debate far beyond the usual arguments and demonstrates that the discipline of Creative Writing developed as a series of pedagogic responses to the long-standing 'crisis' in Literary Studies. He traces the emergence of Creative Writing alongside the New Criticism in American universities; examines the writing workshop in relation to theories of creativity and literary criticism; and analyses the evolution of Creative Writing pedagogy alongside and in response to the rise of 'Theory' in America, England and Australia.

Paul Dawson's thoroughly researched and engaging book provides a fresh perspective on the importance of Creative Writing to the 'New Humanities' and makes a major contribution to current debates about the role of the writer as public intellectual.

Paul Dawson is a lecturer in Creative Writing at the University of New South Wales.

Creative Writing and the New Humanities

Paul Dawson

Routledge
Taylor & Francis Group

LONDON AND NEW YORK

First published 2005
by Routledge
2 Park Square, Milton Park, Abingdon,
Oxon OX14 4RN

Simultaneously published in the USA and Canada
by Routledge
270 Madison Ave, New York, NY 10016

Routledge is an imprint of the Taylor & Francis Group

© 2005 Paul Dawson

Typeset in Baskerville by
Florence Production Ltd, Stoodleigh, Devon
Printed and bound in Great Britain by
TJ International Ltd, Padstow, Cornwall

British Library Cataloguing in Publication Data
A catalogue record for this book is available
from the British Library

Library of Congress cataloguing in Publication Data
Dawson, Paul, 1972–
    Creative writing and the new humanities/Paul Dawson.
        p. cm.
    Includes bibliographical references and index.
    1. English language – Rhetoric – Study and teaching.
    2. Creative writing (Higher education)   3. Humanities –
    Study and teaching.   I. Title.
    PE1404.D386 2005
    808'.042071 – dc22   2004011298

ISBN 0–415–33220–6 (hbk)
ISBN 0–415–33221–4 (pbk)

For Vanessa

Contents

Acknowledgements   ix

Introduction: building a garret in the ivory tower   1

1   From imagination to creativity   21

2   Disciplinary origins   48

3   Workshop poetics   87

4   Creative Writing in Australia   121

5   Negotiating Theory   158

6   What is a literary intellectual?   180

Conclusion: towards a sociological poetics   205

Notes   215
Bibliography   218
Index   245

Acknowledgements

This book is based on a doctoral thesis written at the University of Melbourne. I would like to thank Professors Ken Ruthven and Chris Wallace-Crabbe for their supervision throughout my candidature. My thanks go to the following people for their help with this project at various stages throughout the years: Denise Anderson, Ruth Blair, Anne Brewster, Scott Brook, Suzanne Eggins, Nicholas Horne, Peter Kuch, Jan McKemmish, Diane Parker, Kate Parker, Fiona Ring, and Liz Thompson. I am grateful to the academic readers for Routledge, whose comments were encouraging and very useful in helping me revise my manuscript for publication. Most of the ideas in this book were originally tested over seven years of conferences for the Australian Association of Writing Programs. The response from participants at these conferences provided an invaluable forum to test and develop my ideas. I am indebted to my parents, Helen and David Dawson, for their support. Finally, my greatest acknowledgement must be reserved for my wife, Vanessa, whose unwavering support is a daily blessing, and for whom my love is boundless.

Sections from this book have been published in different form in *Cultural Studies Review*, *Westerly*, and *Southern Review*. A condensed version of Chapter 4 originally appeared in 'Creative Writing in Australia: The Emergence of a Discipline', *TEXT* 5.1 (2001) <http://www.gu.edu.au/school/art/text/april01/dawson.htm>. Sections of Chapter 3 and the conclusion originally appeared in 'Towards a Sociological Poetics', *TEXT* 7.1 (2003) <http://www.gu.edu.au/school/art/text/april03/dawson.htm>.

Introduction

Building a garret in the ivory tower

Once seen as a peculiarly American phenomenon, Creative Writing has developed an increasingly international presence in the last decade. Writing programmes are now entrenched and growing in Australian and British universities, have a strong presence in countries such as Canada and New Zealand, and are also developing in Asia-Pacific countries. Owing to its immense popularity with students, and a growing sense of professional awareness amongst teachers, Creative Writing has increasingly and inevitably become the subject of research interest, as academics draw upon current literary and cultural theory to develop new pedagogical methods, and to examine the role of Creative Writing in the contemporary humanities. Despite this popularity and interest, perceptions of Creative Writing both within and outside the academy continue to be framed by an outmoded scepticism. Since the inception of writing programmes the most prominent discussions about Creative Writing have been concerned with its legitimacy as an academic discipline. These discussions have tended to revolve around a simplistic polemic, manifested in the perennial question, *can writing be taught?* and its corollary, *should it be taught?* As a result much that has been written about writing workshops assumes the form of either a denunciation or an apologia.

The question of whether writing can be taught not only manifests a concern about the limits of education, but continues the debate about the relative merits of native talent and acquired skill which has occupied commentators on literature since antiquity. Today's version of this ancient debate is played out entirely in regard to writing workshops, acquiring a hitherto unheard of institutional context. This raises the question of whether writing *should* be taught, a question which betrays an anxiety about the location of attempts to teach writing: the university. The debates which revolve around these questions rest upon a conception of Creative Writing as a formal institutionalised apprenticeship for literary aspirants and as a sort of surrogate patronage system for established authors. Such an understanding is founded on the assumption that the social practice of writing, the ostensibly placeless activity of literary production, has been somehow absorbed or colonised by the academy, typically after the Second World War. This narrative of absorption has led to an institutionalisation of the traditional rivalry or animosity between writers and critics, a professional division which, in America, Christopher Beach characterises thus: '*PMLA* and *Critical Inquiry* versus *Poets and Writers* and *AWP Chronicle*, PhD versus MFA, literature faculties versus creative writing faculties' (1999: 31). This perpetuates an intellectual and theoretical division between the creative practice of writing and the scholarly or critical study of literature. 'To this day,' David Galef claimed in 2000, 'a tacit war exists between literary critics and writers, though both usually publish and teach within the same department' (169).

In order to overcome this divide and circumnavigate unproductive debates about whether writing can or should be taught, it is necessary to reconceptualise Creative Writing, in terms of both its historical origins and its current state as an academic discipline. Creative Writing functions as a discursive site for continuing debate over some of the foundational questions of literary studies: what is literature, what is the nature of the creative process, and what is the relationship between the creative and the critical? It is possible, then, to see the pedagogical strategies which underpin writing workshops themselves as responses to these foundational questions. As a result I intend to approach Creative Writing not as a practice (creativity), or as a synonym for literature, but as a discipline: a body of knowledge and a set of educational techniques for imparting this knowledge. If the historical examinations of the discipline of English which accompanied the 'crisis' in English Studies throughout the 1980s came to any conclusion, it was that English has never been a stable discipline, and has always been riven by internal conflict. The history of Creative Writing needs to be seen as a series of educational responses to this perennial 'crisis' in English Studies, rather than an apprenticeship which developed alongside and largely untouched by Literary Studies.

There are three crucial turning points in the history of English Studies which I shall demonstrate have borne upon the development of Creative Writing. The first is the debate between scholarship and criticism in American universities in the early part of the twentieth century. This was a result of attempts to replace historical and philological research in departments of English with a literary criticism that evaluated literature in terms of its aesthetic qualities, and enabled the academic study of contemporary (Modernist) literature. It saw the professionalisation of criticism by divorcing it from the public act of reviewing, and the institutional entrenchment of the New Criticism as a pedagogical practice by the middle of the century. The second is the rise of 'Theory' as an international *lingua franca* in the humanities: that collocation of anti-humanist discourses, imported from largely Continental extra-literary disciplines, which was deployed to challenge the authority of 'practical criticism' in English Studies and its construction of literature as a privileged aesthetic category.

'The lurid rhetoric of crisis', Jonathan Culler wrote in 1988, 'seeks to transform our situation from a hapless, even ridiculous diffusion to a decisive, focused condition of choice' (43). This rhetoric of crisis, so prevalent from the 1970s to the 1990s, where Literary Studies was continually described as a discipline in chaotic flux, became an enabling device, charting the path towards a disciplinary refiguration of English Studies. If a crisis is a turning point, then the anxiety generated by Theory can be said to have passed to the extent that we now exist in a post-Theory academy, evidenced by books such as *Post-Theory: New Directions in Criticism* (1999), *What's Left of Theory?* (2000) and *After Theory* (2003). This does not mean that we are comfortably posterior to this crisis, but that its effects are now being worked through.

For instance, the 'canon debate', which was a product of the curricular revisions effected by the crisis in English Studies, lies at the heart of the so-called 'culture wars' that raged throughout the 1990s. In his book *Beyond the Culture Wars* (1992), Gerald Graff saw a resolution to the canon debate in 'teaching the conflicts'. This emphasis on *teaching* rather than on criticism demonstrates the shifting nature of crisis, from disciplinary challenge to institutional revision. The result of the culture wars has been that a sense of crisis is now generated not only by internal intellectual debate (the need to move beyond Theory, embodied in the interdisciplinary enterprise of Cultural Studies), but also by external challenges. These challenges have taken the form of anti-political correctness media campaigns which flared in the early to mid-1990s, but still simmer in the division between academia and the public sphere, as well as institutional pressures which have affected the university as a whole.

Since the 1980s, dwindling public funds have forced university administrations to develop executive models based on the private business sector. Marginson and Considine have called this new model the Enterprise University, an institution which 'joins a mixed public-private economy to a quasi-business culture and to academic traditions partly reconstituted, partly republican, and partly broken' (2000: 236). The 'corporatisation' of universities has generated a schism between their academic and adminstrative sections, such that research and teaching are now compelled to adapt to a growing culture of managerialism and economic accountability, as well as responding to the demand for vocational outcomes for students and a declining job market for academics. The effects on the humanities of these institutional changes can be seen in books such as *Higher Education Under Fire: Politics, Economics, and the Crisis of the Humanities* (1995), *The University in Ruins* (1996) and *Day Late, Dollar Short: The Next Generation and the New Academy* (2000). The crisis resulting from these internal and external challenges tends to revolve around the notion of a public intellectual, a figure which must be seen less as the product of nostalgic yearning for a mythical public sphere than as a discursive site around which debates about the role of the humanities in a public institution circulate.

My aim is to locate the disciplinary development of Creative Writing within this history of crisis. Creative Writing first developed disciplinary identity in American universities alongside the New Criticism, in mutual opposition to scholarship in English Studies. Writing programmes expanded at the same time as the rise of Theory, but became entrenched in opposition to it as a means of retaining this disciplinary identity. This is because Theory called into question the privileged category of literature, the *raison d'être* of Creative Writing. D.G. Myers has produced the only substantial account of this history, with his book *The Elephants Teach: Creative Writing since 1880* (1996), and to a large extent I shall not question his research. Myers's history, however, ends with the *discipline* of Creative Writing turning into a collection of *programmes*; with its 'professionalisation' in the 1970s as an 'elephant machine', a production line which produces not writers, but more teachers of writing and more writing programmes. This narrative serves ultimately to align Myers with standard critiques of writing workshops. Apart from displaying a sympathy for Creative Writing's 'original' intention of combining the study of literature (criticism) with its practice (creativity) for a humanistic understanding of literature 'for its own sake', Myers's nostalgia is apparent in his discontent with an academy 'sicklied o'er with the pale cast of "theory"' (1996: xiii). In other words he does not provide an up-to-date account of Creative Writing. Nor does he suggest possibilities for its future, except that Creative Writing can somehow help repair a three-way schism in the academy between writing programmes, composition and critical theory if it recovers its original integrative function.

In order to show how Creative Writing might be able to negotiate the upheavals in disciplinary knowledge and curricular structure since the advent of Theory and Cultural Studies, I will turn to the development of the discipline in Australia. This did not begin until the end of the 1960s, occurring *alongside* the introduction of Theory to Australian universities as part of an interdisciplinary challenge to existing literary education, and developing in a far more haphazard fashion than in America. This history provides a useful case study of the international emergence of Creative Writing in the decades since the rise of Theory. My aim is to examine how the relationship of Creative Writing to English Studies suggested by this history might point to ways in which the discipline can adapt more successfully as a site of intellectual work in the 'post-Theory' academy, known in Australia as the 'New Humanities'.

In order to situate Creative Writing within a discipline that has shifted from 'practical' criticism to 'oppositional' criticism, and an institution which now speaks of producing public intellectuals rather than disinterested scholars, and in order to promote the importance of literary works to disciplinary knowledge and to public debate, I feel that writers need to be conceived as intellectuals alongside others in the academy. What form a literary intellectual might take in the age of postmodernity and in an era of blurred generic boundaries and hybridised genres, and what role Creative Writing can play in the formation of literary intellectuals is, ultimately, what this book hopes to explore.

I do not wish to assert that Creative Writing has not had a genuine impact on the profession of authorship (by offering employment and training to writers) or on the production of literature (through its impact on publishing). I am suggesting, however, that this understanding does not adequately describe its operation as an academic discipline or its relationship to literary studies. Instead of resting on an assumption that writers were absorbed by the academy, the account of the historical origins of Creative Writing which I shall provide is a means of enquiring into *how* it came to serve the needs of writers in terms of apprenticeship and patronage, into what institutional and theoretical negotiations were required for its establishment. This historical investigation is also a methodological device for reconceptualising Creative Writing as an academic discipline in order to explore more comprehensively its relationship to English Studies.

If Creative Writing is not to be seen as the institutional absorption of literary production into the academy, but as an academic discipline which developed as a series of pedagogical responses to the perennial crisis in English Studies, then we must ask different questions from the ones we are asking: (1) instead of asking whether writers need formal training or whether teaching the craft is helpful for writers, and instead of producing more handbooks on the craft of writing, we must ask what are the theoretical underpinnings of the practical writing workshop, what are the assumptions about literature which allow writing instruction to take place; (2) instead of questioning the academic rigour of the writing workshop, we must ask what constitutes knowledge in Creative Writing, and how does work produced by teachers and students in Creative Writing (i.e. their 'research') contribute to knowledge in Literary Studies – and this also means asking what is the function of literature in modern Literary Studies; (3) instead of bemoaning a split between writers and critics we must ask what position of literary authority can the writer assume in the academy, not as an artistic practitioner, but as an intellectual? In order to clear a conceptual path for these questions, however, we must explore the assumptions about Creative Writing which organise our current understanding of the discipline.

Can writing be taught?

The question, *can writing be taught?*, tends to be posed as a challenge rather than as a genuine enquiry; a challenge which threatens to damn the foundational premise of Creative Writing by daring the addressee to answer in the affirmative. This display of pedagogical anxiety about a university subject has overshadowed an earlier one, expressed in the question *can literature be taught?* In his inaugural lecture in 1913 as the first Professor of English at Cambridge University, Sir Arthur Quiller-Couch reminded his audience that 'some doubt does lurk in the public mind if, after all, English literature can, in any ordinary sense, be taught' (1946: 13–14). He pointed out that 'by consent of all, Literature is a nurse of noble natures, and right reading makes a full man', and that the study of literature found a place in universities due to the conviction that 'Literature is a good thing if only we can bring it to operate on young minds' (12). The rise of English Studies was dogged by the pedagogical challenge of how to bring literature to operate on the minds of students. The study of literature was first conducted as historical and linguistic scholarship precisely because of anxiety about whether it could be taught in any rigorous academic fashion. The catchcry of criticism in its struggle to replace scholarship as the dominant mode of teaching literature was that it promoted the study of literature *as* literature, that is, as an art. For John Crowe Ransom, 'the students of the future must be permitted to study literature, and not merely about literature' ([1937] 1984: 95). The institutionalisation of criticism in the university gave English departments an independent disciplinary existence because it provided a successful means of teaching literature. The answer to the question of whether literature could be taught, however, was that students were taught how to write *criticism* of literature rather than to absorb scholarly knowledge about it. If this is the case, Creative Writing might thus be seen as the teaching of literature *as writing*.

But the question *can writing be taught?* has an older and non-institutional heritage: it is the twentieth-century version of the ancient aphorism, *poeta nascitur non fit*, or, 'poets are born, not made', recast as a sceptical question. In his *Art of Poetry*, Horace writes that

> The question has been asked whether a fine poem is the product of nature or of art. I myself cannot see the value of application without a strong natural aptitude, or, on the other hand, of native genius unless it is cultivated – so true is it that each requires the help of the other, and that they enter into a friendly compact with each other.
>
> (1965: 93)

What Horace is suggesting here is that a poet must possess natural talent, although this talent needs to be cultivated. While he emphasises the importance of labour and study, he does not argue that 'art' can lead to the development of talent. According to William Ringler, a commentary on this work around the year 200 by the Latin grammarian Pseudo-Acro provides the origin of the phrase *poeta nascitur non fit*. It enters the English language in the Elizabethan period through the influence of Continental writings; although, as Ringler points out, it does not appear in this 'precise order of words' (1941: 497) until the time of Coleridge, who uses it in his *Biographia Literaria* to explain the qualities of the imagination. For Ringler, the 'appearance or non-appearance' of this phrase 'in the critical works of any period serves as a barometer indicating the presence or absence of ideas concerning inborn talent or genius' (503). While the phrase is familiar to readers today, it is more common to see its variation, 'you can't teach writing' or, in its interrogative form, 'can writing be taught?' The simple reason for this is that the latter is always brought up in reference to Creative Writing programmes, which did not exist before the twentieth century.

What is the relationship between *poeta nascitur non fit* and 'can writing be taught?', and what is the reason for this change in phraseology? Immanuel Kant shifts the ancient debate about the role of art and learning in the production of poetry by suggesting, not only that poetry is a product of genius, but that it is defined by the fact that it cannot be taught. In his *Critique of Judgement* Kant argues that genius 'cannot indicate scientifically how it brings about its product, but rather gives the rule as *nature*' ([1790] 1952: 169). The prime characteristic of genius, then, is originality, and its opposite is imitation. By describing learning as a form of imitation Kant is able to distinguish between fine art and science. Science, as a form of learning, differs by degree from imitation, but differs in kind from the original genius which guarantees fine art. Whereas the work of even a brilliant scientist such as Newton can be learned, 'we cannot learn to write in a true poetic vein, no matter how complete all the precepts of the poetic art may be, or however excellent its models' (170). Newton could make 'intuitively evident and plain to follow' all the steps which led to his great discoveries. No poet, however, 'can show how his ideas, so rich at once in fancy and in thought, enter and assemble themselves in his brain, for the good reason that he does not himself know, and so cannot teach others' (170). Here Kant is inverting Plato's criticism of poets by celebrating their lack of knowledge, making this a guarantee of genius. The difference between science and art, then, is manifested in terms of pedagogy. And this is why science can continue to make advances in knowledge, while works of art do not become progessively greater.

What must be noted here, however, is that while someone may learn how a scientific theory was produced, this does not mean they will be capable of producing one themselves. We cannot make a Newton any more than we can make a Shakespeare. The question of whether writing can be taught, then, is really a question of what can writers, *as writers*, tell us about literature? To assert that writers cannot explain their creative process is to assert that writers cannot tell us anything about literature, they can only write it.

While the phrase 'poets are born, not made' refers to the industry of the poet, the debate over whether writing can be taught places emphasis on the pedagogy of the instructor; it is the same argument, but with a different emphasis. This debate, and phrase, takes shape in a form familiar to us with the exchange between Sir Walter Besant and Henry James at the end of the nineteenth century. Walter Besant was a minor British novelist and man of letters who founded the Royal Society of Authors and did much to champion the profession of authorship. In 1884 Besant delivered a lecture at the Royal Institution entitled 'The Art of Fiction'. His first point was that fiction, like painting, sculpture, music and poetry, should be considered an art form. Like these arts, he said, fiction 'is governed and directed by general laws; and . . . these laws may be laid down and taught with as much precision and exactness as the laws of harmony, perspective, and proportion' (1884: 3). Of course, like all art, 'no laws or rules whatever can teach it to those who have not already been endowed with the natural and necessary gifts' (4). Besant was not a literary critic, however. He wanted to improve the position of the author in society. He claimed that novelists enjoy no national distinctions or honours as in every other profession or art. They have no associations, no 'letters after their name' (5). Even those who appreciate the novel could not bring themselves to afford it the distinction of an art form. He says:

> How can that be an Art, they might ask, which has no lectures or teachers, no school or college or Academy, no recognised rules, no text-books, and is not taught in any University? Even the German Universities, which teach everything else, do not have Professors of Fiction, and not one single novelist, so far as I know, has ever pretended to teach his mystery, or spoken of it as a thing which may be taught.
>
> (7)

Besant decried the idea of the time that anyone could sit down and write a novel, their skills being 'acquired unconsciously, or by imitation' (7). His earnest exhortation was that for those who are 'attracted to this branch of literature . . . it is their first business to learn' the 'laws, methods and rules' which govern the genre (7). According to David Lodge, 'if anyone deserves the title "Father of Creative Writing Courses" it is he' (1996: 173). Besant was not, of course, advocating a Creative Writing degree. His point was that if the novelist's craft was taught in a university, by writers, then, as with other arts, fiction would have greater credibility in the public sphere. The presence of a university in the realm of literature would influence public perception of authors and hence increase their professional and social standing. Nonetheless, he hoped that 'one effect of the establishment of the newly founded Society of Authors will be to keep young writers of fiction from rushing too hastily into print, to help them to the right understanding of their Art and its principles, and to guide them into true practice of their principles while they are still young' (1884: 27). What makes Besant's lecture different from an *ars poetica* of previous centuries is that it is backed up by an institution devoted to the professional status of authors.

This lecture inspired Henry James's famous riposte of the same name, in which he claimed that while fiction is indeed an art form, its laws cannot be laid down; the novel is an organic form incapable of dissection and the only rule to be observed by the novelist is that it be interesting. James employs a Kantian line when he claims that the novelist's 'manner is his secret, not necessarily a jealous one. He cannot disclose it as a general thing if he would; he would be at a loss to teach it to others' ([1884] 1972: 33). In 1899 Besant published *The Pen and the Book*, 'written for the instruction and the guidance of those young persons, of whom there are now many thousands, who are thinking of the Literary Life' (v). Everything from a writer's lifestyle to the editing and publishing procedures are covered in this book. 'In treating of Imaginative Literature,' Besant writes, 'one thing is most certain that, without the gift, it cannot be taught' (73).

In his 1902 book, *A Study of Prose Fiction*, Bliss Perry mused over 'the question first brought before the public by Sir Walter Besant's lecture upon "The Art of Fiction," namely, whether that art can be taught' (296). The debate over whether writing can be taught takes shape out of practical rather than philosophical concerns (such as those which occupied Kant). It develops when formal attempts to teach writing begin at the end of the nineteenth century; either by laying down guidelines for technique in handbooks, or criticising manuscripts in workshops. It is a self-conscious debate, an attempt by teachers of writing to pre-empt scepticism about their pedagogical enterprise, a scepticism encapsulated in the phrase 'poets are born, not made'. At the same time that Besant was writing, handbooks on play-writing and especially short-story writing were beginning to emerge in America. These were anticipated by an English text, *Playwriting: A Handbook for Would-Be Dramatic Authors*, in which the anonymous 'Dramatist' set the tone for following handbooks when he claimed that 'I could roll off fifty or a hundred neatly-turned instructions for you here, but they would no more teach you to write a play than a treatise on navigation would help a landsman to handle a yacht. Beyond a few rudimentary hints and technical rules, which we will discuss hereafter, nothing can be taught, no help can be given' (1888: 12). In 1929 Stewart Beach prefaced his book, *Short*

Story Technique, with this defensive claim: 'It is often asserted that short-story writing cannot be taught, and I am so thoroughly in agreement with the statement that I feel this book requires some word of explanation' (iii). By 1960 Archibald Macleish could write with a certain degree of playfulness, '[e]verybody knows that "creative writing" – which means the use of words as material of art – can't be taught' (88).

The irony of the debate over whether writing can be taught, which was triggered by the rise of Creative Writing, is that most writing courses themselves tend to operate with the notion of innate talent, claiming only that talent can be nurtured in a sympathetic environment: a community of writers where the practical skills of literary craft can be taught, and where students can become better readers of literature and better critics of their own work. In fact, it is common for classes in Creative Writing to regulate enrolment numbers by requiring the submission of a folio which displays creative potential. The first Writers' Workshop at the University of Iowa, held at a summer school in 1939, was 'open only to students who can present evidence of their ability to participate' (Iowa University 1939: 1). The official position of the Workshop is still characterised in these terms: 'Though we agree in part with the popular insistence that writing cannot be taught, we exist and proceed on the assumption that talent can be developed, and we see our possibilities and limitations as a school in that light.'[1] If writing cannot be taught, however, of what worth is Creative Writing to aspiring writers and to the study of literature? This leads to our second question.

Should writing be taught?

There are two sides to the debate about whether Creative Writing should be taught in universities: the first is a concern about the external influence of writing programmes on literary culture; the second about its internal relationship to academic research and teaching. Workshops are often considered to have a homogenising effect on students' work, thus inhibiting genuine creativity (in other words, original and individual expression). This is because critical decisions about a manuscript are arrived at by class consensus, supposedly influencing students to write in order to please their tutor and peers. The other reason is that 'workshopping' operates negatively, by warning students to avoid certain practices, such as adjectival floridity, and hence promotes an easily teachable style of writing. 'We teach how not to write', Richard Hugo claims (1979: 64).[2]

The first side to the question 'should writing be taught?' concerns both the usefulness of writing programmes for aspiring writers and their influence on the publishing industry and the general state of literature. Creative Writing is blamed on the one hand for giving false hope to aspiring writers, since most graduates do not go on to become successful authors. On the other hand Creative Writing is blamed for producing too many authors, to the extent that graduates of writing programmes dominate mainstream literary culture in America. In a sense, the doubt generated by the question of whether writing can be taught is ironically answered in the affirmative by this concern. What enters here are questions of *value*; work *is* being successfully produced and published, but it lacks literary quality. This is evidenced by the prominence of Creative Writing as a scapegoat in contemporary debates about the 'death of poetry' in America.[3]

The most common complaint arising from these debates is that the 'workshop' poem which dominates contemporary poetry is a bland and unambitious free-verse lyric focused on an epiphanous moment of quotidian experience, with an autobiographical association encouraged between the speaker and the poet. It is also argued that despite the fact that more poetry is being published than ever before, it does not address the general reader, but rather is confined to an audience within the professional industry of writing programmes and their attendant readings, prizes, publishing houses and tenure-track jobs.

The workshop poem has also been the target of avant-garde movements, with both Language poets and the New Formalists defining themselves in opposition to the mainstream American poetry produced and perpetuated by Creative Writing. Spokespersons for these movements argue not only that writing workshops produce outmoded free-verse confessional lyrics, but that they are at the hub of an exclusionary network of publishing and grant-funding departments. Two recent books on the state of contemporary American poetry, Vernon Shetley's *After the Death of Poetry* (1993) and Christopher Beach's *Poetic Culture* (1999) accept this characterisation, seeing the future of poetry in a move away from the deleterious effects of writing programmes.

The same complaints are made in regard to fiction. In 1983 *Granta* devoted an issue to what it called 'dirty realism'. This phrase was used in the editorial by Bill Buford to describe the 'fiction of a new generation of American authors' who wrote about 'the belly-side of contemporary life' (5). This generation, Buford claims, were influenced by writers such as Raymond Carver and Frederick Barthelme who dealt with the minutae of life in 'a flat, "unsurprised" language, pared down to the plainest of plain styles' (5). By the 1990s complaints were being levelled at writing workshops for producing a new generation of writers influenced by Carver and writing technically competent but bland and soulless minimalist prose, with largely objective realist observations about the minutiae of everyday existence. John W. Aldridge's 1992 book, *Talents and Technicians*, is perhaps the best known of these critiques. What lies behind all these criticisms is the assumption that writing cannot really be taught, and hence should not be.

The second side to the question, 'should writing be taught', involves an anxiety about the effects of writing workshops on university education, manifested in concerns about academic rigour. Where once English was criticised for its vague *belle lettrism* and dismissed as mere chatter about Shelley, a poor man's classics, or a woman's subject, Creative Writing now operates as the soft alternative to an increasingly rigorous Literary Studies. Recalling his early teaching career, Theodore Weiss claimed that one occurrence which was considered 'barbaric and outrageous – after all, what studious length of years, what scholarship, research, rigors, had hallowed it? – was the intrusion into the university of the creative writing workshop' (1989: 150). Wilbur Schramm, first director of the Iowa Writers' Workshop, was compelled to defend the discipline as 'comparable both in quality and in severity with the discipline of any other advanced literary study. The graduate student would not find a good play, or novel, or book of verse an easy substitute for the usual thesis or dissertation' (1941: 190).

As writing programmes expanded throughout the 1970s and 1980s, however, opposition came not from scholarship or criticism but from Theory. In 'English departments all across the United States at the present moment,' Donald Morton and Mas'ud Zavarzadeh claimed in 1988, 'a political rapproachment is being negotiated between traditional humanist scholar-critics and creative writers' (160). Writing workshops, they argue, 'are founded upon a set of assumptions that have all been put in question by postmodern critical theory' (155). This set of assumptions is said to ensure the workshop's complicity in the maintenance of the capitalist state. However, there is not so much a demonstration of political commitment as there is of professional castigation at work in their claim that ideas such as 'voice' or 'originality' are academically outmoded, and in their provision of a long list of theorists which students ought to read. Eve Shelnutt, a teacher of Creative Writing herself, claimed that writing workshops shelter students from 'the broader intellectual life of the university' (1989: 9), discouraging them from seeing themselves as thinkers, and

refusing to come to terms with exciting changes in literature departments, specifically those wrought by poststructuralist theory. Concerns
in Australia about the academic rigour of Creative Writing are
currently manifested in debates about the incommensurability of
'creative' work with standard definitions of research as they relate
to university funding and postgraduate study.

What is at stake here is not only the nature of creative work, but
ideas of its proper place. Wordsworth's 'The Prelude' is instructive
here because it opposed nature to the academy as the best teacher
of the poet. In the third book, 'Residence at Cambridge', Wordsworth
writes of 'A feeling that I was not for that hour, / nor for that place'
([1850] 1950: 509). Instead, he called on the earth and sky to 'teach
me what they might; / Or, turning the mind in upon herself, / Pored,
watched, expected, listened, spread my thoughts' (509). In other
words, while the university is a place of learning, the imagination
which Wordsworth seeks to develop through nature cannot be taught.
One could argue that this is Wordsworth's own peculiar experience,
but he of course is a crucial part of the canon, a representative writer
the study of whom perpetuates Romantic concepts of creativity in
the academy.

The fact that English is constructed as the professional domain of
the critic contributes to the idea that the academy is an anomalous
location for writers. If the writer cannot contribute to disciplinary
knowledge, a critic might ask, what is the point of Creative Writing?
It is little wonder, then, that the *presence* of writers and of a professionalised discipline for their reproduction within the academy is
a major source of consternation in discussions about Creative
Writing. Not only are writing programmes seen as anomalous, but
the work they produce, literature, has traditionally been perceived
as *placeless*.[4] Regardless of writers' occupations, their 'creative' work,
supposedly, is not tied to their specific location (even though experiences of this may form the basis of their writing) because it is
generated by their creative impulse and addresses an abstract general
audience. Hence when writers become physically located within the
university and their 'creative' work (as the equivalent of academic
research) is produced to *maintain* this position, literature itself is seen
to be tied to an institution. What requires challenging here, if we
are to examine ways in which Creative Writing can contribute to
intellectual work in the contemporary humanities, is the pervading
influence of the two metaphors which encapsulate popular under-
standings of the location of both writers and academics: the garret
and the ivory tower.

The garret and the ivory tower

A garret is the clichéd writer's retreat. It conjures up images of a solitary author eking out a bohemian existence in order to gain the distance necessary to comment upon his or her surroundings or simply to indulge a creative impulse. The metaphor of the garret assumes that writing takes place outside society before it is released into the public sphere for critical scrutiny, via the machinations of the publishing industry. The word came to be associated with poets in the mid-seventeenth century, around the time that Grub Street acquired its reputation as a place for literary hacks in England. As a result it has always been associated with hardship and penury. Thomas Brown (1663–1704) self-parodies his profession in 'The Preface' by drawing attention to the harshness of the poet's life, forced to scribble 'Dogg'rel and News' for a living:

> I am closely block'd up in a Garret,
> Where I scribble and smoak,
> And sadly invoke
> The powerful assistance of CLARET,
> Four Children and a Wife,
> Tis hard on my Life,
> Beside my self and a Muse,
> To be all cloath'd and fed.
> <div align="right">(<i>Literature Online</i>)</div>

Despite its operation as a cliché (see 'The Poetaster' by John Byrom), there has always been a certain romanticism attached to the garret. This is made explicit in Mark Akenside's 'The Poet . . . A Rhapsody' (1737). In this poem Akenside draws attention to the fate 'of the Muse's son, / Curs'd with dire poverty! poor hungry wretch!', before going on to suggest that manual labour is impossible for the poet: 'Oh! he scorns / Th' ignoble thought; with generous disdain, / More eligible deeming it to starve, / Like his fam'd ancestors renown'd in verse' (1996: 395). In the eighteenth century the word 'garreteer' developed, to mean 'an impecunious author or literary hack' (*Oxford English Dictionary* (*OED*)), but Akenside's poem demonstrates that the inhabitance of a garret can be seen as a mark of poetic authenticity: 'These are his firm resolves, which fate nor time, / Nor poverty can shake. Exalted high / In garret vile he lives' (395).

Perhaps the most extreme and romantic account of the self-sufficiency of the writer is a poem by Emily Dickinson written circa 1863:

Publication – is the Auction
Of the Mind of Man –
Poverty – be justifying
For so foul a thing

Possibly – but We – would rather
From Our Garret go
White – Unto the White Creator –
Than invest – Our Snow –

Thought belong to Him who gave it –
Then – to Him Who bear
Its Corporeal Illustration – Sell
The Royal Air –

In the Parcel – Be the Merchant
Of the Heavenly Grace –
But reduce no Human Spirit
To Disgrace of Price –

(1970: 348–9)

In this poem the garret is linked to creativity (it is where the writer composes), and to poverty (the writer is isolated and unrewarded by society). This isolation, however, is the guarantee of poetic creativity. The garret is opposed to publication (which is equated not with dissemination, but with commercialisation), 'the Auction of the Mind of Man'. Poetry is a private circular communion with God, and hence is its own reward. We can see here from its origin as a physical space in which the writer composed (a space which provided cheap rent on Grub Street and a haven above the din of industrialised cities) the garret has come to denote a metaphorical space for the creativity of the isolated author.

How does this idea of the garret relate to the clichéd domain of the academic? 'One of the most enduring popular myths of humanities research', according to Meaghan Morris and Iain McCalman, 'involves an egghead in an "ivory tower"' (1988: 1). The ivory tower denotes a physical space or state of mind which is removed from the practicalities and harsh realities of everyday life. As a cliché, claims Masao Miyoshi, it 'is as taken for granted as the university itself' (2000: 50). Its connection to the academy brings up associations with both the idea of pure or basic research, where universities operate as a haven for the pursuit of knowledge for its own sake, and the

Arnoldian concept of disinterestedness, where the free play of the critical mind can operate in isolation from political partisanship or civic responsibility in order to aid its development towards a state of culture. Rather than commenting upon or representing society, this view of the academic is one of an intellectual figure unconcerned with the world or with seeking a public audience, eschewing emotions or personal involvement for the objectivity of research.

While the idea of pure research and disinterestedness embodies ostensibly noble intentions, the phrase 'ivory tower' is generally invoked as a negative description. From whence does it originate? First employed by Saint-Beuve in the late nineteenth century, it gained widespread use throughout the twentieth (according to the *OED*). The idea of a tower is simple enough – a lofty height removed from daily hustle where one can contemplate or experiment idly. But why ivory? Miyoshi claims that there exists no explanation for 'the choice of ivory for indicating seclusion from the world or shelter from harsh realities' (2000: 50), proposing a connection between academia and the ivory trade in Africa, for ivory is contraband, and thus between the university and colonialism (50). The fact that no one has detected this 'connection', according to Miyoshi, 'might reaffirm the devastatingly accurate denunciation implanted in the phrase' (50). This is not a connection, it is a fanciful association. The rarity of ivory might suggest the rarefied nature of academic research, but it is the colour of ivory rather than its matter which provides a better indication for its use.

While Saint Beuve is credited with the origin of the phrase in its current context, it does appear in the Old Testament Song of Songs, as a metaphor for the fairness of the neck of Solomon's lover. It also appears in English poems of the Augustan period which were based on the Song of Solomon. In his *Divine Poems* (1632), for instance, Francis Quarles wrote: 'Thy Necke doth represent an Ivory Tower, / In perfect pureness, and united power' (*Literature Online*). Ivory, then, represents whiteness, purity, divinity. There is no real connection between this archaic metaphor and the current one, but the notion of purity attached to whiteness no doubt suggests the use of ivory to indicate pure research or detached intellectual work unsullied by social demands. One can remember here Dickinson's description of the garret as a 'white' space where poetry, or 'snow', is produced for its own sake, unsullied by publication. In fact, I would argue, this demonstrates that the ivory tower and the garret are parallel and permeable metaphors for the academic critic and the writer. In describing his journey from a poor family to Greenwich Village to a university posting, David Madden claimed that 'I have gone then from the smokestack of poverty to the garret of Manhattan to the Ivy Tower, but I am happy as a Holy Roller to testify that I have never left the Ivory Tower of art' (1989: 181).

Irving Babbitt points out that the 'empire of chimeras', which referred to the independent workings of the imagination in eighteenth-century discussions of original genius, 'was later to become the tower of ivory' ([1919] 1955: 45). Babbitt provides no evidence to suggest a linguistic connection or phraseological development; rather he is connecting the two ideas. The empire of chimeras is removed from the world and from common reason because it is the domain of the imagination. In his 'Conjectures on Original Composition' Edward Young discusses the 'creative power' of genius which may 'reign arbitrarily over its own empire of chimeras' in 'the fairy land of fancy' ([1759] 1947: 283). While Young was exalting the original qualities of genius he nonetheless uses this phrase when warning against the danger of indulging too greatly in the imagination. It is obvious, then, that the tower of ivory performs the same function today as the archaic phrase did in an earlier time. Furthermore, of the earliest usages of the phrase provided by the *OED*, less than half refer to the university. The university becomes a literal embodiment of a state of mind as easily occupied by the artist as by the academic.

A good example of how the ivory tower is connected to the garret is a 1751 issue of *The Rambler*, in which Samuel Johnson undertook the task of 'communicating to the public, the theory of a garret' (1971: 102). Here he draws attention to the literal qualities of the garret, which is, of course, an attic or a room in or near the roof of a house. 'That the professors of literature generally reside in the highest stories, has been immemorially observed' (103). Johnson discusses the Muses on Olympus, and Lucretius's fondness 'for a garret, in his description of the lofty towers of serene learning, and of the pleasure with which a wise man looks down upon the confused and erratic state of the world moving below him' (103–4). He goes on to argue that 'the garret is still the usual receptacle of the philosopher and poet', but that this is only due to imitation of ancient custom 'without knowledge of the original reason for which it was established' (104). It is generally believed, Johnson claims, that the garret affords the best working place for 'the wits' because it can be rented cheaply, or because it is the remotest room of a house, and thus free from distraction (104). The universal practice of working in a garret, however, according to Johnson, is because the faculties of the mind are made sharper by the elevation which a garret provides, and the clarity of the air which accompanies it. One may question the seriousness of Johnson's prose, but it is obvious nonetheless that the garret operates here as an embodiment of the same state of mind as the positive elements of the ivory tower. In other words, in many instances the garret and the ivory tower are interchangeable. The obsolete Middle English definition of garret is of a watchtower or turret projecting from the parapet of a fortress (*OED*). This carries many metaphorical associations. The writer is cut off from society, defending his or her integrity against it, but also is able to observe the world from on high.

Why, then, does tension exist between the two? For a start, unlike the ivory tower, the garret is not removed from the harsh realities of the world. As we have seen with the poetic line from Akenside to Dickinson, this is a badge of pride for poets, a symbol of their unwillingness to conform to society. From Grub Street to Greenwich Village the garret is associated with penury and bohemianism. It is pertinent that Albert Parry's 1933 account of American bohemianism is entitled *Garrets and Pretenders*. The pretenders are those who assume the mantle of bohemianism in order to gain artistic or intellectual credibility. Creative Writing is seen as the modern-day garret; it has become 'a campus version of bohemia', according to Malcolm Bradbury (1992: 7), and 'today's Paris of the 20s', according to Claire Messud (1991: 14). This becomes the grounds on which it is criticised when the garret is seen as too much like the academic ivory tower. Ted Solotaroff claims that for today's generation of writers raised and housed in writing programmes, teaching provides 'a comfortable life and free time' (1985: 266), and study provides 'unreal' conditions: 'the graduate writing programme makes the next stage – being out there by oneself in the cold – particularly chilling' (267). It is the security that writing programmes afford which is seen as a compromise of an author's integrity.

Yet when Bradbury established England's first Creative Writing degree at the University of East Anglia in 1970 he claimed that 'a course of this kind, conducted from the distance of an academic environment, distinct from the commercial marketplace, could have some impact on the state of serious fiction in Britain' (1992: 7). Bradbury here is not only employing the Arnoldian argument of disinterestedness and promoting the benefits of the ivory tower, but is also aligning himself with the romanticisation of the garret from Akenside to Dickinson by arguing that Creative Writing provides a haven from the need for ignoble labour and from commercial pressures. In fact, concerns about the absorption of writers by the university are only a rehash of complaints about the professionalisation of criticism and the institutionalisation of intellectuals.

This book, then, is ultimately not an account of how a garret was built in the ivory tower, but an argument against the pervasiveness of these metaphors and the assumptions about Creative Writing *and* Literary Studies which they underpin. That Creative Writing operates largely within departments of English or Literary Studies, yet is somehow seen as separate to that domain of academic activity, as practice rather than theory, primary rather than secondary, research equivalence rather than research, embodied in a split between the creative and the critical, the writer and the critic, is a division I wish to negotiate, rather than collapse. Hence the active construction of 'Building a Garret in the Ivory Tower'. It has not yet been built. For Morris and McCalman (1998), the myth of the ivory tower masks the operation of the contemporary academy as a public institution with responsibilities to and interrelations with a range of forums in the broader community. And it is this myth, they argue, which produces the romanticised ideal of a 'public intellectual' who can break free from the introspective constraints of academia and address a general audience. This is only one example of ways in which the modern humanities is responding to both external financial and internal theoretical pressure to redefine itself as an interdisciplinary enterprise which is engaged with rather than cut off from society. The challenge for Creative Writing, as an academic discipline and as an institutional site for writers, is to negotiate not only the (metaphorical) demands of the garret and the ivory tower, but also the real institutional conditions of the university and its relationship to the public sphere.

1 From imagination to creativity

The phrase 'creative writing' has several meanings. It operates as a synonym for literature; for published works of fiction, poetry and drama. It is also the name given to a subject or course of study in which students produce writing which is generally considered 'creative'; that is, writing in the aforementioned literary genres. Hence a division can be made between creative writing as literature and creative writing as 'pseudo-literature' – as Robert Scholes calls it in *Textual Power* (1985: 5) – since the creative writing produced by students is recognised by academic credit rather than publication and general circulation, although it aspires to the status of literature.

Creative writing does not have to refer specifically to 'literary' works, however, but to any writing which is 'creative', i.e. original, unconventional, expressive, etc. It is sometimes seen in opposition to literature. Kevin Brophy, for example, questions attempts to duplicate mainstream literary forms in the writing workshop. He sees creative writing as a practice, as 'a pursuit of creativity', which can free writers from the traditional and established genres of the 'recent modernist literary canon' – novels, plays and poems – and thus from concepts of authorship as an elitist and solitary practice (1998: 34). In schools creative writing is often described as the free expression of a child's personality, the verbal enunciation of their individual creativity. In *Creative Writing in the Primary School*, the school teacher A. Chapple defines 'creative writing' as 'that written expression in which children put down their own ideas, thoughts, feelings and impressions in their own words. It is writing that is original as opposed to imitative. It is sincere, personal expression that is flavoured by the personality of the child' (1977: 1).

It is my intention to approach Creative Writing as a discipline, that is, as a body of knowledge and a set of pedagogical practices which operate through the writing workshop and are inscribed within the institutional site of a university. In order to understand how the discipline of Creative Writing developed, however, it is first necessary to understand how the phrase 'creative writing' developed and came to incorporate all the meanings listed above. My aim in this chapter is to provide an account of the historical development of the word 'creative', the phrase 'creative writing', and the word 'creativity' as it is these words and their associations which organise our understanding of writing programmes. My argument is that the discipline of Creative Writing is a distinctly twentieth-century phenomenon, made possible by the transition in the common parlance of literary criticism from the faculty of imagination to that of creativity, and by the importance of this concept of creativity to the rise of modern English Studies.

It is beyond the scope of this study to provide a history of the complex notion of the imagination. I would like to briefly sketch, however, the historical trajectory of the word as it shifted from a largely passive mental faculty to become the central focus of Romantic theory by virtue of its reconceptualisation as a creative faculty. My concern here is with how the developing notion of man's 'creative power' caused interest in the imagination to shift by the end of the nineteenth century to 'creativity', precisely because its associations had outgrown the word, and how this shift enabled a democratisation of concepts of authorship in particular and human productivity in general. This was not merely a semantic transition. Despite the emphasis placed on the imagination by the Romantics, not just as the source of poetry, but as a divine presence in man and the active agent of all human perception, the word still retains ambiguous connotations. Confronted with evidence of an erroneous recollection or an inaccurate memory, one will say, 'it must have been my imagination'. When challenging a false assertion one claims that 'you're imagining things'. The imagination can distort the future by the negative projection of possible outcomes, or can play tricks on the senses. 'A paranoid, overactive imagination was a sure sign of stress' (1999: 191) writes Tara Moss in the recent Australian crime thriller, *Fetish*.

Creativity, on the other hand, designates the ability to create; to produce something new and original, to provide innovative changes to anything which is routine or mechanistic. Its products are the unique expression of each individual, without any association with the senses and their capacity to fool the mind. The source of creativity comes wholly from within man without associating, compounding or unifying imported sensory data and without the internalisation of the divine spirit. Creativity is the productive imagination fully secularised and divested of any ambivalent connotations. 'No word in English',

Raymond Williams points out in *The Long Revolution*, 'carries a more consistently positive reference than "creative"' (1965: 19). The word 'creative' entered our language at the end of the seventeenth century. In order to understand how and why, we must be aware of how the imagination was perceived at this time, for it is the imagination which the idea of creative power modifies and ultimately supplants.

The reproductive imagination

The most common understanding of the imagination in the seventeenth century was as the mental ability to reproduce images previously apprehended by the senses. It was also the part of the mind capable of producing wild, irrational ideas or images with no corresponding object in reality, and of inducing delusion by tricking the senses. These two strands of thought are illustrated by the philosophy of Thomas Hobbes and Francis Bacon. Their work challenged the classical theory of poetry as a madness and heat fuelled by divine inspiration, and appears to have had profound influence on the literary criticism of the time.

Hobbes, in *Leviathan*, describes the faculty of imagination as 'memory' ([1651] 1968: 89) or 'decaying sense' (88). This 'decaying sense' is a neutral description rather than a negative one; it refers to what happens to the imprint of a sensory impression upon the mind after the object apprehended is no longer in sight and others take its place. Here we can see that Hobbes is representing the imagination as a reproductive faculty; it does not generate anything new from within the mind, but retains what was perceived of the external world. Hobbes goes on to explain that there are two levels to this faculty. The recall, or straightforward mental reproduction, of a previously apprehended object is '*simple Imagination*'; as when one imagineth a man, or horse, which he hath seen before. The other is *Compounded*; as when from the sight of a man at one time, and of a horse at another, we conceive in our mind a Centaure' (89). It is this compound imagination which the poet works with.

John Dryden, England's first official poet laureate and the pre-eminent literary critic of the time, provides an account of the use of imagination in poetry, similar to Hobbes's simple imagination, in the preface to *Annus Mirabilis*. Here Dryden describes the composition of poems as a production of wit. This wit consists of the 'faculty of imagination in the writer . . . which searches over all the memory for the species or ideas of those things which it designs to represent' ([1667] 1900: 14). As he continues, however, the imagination is given more scope than mere recall. It incorporates Hobbes's compound imagination as a faculty which can piece together elements from memory, but it is expanded to encompass a series of compositional stages (invention, fancy, and expression) organised around similar principles to those of classical rhetoric (inventio, dispositio, elocutio, memoria, actio).

A concurrent idea of the imagination in poetry emphasises the ambivalence felt towards this faculty, because of its capacity to produce images and ideas which do not exist in nature, and hence places the imagination in opposition to reason. Francis Bacon, in *The Advancement of Learning*, had effected this philosophical division between reason and imagination. 'The parts of human learning', he wrote, 'have reference to the three parts of man's understanding, which is to the seat of learning: History to his memory, Poesy to his imagination, and Philosophy to his reason' ([1605] n.d.: 89). Poetry is considered 'feigned History' and tries to fashion accounts of events which are more satisfying than those which actually happened. For Bacon the imagination is an agent or messenger which operates between the two provinces of sense and reason (121). Poetry 'doth truly refer to the imagination, which, not being tied to the laws of matter, may at pleasure join that which Nature hath severed, and sever that which Nature hath joined, and so make unlawful matches and divorces of things' (89).

After Bacon, there appears to be much concern in effecting the right balance between imagination and reason in the production of poetry. Throughout the seventeenth century we see claims, such as those by Thomas Rymer, that the poet's imagination had to be reined in by reason or judgement. 'Reason must consent and ratify whatever by fancy is attempted in its absence,' Rymer wrote, 'or else 'tis all null and void in law' ([1678] 1908: 185). The reason why poets were encouraged to keep their wild imagination in check was that poems were required to meet certain objective (classical) standards. A 'Poet is not to leave his reason,' Rymer asserted, 'and blindly abandon himself to follow fancy, for then his fancy might be monstrous, might be singular, and please no body's maggot but his own; but reason is to be his guide, reason is common to all people, and can never carry him from what is Natural' (192). It is important to note that the imagination was still considered essential to the composition of poetry. The concern was with the correct balance between this faculty and that of reason. John Sheffield, in 'An Essay Upon Poetry', writes: 'As all is dullness, when the Fancy's bad, / So without Judgement, Fancy is but mad' ([1682] 1908: 287).

Poetic creation

The notion of man as a creative being is a product of Renaissance humanism, originating in Italy. 'We speak now of the artist's activity as "creation",' Raymond Williams comments in *The Long Revolution*, 'but the word used by Plato and Aristotle is the very different "imitation"' (1965: 19–20). Since antiquity poetic production had been referred to as *mimesis*, or imitation of nature, based on the authority of these two philosophers. The Renaissance introduced the idea of poetry as *creation*. The creation of a world in the poet's mind, of a heterocosm, was considered analogous to the divine act of creation by God. '"There are two creators," wrote Torquato Tasso (1544–95), "God and the poet"' (R. Williams, 1988: 82).

This concept of the poet as creator was introduced to Elizabethan England by Sir Philip Sidney in *An Apology for Poetry*. Sidney follows the authority of Aristotle in claiming that poetry is an art of imitation, and that it is a higher art than history because it is closer to philosophy and its capacity to represent universal truth. He claims, however, that poetry exceeds even philosophy in terms of efficacy, and is in fact the 'Monarch' of all human sciences because it presents knowledge and ideas in a palatable and pleasing form. He parts company even further with Aristotle when he abandons any pretensions to mere imitation of nature: 'the poet, disdaining to be tied to any such subjection, lifted up with the vigour of his own invention, doth grow in effect another nature, in making things either better than Nature bringeth forth, or, quite anew, forms such as were never in Nature' ([1595] 1922: 7).

Sidney was aware of the potential blasphemy of this 'saucy' comment (8), for it seems to put the poet on the same level as God by comparing poetry to the divine act of Creation. He defends this comparision, however, by claiming that inspiration is a gift from God and the artistic product is a celebration of his glory. So instead of being inspired, being breathed into by divine power and becoming possessed with a mad poetic frenzy, the poet composes with a power *like* that of God. This power, rather than the ability to imitate nature, is a power to create another nature, one far more pleasing or so unlike the natural world as to justify the comparison of the poet with god. What the poet imitates is not natural phenomena but that which produced them – God's creative power.

It is notable that Sidney does not employ the word 'create', and this is because of the aforementioned potential for blasphemy. For instance, in a poem of 1592, entitled 'Of the Soul of Man and the

Immortalitie Thereof', John Davies writes that 'to create, to God alone pertaines' (Chadwyck-Healey English Poetry Full-Text Database). Instead Sidney talks of the vigour of the poet's invention. As Logan Pearsall Smith explains, the 'term *invention*, which criticism had inherited from classical rhetoric, served for a long time as a name for that finding in Nature of something new to copy which was called *originality*' (1925: 89). As the connection between invention and originality became stretched, Smith argues, 'create' became an 'alternative word' for 'invent' (91). It may also be noted that rather than a compositional act which required the discovery of a topic to be worked up for presentation, invention became an innate quality, the mental faculty responsible for originality.

The introduction of the analogy between the poet and God enabled the use of the words 'create' and 'creation' in reference to poetry. What did it mean to be creative? Originally this was the capacity to produce figures or characters in poetry for which there was no correlation in nature. In the preface to *Troilus and Cressida*, Dryden wrote that, with the character of Caliban, Shakespeare 'seems there to have created a person which was not in Nature, a boldness which, at first sight, would appear intolerable; for he makes him a species of himself, begotten by an incubus on a witch' ([1679] 1900: 219). Dryden defends this possible impropriety by use of the Hobbesian compound imagination. In the same way that a centaur is fashioned out of the image of a man and a horse, so Caliban is conceived out of 'an incubus and a sorceress', beings in which 'at least the vulgar still believe' (219). The ability to produce things which did not exist in nature gradually came to be seen not as delusion, or the workings of wild fancy which needed governing by reason, or as Hobbesian compounded imagination, but as original creation, analogous with that of God. And this creation gained respectability because rather than the fanciful inventions of mediaeval and Elizabethan romances, it applied to the work of Shakespeare, the greatest of English writers. This view was popularised by Joseph Addison in his series of essays 'The Pleasures of the Imagination' which appeared in *The Spectator* in 1712.

Creative power

When the adjective 'creative' entered the language the poet's faculty of invention ceased to be metaphorically associated with Creation and became etymologically linked. That the word 'creative' signifies an internalisation of divinity is obvious when the context of its first appearances is examined. The *Oxford English Dictionary* and Raymond Williams (1988) cite Ralph Cudworth as the first to use the word. *The True Intellectual System of the Universe* (1678) was written to refute the arguments of atheism, and within it Cudworth talks of the 'Divine, miraculous, creative power' of God (qtd in R. Williams 1988: 83).

The first use of the word in reference to man's poetic ability appears to be in 1700 in the poem, 'To Amasia *speaking* an Extempore Verse', by John Hopkins. In this poem Hopkins praises his muse, Amasia, by comparing her to God: 'You, like creative Heav'n your Labours Frame; / You spoke the Word, and at your Breath they came'. This simile becomes a concrete description in another poem in the same collection, 'Love in Idea', where he talks of 'Creative fancy ever springing more' (Chadwyck-Healey English Poetry Full-Text Database). Three years later Sarah Egerton eulogised Dryden's 'creative strains' in 'An Ode on the Death of Mr. Dryden' ([1703] 1987: 75).

According to Raymond Williams (1988) and Logan Pearsall Smith (1925) the minor English poet David Mallet was the first to use the word 'creative' in relation to the powers of the poet. In 1728 Mallet opened his long poem, *The Excursion*, with: 'Companion of the Muse, Creative Power, Imagination!' (qtd in R. Williams, 1988: 83). While the work of Hopkins and Egerton seems to suggest earlier uses of the word, this would appear to be its first association with the imagination. We must remember Hopkins's 'creative fancy', however, for fancy at this stage was interchangeable with imagination. Addison, for example, used the two terms 'promiscuously' in *The Spectator* in 1712 (1982a: 368).

The word 'creative' became established in general usage by the mid-eighteenth century. And it is the concept of man's creative power which motivated speculations about original genius, as opposed to imitative talent, that began to appear at this time. The doctrine of original genius provided a conclusive answer to the debate between the merits of the Ancients and the Moderns which had occupied so much criticism in previous centuries. Modern poets had to be less slavish in their following of the ancients if they were to attain the same heights; they had to emulate the genius of the ancients rather than imitate their writing. As a result the grounds for critical evaluation shifted from the classical learning of poets (evidenced in their adherence to 'rules' such as the ancient unities) to their capacity for originality.

Joseph Addison prepares the ground for this shift in number 160 of *The Spectator* (1711), and in *Tom Jones* Henry Fielding outlines with disdain its growing influence ([1749] 1992: 523). A number of treatises on the concept of original genius emerged in the latter half of the eighteenth century, the most influential of which was Edward Young's *Conjectures on Original Composition*. 'Imitations are of two kinds,' Young claimed, 'one of nature, one of authors. The first we call originals, and confine the term imitation to the second' ([1759] 1947: 273). What Young means by imitating nature is different from what Aristotle means, however, for he is referring to a personal experience of nature achieved by introspection, rather than an objective representation of universal forms.

Young plays down the importance of learning and upholds the native force of mind of genius. 'Genius is a masterworkman, learning is but an instrument' (279). Genius 'can set us right in composition, without the rules of the learned' (280). To prove that genius, the only mind from which originality can come, is not rare, Young claims that there may be many geniuses unknown to us. 'There might have been more able consuls called from the plough than ever arrived at that honour: many a genius probably there has been which could neither write nor read' (282).

Original genius is the culmination of a gradual conflation of the classical theories of the source of poetry: divine inspiration and natural talent. Genius, which originally meant an attendant spirit, became, according to Young, 'that God within'; an innate quality rather than an external inspiration. But because it is original or creative, it has the same characteristics of inspiration: an ease of composition, often spontaneous and frenzied, accompanied by an inability to explain its function. Where Young's work differs from ideas of the previous century is in his psychologising of genius, and his attempt to encourage it. 'Born originals,' he asks, 'how comes it to pass that we die copies?' (285). The culprit is that 'meddling ape Imitation' (285). What makes us original is our own unique individuality rather than the capacity to imagine beings which do not exist in nature. 'Therefore dive deep into thy bosom,' he exhorts, 'learn the depth, extent, bias, and full fort of thy mind. Contract intimacy with the stranger within thee' (288–9). This is an exhortation to strike away from imitation and pursue an individual vision which expresses the unique personality of the poet. 'Nor are we only ignorant of the dimensions of the human mind in general, but even of our own' (287). It is this sort of introspection which will lead to the idea of creativity as an expression of individuality and the twentieth-century search for the 'genius within'.

Throughout the eighteenth century the word 'creative' was most often used in the phrase 'creative power'. Creative power was the capacity of a poet's imagination to mimic the divine act of Creation by producing in fiction characters which did not exist in nature, or events and ideas which had not previously been contemplated. Hence, to be creative meant to be original. However, to be original was the mark of genius, and only a gifted few could claim that distinction. According to William Duff, a 'creative Imagination' is 'the distinguishing characteristic of true Genius' ([1767] 1995: 48). By being associated with the creative ability of God the supernatural products of the imagination, such as Shakespeare's fairies and witches, are regarded with admiration rather than suspicion. By being linked with a mental faculty, the creative power of the poet ceases to operate as a metaphor, or an analogy with God, and becomes an innate quality of man. The faculty of imagination then becomes liberated from its passive sensory function and is given a productive rather than merely reproductive function. Furthermore, the concept of inspiration, or divine possession, becomes internalised, so that creative power springs from within rather than being breathed in from without.

It can be seen from this brief survey of eighteenth-century theories of original genius and their emphasis on the creative power of the imagination, how the phrase 'creative writing' will become associated with a lack of necessity for learning of any kind, with an ease of composition reliant on natural ability rather than the study of precepts, and with a sense of self-expression. This is why when a course of study labels itself Creative Writing there are going to be complaints that writing cannot be taught, and that a university, a place of higher learning and of work, would seem antipathetical to the very concept of creative power.

The creative imagination

It is with that movement we call Romanticism that the imagination is recast as a creative faculty, associated with passion and divinity, and superior to that of reason. If reason is common to all men it must follow a single pattern, but each person's imagination is idiosyncratic and individual. Poetry, in the Romantic view, was not the product of a lively imagination kept to nature by reason; it provided access to a higher truth via the unique imagination of the original genius, although this imagination differed in degree only from that which all men possess. The Romantic 'revolution', then, placed poets at the vanguard of an attack on the mechanised and scientific view of society generally associated with John Locke and Isaac Newton, and embodied in the aridity of an increasingly industrialised society.

William Blake, that prophet of the Imagination, provided the ultimate Romantic response to the earlier philosophic concepts of Hobbes when he claimed that 'Imagination has nothing to do with Memory' ([1826] 1972: 782). The Imagination, for Blake, consisted of Vision and Inspiration, and was 'the Divine Body in Every Man' ([circa 1820] 1972: 773). The poet's supreme power was God's creative spirit within man. Rather than being inspired by divinity, the poet expires the divinity which animates every man, but which only the poet can fully access. So rather than a faculty responsible for producing unnatural fictions, the creative imagination becomes the source of visionary truth.

Coleridge provides the philosophical rigour for Blake's visionary concept of the imagination in his *Biographia Literaria* (1817). One of the major preoccupations of this book is a rehabilitation of the imagination as a productive or creative faculty by combining Coleridge's twin interests in poetry and philosophy. His first step was to reject the law of association which dominated British empirical philosophy from Hobbes through Locke and Hume to Hartley. For these philosophers, Coleridge complained, the mind was a passive agent animated by the input of external sensory data. As Locke wrote of the mind, the 'senses at first let in *particular* ideas, and furnish the yet empty cabinet' ([1690] 1964: 89). Coleridge's complaint is that the human will, in this theory, is considered subordinate to the 'blind mechanism' of the chain of associations, which is generated when objects enter the mind and are stored in the memory with a causal relationship ([1817] 1956: 68). If taken to its natural consequences, Coleridge argues, the law of association would assert that the 'inventor of the watch did not in reality invent it; he only look'd on, while the blind causes, the only true artists, were unfolding themselves . . . So must it have have been with Mr. Southey and Lord Byron, when the one fancied himself composing his *Roderick*, and the other his *Childe Harold*' (69).

Coleridge's polemic may be prone to caricature, but it nonetheless establishes the grounds upon which he wishes to refurbish the imagination. With Coleridge the imagination no longer performs a passive function and compounds, associates or aggregrates images of external objects; it is an active mode of perception. This reconceptualisation of the imagination is achieved by relegating functions it was commonly held to perform to that of fancy. 'The fancy is indeed no other than a mode of memory emancipated from the order of time and space,' he claims, so 'equally with the ordinary memory it must receive all its materials ready made from the law of association'

(167). The imagination, thus liberated from associationism, becomes a 'shaping or modifying power' (160). This helps us to understand Coleridge's notorious definition of imagination:

> The imagination then I consider either as primary, or secondary. The primary imagination I hold to be the living power and prime agent of all human perception, and as a repetition in the finite mind of the eternal act of creation in the infinite I AM. The secondary I consider as an echo of the former, co-existing with the conscious will, yet still as identical with the primary in the kind of its agency, and differing only in degree, and in the mode of its operation. It dissolves, diffuses, dissipates in order to re-create; or where this process is rendered impossible, yet still, at all events, it struggles to idealize and to unify. It is essentially vital, even as all objects (as objects) are essentially fixed and dead (167).

Here the Renaissance analogy between poetic and divine creation is extended to all imagination. The 'infinite I AM' is God, a 'self-comprehending and creative spirit' (114). Hence, in duplicating this, perception is not only a passive reception of objects through the senses, but an active creation of them too. Nature is not only something external to us which we behold through our senses and then is mediated in our minds by our imagination, but is also something which we shape and modify in the act of perception via our imagination. Thus, because imagination partakes of divine creation, nature (God's creation) is something which also operates on our minds from *within*.

The 'secondary imagination' is an echo of the former in the sense that it reduplicates the primary act of perception via the *conscious* will. It differs in its 'mode of operation' because the mode of operation is not general perception, but poetic creation. The poetic imagination, then, differs in degree from the primary because it is an echo of the original. It is a more localized operation of the imagination, but at the same time is more heightened. Poetry, thus, does not imitate, it *recreates* the act of perception by giving new light to 'fixed and dead' objects, thus showing how the faculty of imagination operates in general human perception.

This is corroborated by Coleridge's account of the purpose of his poetic collaboration with Wordsworth in the *Lyrical Ballads*. While Coleridge's plan was to use the 'modifying colours of the imagination' to give a 'semblance of truth' (169) to 'persons and characters supernatural' (168), Wordsworth's was to 'give the charm of novelty to things of every day, and to excite a feeling analogous to the supernatural, by awakening the mind's attention from the lethargy of custom and directing it to the loveliness and the wonders of the world before us' (169). By consciously using his imagination the poet is demonstrating that the world is not something fixed and dead which we passively perceive, but something which we create, and only becomes dead by virtue of the 'lethargy of custom'. In other words, by asking the reader to indulge in a 'willing suspension of disbelief' (169), the Romantic poet is promising access to a higher realm of truth, a world beyond that which we see through a 'film of familiarity' (169), a world in opposition to the 'mechanic school' (152) of Newton and Locke, a world which is created by the imagination as much as it is perceived.

What makes poetic genius creative, what activates the imagination, is the passion of the individual poet. For Coleridge, to be creative meant to be original, but unlike the scientific concept of a discovery of something which already existed but was unknown, original meant something new which sprang from the unique personality of the artist in the form of his passion. He argued that the question 'What is Poetry? Is so nearly the same question with, what is a poet? That the answer to the one is involved in the solution of the other. For it is a distinction resulting from the poetic genius itself, which sustains and modifies the images, thoughts and emotions of the poet's own mind' (173). While the imagination had tended to be seen as a faculty which the poet could *employ* for his work, the creative imagination came to be the faculty which the poet *expressed* through his poetry. This is evident when Shelley talks of 'the direct expression of the inventive and creative faculty itself' ([1821] 1963: 184). The poet's imagination is therefore the centre of his personality.

Creative writing

While the doctrine of original genius assumes that only a certain gifted few possess the creative imagination necessary for the production of great poetry, Coleridge's assertion that it differs in kind rather than degree from the primary imagination, which is the agent of *all* human perception, that is, a faculty common to all men, suggests the possibility of extending creative power to all men. We must look to America for the beginning of a democratisation of creative power and for the development of the phrase 'creative writing'. This begins with 'The American Scholar', an oration delivered by Ralph Waldo

Emerson in 1837. Emerson claimed that America has 'listened too long to the courtly muses of Europe' (1907: 860) and that the time had come 'when the sluggard intellect of this continent will look from under its iron lids, and fill the postponed expectation of the world with something better than the exertions of mechanical skill' (847). It was through the development of creative power that this expectation would be fulfilled.

For Emerson the true scholar is he who engages directly and personally with nature and experience before committing his perception to the page. A book is merely the record of this sacred thought, of this 'act of creation' (850). He condemns as bookworms those whose thoughts proceed from the received wisdom of the record rather than 'their own sight of principles' (850). Books, he claims, 'are for nothing but to inspire', and what they inspire is the active soul, the genius which is 'not the privilege of here and there a favourite, but the sound estate of every man' (851). This democratisation of genius is not surprising given that the American Declaration of Independence had claimed a scant fifty years before that all men are born equal. Emerson retains the Romantic distinction between original and imitation, but originality is understood as the experience of nature rather than of books, as opposed to the expression of a unique poetic sensibility. So, unlike the doctrine of original genius as the ability of a gifted few, Emerson claims that genius is an innate quality of every man which can be awakened. 'There are creative manners, there are creative actions and creative words; manners, actions, words, that is, indicative of no custom or authority, but springing spontaneous from the mind's own sense of good and fair' (851).

In his attack on the tendency of American colleges to educate by drills rather than to create by setting 'the hearts of their youth on flame' (852), Emerson condemns the tendency to see books as a repository for historical fact and lexical curiosities rather than the expression of individual genius. 'There is then,' he writes, 'creative reading as well as creative writing' (852). According to D.G. Myers, it is this passage which contributes the phrase 'creative writing' to the language (1996: 31). It seems to me, however, that in this context the two words do not fit together as a phrase; there is no sense of naming here, there is no *thing* being labelled, and it is not reproduced elsewhere in Emerson's work. Furthermore, the subject of the sentence is 'creative reading'. Emerson's point is that while it is taken for granted that writing can be creative, reading must also be creative if we are to employ books productively. Nonetheless, it is obvious here that Emerson was not making a generic distinction between types of writing. Creative writing is defined as a *practice*, the operation of individual thought derived from first-hand experience of nature and life.

The phrase 'creative writing', however, has also come to operate as a synonym for literature, for published works of fiction, poetry and drama. In surmising when and why these genres came to be called creative, Myers asserts that 'the teaching of creative writing came first, historically preceding the fiction and verse that are now called 'creative' and helping to determine the very categories by which this writing would be characterized and defined. The academic and not the literary usage is thus the primary meaning of the term' (1996: xiii). This cannot be sustained, however. It is Wordsworth who appears to have first employed the term 'creative' as a generic definition of literature, before the development of Creative Writing. In an untitled sonnet addressed to B.R. Haydon in 1815 he writes:

> High is our calling, Friend! – Creative Art
> (Whether the instrument of words she use,
> Or pencil pregnant with ethereal hues,)
> (1950: 207)

So for Wordsworth there is a certain *type* of writing which is creative. And this is the type of writing which is an art form alongside painting: that is, poetry. Furthermore, the phrase 'creative writing' was in operation as a synonym for literature before it was first used to label a course of study – which, according to Myers, was in 1925 (1996: 103). In 1919 Irving Babbitt made a distinction 'between two types of imagination – the ethical type that gives high seriousness to creative writing and the Arcadian or dalliant type that does not raise it above the recreative level' (1955: 275). In other words, Babbitt is using the phrase 'creative writing' to describe 'high' literature. To understand why the phrase 'creative writing' came to be used to denote literary works one must examine how the word *literature* came to define 'creative' works.

Poetry, as Peter Widdowson points out, was originally 'the generic term for what we know as literature', and this included 'poetic drama and prose romances, fables and sagas' (1999: 26). Despite this, poetry has always been associated with verse. In his *Poetics* Aristotle claimed that there is 'an art which imitates by language alone' (1984: 2316) and no name exists for this art, whether it is a Socratic dialogue or a mime or a metrical composition. He says, however, that anything written in verse is commonly called poetry, regardless of whether it is an art of imitation or a scientific treatise. So even though poetry is to be defined as imitation rather than verse, he acknowledges its general usage. In this case poetry has generally been understood to fall within the genres of dramatic, epic or lyric. Widdowson quotes Sidney's *Apologie for Poetry* to demonstrate the generic quality of the word poetry, but Sidney's point, that many excellent poets have never versified and many versifiers ought not to be called poets, demonstrates that he is attempting to address the persistent association of poetry with verse. Indeed, Sidney claims that verse is the 'fittest raiment' for poetry ([1595] 1922: 10). Samuel Johnson defined poetry in his 1775 dictionary as metrical composition, and a poet as an inventor, an author of fictions and one who writes in measure (1986: 195). As late as 1821 Shelley claimed in his *Defence of Poetry* that Plato and Bacon were poets and that poetry is not merely an art but an expression of the imagination in all aspects of society, or an ability to apprehend the eternal truth of existence. However, poetry 'in a more restricted sense expresses those arrangements of language, and especially metrical language, which are created by that imperial faculty, whose throne is curtained within the invisible nature of man' (1963: 164). So, unlike Widdowson, I do not see a specialisation of poetry as verse occurring from the mid-seventeenth century and gaining speed early in the nineteenth, but continuing attempts to define poetry more expansively than its popular conception as metrical composition.

The fact that the word 'poetry' or 'poesy' is superseded by 'literature' as a general category for creative works can be attributed partly to the fact that a new word was required to accommodate the novel as it gradually came to be recognised as an art form. Because poetry was generally defined as the imitation of nature, fictional prose romances did not come under the title of poetry, despite their use of the imagination. Henry Fielding, in *Tom Jones*, writes that 'truth distinguishes our writings from those idle romances which are filled with monsters, the productions, not of nature, but of distempered brains' ([1749] 1992: 93). The fact that he wished to distinguish his work from romance by labelling it 'a comic epic poem in prose' ([1742] 1948: xviii) demonstrates that he was searching for the credibility of poetry. Nathaniel Hawthorne, in his preface to *The House of the Seven Gables*, gives this writing a name: 'When a writer calls his work a Romance, it need hardly be observed that he wishes to claim a certain latitude, both as to its fashion and material, which he would not have felt himself entitled to assume had he professed to be writing a Novel' ([1851] 1957: 90). By 1884 Walter Besant was urging, in *The Art of Fiction*, that the novel be recognised as an art form alongside poetry.

Furthermore, while plays were always categorised as poetry, and often referred to as dramatic poetry, the title of A.W. Ward's *History of English Dramatic Literature* (1875) demonstrates that the drama was attaining a separate literary identity. By the time of George Pierce Baker's *Dramatic Technique* (1919) there is no mention of drama as poetry, even in discussion of dramatic poets such as Shakespeare, more than likely because the drama was no longer written in verse and therefore was not considered poetry.

If this explains why another word was required to replace poetry as a general category for creative works, it does not explain why literature was that word. Samuel Johnson's dictionary defined literature as '[l]earning; skill in letters' ([1775] 1986: 131). Johnson himself, in his life of Milton, wrote: 'His literature was unquestionably great. He read all the languages which are considered either as learned or polite' ([1779] 1906: 107). To be possessed of literature was to have acquired polite learning, and Raymond Williams points out that the word originally designated something like our modern understanding of literacy, or 'reading ability and reading experience' (1977: 47).

A phrase in Johnson's life of Addison demonstrates that while poetry, in the eighteenth century, could be considered a part of this polite learning, it could also be distinguished from literature: 'a woman without skill, or pretensions to skill, in poetry or literature' ([1779] 1906: 404). The distinction here shows that poetry is still being defined by its belonging to the province of the imagination, while literature denotes the province of knowledge. It was not until the nineteenth century that literature was gradually narrowed to mean 'creative' works. This specialised understanding of literature develops as poetry is glorified by the Romantics as the embodiment of man's creative power, in opposition to works of science, and hence the most important form of literature. Raymond Williams points out that the word 'literacy' developed in the late nineteenth century as 'literature' was being restricted to its modern sense (1977: 46–7). A reason for this specialisation may be that other forms of literature were themselves becoming more highly specialised; history, philosophy, criticism, all those forms of prose which may have come under the umbrella of literature or *belles lettres*, were hardening into separate disciplines. Barbara and John Ehrenreich describe this process as the beginning of the rise of the 'Professional-Managerial Class' in modern monopoly capitalism (1979: 27).

From the mid-nineteenth century, literature gradually ceased to be employed as a general term and became consciously defined in opposition to criticism. The specific terms of this opposition were first established by Matthew Arnold in his seminal essay of 1865, 'The Function of Criticism at the Present Time'. In this essay Arnold claimed that 'creative power' is exercised in more than just 'the production of great works of literature or art' (1937: 28), which demonstrates a belief that already literature (by which Arnold means poetry) was generally considered 'creative'. The older distinction between imagination and reason was one between two mental faculties necessary for the production of poetry. Arnold's distinction between the critical and the creative assigns the two mental powers to different types of writing. Literature, as a primary artistic product, is creative, and its commentary is critical. He retains this generic distinction between literature and criticism, but immediately sets out to claim use of the creative faculty in the act of criticism. While there is some ambiguity in this essay, for literature can at times be understood as a body of writing more general than just poetry, criticism is ultimately not so much commentary as a free play of the mind in search of knowledge, from which creative literature can draw.

In 1907 George Saintsbury's *A Short History of English Literature* could still include the prose of Francis Bacon and periodical essays of the great reviews and quarterlies, although it is to be noted that poetry was no longer a general category, but one class of literature. The annexing of the word literature to denote a certain type of writing associated with the fine arts, rather than with general learning, finds its completion in the efforts of English or literary studies to define an object of study. In *The Teaching of English in England*, known as the Newbolt Report and regarded as a defining moment in modern English studies, it is claimed that 'literature, and in particular poetry, is the finest of the fine arts' (Newbolt, 1921: 204). Literature 'is an art; and art is a different thing from either science or speculation, the mainsprings of philosophy' (206). It is obvious here that poetry has become subsumed in a broader category of literature, but that the word 'literature' has been narrowed to denote the Romantic concept of poetry. Literature, moreover, is defined in opposition to other possible definitions of what it could be and becomes interchangeable with English (as a discipline): 'We believe, therefore, that formal grammar and philology should be recognised as scientific studies and kept apart (as far as that is possible) from the lessons in which English is treated as an art, a means of creative expression, a record of human experience' (11). This practice of academic definition culminates with Wellek and Warren's 1949 textbook, *Theory of Literature*, in which they state: 'We must first make a distinction between literature and literary study. The two are distinct activities: one is creative, an art; the other, if not precisely a science, is a species of knowledge or of learning' (1963: 15). This is precisely so that the object of critical scrutiny in something called Literary Studies could be defined.

The reason why creative writing becomes a popular synonym for literature is that it helps define literary works in opposition to something called criticism. For instance, arguing in a 1921 article in *The New Republic* against 'all the heavy effort' to make a science of criticism, H.L. Mencken claimed that the critic's 'choice of criticism rather than creative writing is chiefly a matter of temperament . . . with accidents of education and environment to help' (249). And in his 1929 essay, 'Experiment in Criticism', T.S. Eliot claimed, in an implicit reference to the terms established by Arnold, to be 'more than skeptical of the old superstition that criticism and "creative writing" never flourish in the same age . . . "Creative writing" can look after itself; and certainly it will be none the better for suppressing the critical curiosity' (1962: 616).

As Williams points out, the difference between the words 'literature' and 'poetry' is that literature came to mean a body of printed works to be *read*, whereas poetry, which comes from the Greek 'to make', by etymology and by critical description, retained an active sense of making (1977: 47). Creative Writing, I suggest, offered an alternative to the word 'literature' in the sense that it emphasises process rather than product. Thus the logic behind studying Creative Writing as opposed to studying literature does not have to be that one writes as opposed to reads, nor that one produces a creative fiction rather than a non-creative essay. The object of study in a Creative Writing class, whether it be a published work of literature or a student manuscript, is scrutinised in terms of the process of its making, rather than as a literary artefact. That is, the distinction is not between what students produce, but what they study: text as process rather than text as product. The phrase also refers to post-Renaissance ideas of the creation, rather than imitation, of the poet or novelist. Fiction, in fact, is most often referred to as creative writing, as if to give the novelist a cachet similar to that of the poet. 'Publication in the Northern Territory for creative writers and poets is a vexed issue,' Marian Devitt wrote in 1998 (33).

'Creative writing' was also a phrase which came to embody the Romantic revolt against industrialisation and empirical philosophy

in the name of man's creative spirit. Thus when F.R. Leavis calls
Lawrence a 'great creative writer', he is not just saying that Lawrence
is a good novelist, but that his writing gives us 'faith in the creative
human spirit and its power to ensue fulness of life' ([1955] 1964: 15).
This is precisely the sort of Romantic ideal embodied in the modern
understanding of Literature; an ideal carried on by the critical
tradition from Arnold to Leavis.

According to Williams, the process of specialisation by which the
meaning of the word 'literature' was narrowed to cover only 'creative'
works was 'in part a major affirmative response, in the name of an
essentially general human "creativity", to the socially repressive and
intellectually mechanical forms of a new social order: that of capitalism, and especially industrial capitalism' (1977: 50). While this
process began with the Romantics, the term 'literature' was not
specialised until later, Williams argues, when it was pitted 'against
the full pressures of an industrial capitalist order, the assertion became
defensive and reserving where it had once been positive and absolute.
In "art" and "literature", the essential and saving *human* qualities
must, in the early phase, be "extended"; in the latter phase,
"preserved"' (50). This latter phase is undoubtedly a reference to the
work of Leavis.

The challenge of 'creativity' to modern life which the Romantics
issued was taken into British universities, not as a call to produce
more poetry, but in the form of criticism and its creative judgement
of literary works committed to Life. It was an essentially defensive
move against industrial society. In a 1967 lecture entitled 'Literature
and the University', Leavis claimed that 'Blake was the human protest
on behalf of life against the repression of creativity represented by
the prevailing ethos of the 18th century' (1979: 52). He then argued
that the 'civilization we live in presents a more formidable menace
to life' (52). Rather than the mechanised philosophy of Newton and
Locke which Blake opposed, the current challenge to creativity was
what Leavis called the 'technologico-Benthamism' of industrialised
mass civilisation (63).

Leavis argued that poetry matters little in the modern world and
most people don't know how to read it. It is the critic, the person
of 'good sensibility', capable of 'intelligent and sensitive criticism',
who was required to reaffirm human creativity through a particular
way of *reading*. And it was through English Studies, which Leavis
saw as the humane centre of a collocation of specialist disciplines in
the university, that the critic as a teacher could create a cultural
haven in the face of a materialistic, technological society. For Leavis,

criticism was the application of a disciplined and sensitive intelligence to a poem, a personal, creative response to the words on the page. 'What, under the head of Practical Criticism, we call analysis,' he says, 'is a creative, or re-creative, process. It's a more deliberate following-through of that process of creation in response to the poet's words than any serious reading is' (48). While the poet's creative skill is acknowledged, explication of authorial intent is not the aim; the collaborative building of a literary object in which critical minds can meet creatively is the goal.

Leavis's important work, which began in the 1930s, already had a tradition of anti-industrialism in the school system to draw upon. In her book *The Preachers of Culture*, Margaret Mathieson argues that the spirit of anti-industrialism in Romantic literature and criticism underpinned the development of modern English Studies as an alternative to classical education in grammar schools. Not only was it manifested in the Arnoldian view of 'the spiritually educative role of literature' (Mathieson 1975: 62), but it motivated the assimilation of theories of progressive education into the British school system. In fact, Mathieson asserts, the belief that a child's personal growth could be facilitated by self-expression in writing enabled English to assume a central position in the popular school curriculum. H. Caldwell Cook, through his book *The Play Way* (1917), was 'the earliest exponent of creative activity in English' (86). And by the time of the Newbolt Report of 1921, 'experience of literature and creative work in the native language had both come to be seen as vitally important in the development of character' (65).

In America, by contrast, creativity became a symbol of democracy and attempts were made to harness creativity in order to aid and expand capitalist productivity rather than preserve a nostalgic haven against it. This can be seen in a 1925 review article by W. Wilbur Hatfield in the *English Journal*. The first book reviewed is *The Creative Spirit* by Rollo Walter Brown. This is described as a 'big' book, devoted to a grand vision of the role of creativity in any vital civilisation, with chapters on education, religion, science, art, industry and society in general. The ability to invent and produce new things, to be active and pioneering, was essential to prevent stagnation or routine. According to Hatfield, 'the improvement of industrial procedure, social relations, and government action' is less important than 'the reflex influence of this creative effort upon the minds and spirits engaged in it' (1925: 573). The real benefit of creativity is self-expression, and 'this freeing of the spirit of the individual is really the essence of democracy, to which all machinery of government and industrial organization are but the means' (574). The second book reviewed is *Creative Youth*, a seminal work in the development of Creative Writing in high schools, which I shall discuss in Chapter 2. This book is described as a record of 'the activity of this creative spirit in the English classroom' (574). Self-expression through Creative Writing in American schools was thus seen as a democratic practice and as an important contribution to creative life in a progressive industrial society.

The genius within

In 'The Function of Criticism at the Present Time', Matthew Arnold continues Emerson's liberal development of man's creative power by asserting its presence in areas way beyond the field of literary production:

> It is undeniable that the exercise of a creative power, that a free creative activity, is the highest function of man; it is proved to be so by man's finding in it his true happiness. But it is undeniable, also, that men may have the sense of exercising this free creative activity in other ways than in producing great works of literature or art; if it were not so, all but a very few men would be shut out from the true happiness of all men. They may have it in well-doing, they may have it in learning, they may have it even in criticising.
>
> ([1865] 1937: 28)

It is obvious here that Arnold is positing a general creative faculty common to all men, man's 'highest function', for which he has chosen not to use the word 'imagination', perhaps because of its ambivalent connotations in regards to delusion or day-dreaming, and perhaps as a conscious separation from the lack of learning which he inveighed against the Romantic imagination. All that was required was a noun to give this faculty concrete existence.

In his 'Essay, Supplementary to the Preface', Wordsworth writes that imagination 'is a word which has been forced to extend its services far beyond the point to which philosophy would have confined' it, and 'has been overstrained, from impulses honourable to mankind, to meet the demands of the faculty which is perhaps the noblest of our nature' ([1815] 1974a: 210). That faculty is variously referred to by Shelley, in his *Defence of Poetry*, as 'the inventive and creative faculty' ([1821] 1963: 184), the 'poetical faculty' (184) and 'the imaginative and creative faculty' (190). It is not until the latter part of the nineteenth century that the word 'creativity' comes into use, and it comes to replace the overworked and exhausted imagination as a description of that noble faculty of mankind. Fittingly, if one accepts the authority of the *Oxford English Dictionary*, it is in relation to poetry. 'Shakespeare's verse remains unrivalled,' A.W. Ward claimed in 1875, 'due to the spontaneous flow of his poetic creativity' (506).

It is important to note here that Ward does not talk of Shakespeare's imagination or of his genius, but of his creativity. From this point 'creativity' supplants 'imagination' as the noble faculty of mankind. The passage is an echo of Wordsworth's famous line in the 1800 preface to the *Lyrical Ballads*, and puts the same emphasis on ease of writing that Romantic theories of original genius did. Creativity is here defined as something which is directly expressed rather than deliberately constructed. Shakespeare's verse is his thoughts laid bare, not the product of a dramatic craft, and therefore it is *specific* to his genius, to his personality. So in the moment of its naming, the faculty of creativity is associated with what we might today call the unconscious.

'The process by which external inspiration was internalised', Ken Ruthven neatly explains, 'begins with late eighteenth-century speculations about the nature of original genius, and culminates in Freudian psychology in the early years of this century' (1979: 64). The imagination which Romantic artists drew upon, what Shelley called 'that imperial faculty, whose throne is curtained within the invisible nature of man' ([1821] 1963: 164), has been classified by psychoanalysis as the unconscious. In his essay of 1908, 'Creative Writers and Day-dreaming', Freud claims that a 'piece of creative writing, like a day-dream, is a continuation of, and a substitute for, what was once the play of childhood' (1972: 41).

André Breton's adaption of Freud's therapeutic method of 'free association' was instrumental in demonstrating how the unconscious was a wellspring of creativity which could be tapped into via the practice of 'automatic writing' in order to achieve a state of 'surreality'. Unlike the Romantic faith in original genius as the locus of the emancipation of the imagination, and poetry as the expression (and surrealism seems to be a post-Romantic inversion of the law of association, with ideas welling from within rather than being furnished from without), Breton sees automatic writing as a technique which can be made available to everyone. Breton's project to liberate the imagination by directly accessing the unconscious has many similarities with, if not a direct influence upon, certain elements of Creative Writing which seek to democratise the concept of original genius via the unconscious.

This influence can best be demonstrated by Dorothea Brande's bestselling book *Becoming a Writer*. A genius, for Brande, is simply 'the man who by some fortunate accident of temperament or education can put his unconscious completely at the service of his reasonable intention, whether or not he is aware that this is so' ([1934] 1983: 48). All persons are unique, Brande claims, because of their individual experiences, and hence everyone can be an original writer. In order to achieve this originality the 'unconscious must flow freely and richly, bringing at demand all the treasures of memory, all the emotions, incidents, scenes, intimations of character and relationships which it has stored away in its depths' (45). The exercise she prescribes to access the unconscious is similar to the practice of automatic writing, with the same goal of achieving a state of 'surreality': 'what you are actually doing is training yourself, in the twilight zone between sleep and the full waking state, simply to *write*' (73). The unconscious has since been commonly regarded as the source of poetic creativity. By the mid-1960s Anne Sexton was able to claim that '[p]oetry, after all, milks the unconscious' (1985: 85).

The science of creativity

Whereas the imagination became the central focus of aesthetics and poetic theory in the nineteenth century, since the twentieth century explorations of creativity have taken place largely in the domain of psychology. Creativity, in fact, has become a distinct field of study in its own right. Before its emergence as a field of study, according to J.P. Guilford, '[i]f anything at all related to the subject was mentioned in the textbooks, it was under the mysterious label of "imagination" or "creative imagination"' (1968: 137).

Empirical research into the nature of genius began with Alexander Galton's *Hereditary Genius* (1869). 'The interest in what is now commonly termed "creativity",' according to C.L. Burt, 'goes back to Galton's pioneer studies of the intellectual characteristics of men of genius' (1970: 203). Galton attempted to prove that genius is passed on through the genes, thus giving scientific credibility to the assumption of congenital talent, of poets being born rather than made. The branch of study Galton inaugurated attempts to explain what it is that makes genius 'creative', that allows it to introduce new ideas and objects into the world. This takes the form of study of the personality characteristics and individual motivations of famous personages considered to be highly creative or possessed of genius, by virtue of their 'creations'.

Study of the creative *process*, on the other hand, has been highly influenced by Graham Wallas's *The Art of Thought* (1926). Using the testimony of artists and scientists, Wallas divided creative thinking into four stages denoted as: preparation, a period in which material is gathered; incubation, where little work seems to be done because thought is operating at the unconscious level; illumination, where unconscious mental work manifests itself in the spontaneous flash of insight associated with inspiration; and verification, where ideas are tested and organised into coherent form.

A seminal moment in the development of creativity as an area of scientific study was the presidential address of J.P. Guilford to the American Psychological Association in 1949, later published in the association's journal under the title 'Creativity'. Guilford pointed out the 'appalling' lack of research in this area (1968: 70) and, while acknowledging the widespread currency of Wallas's theory, claimed that the 'belief that the process of incubation is carried out in a region of the mind called the unconscious is of no help. It merely chases the problem out of sight' (90). What needed to be understood, according to Guilford, were the mental processes put into action by creativity. He also challenged the assumption that creativity is a product of high intelligence, arguing that intelligence tests from Binet onwards concentrated on predicting scholastic performance, thus neglecting creative potential. 'We must look beyond the boundaries of the IQ,' Guilford argued, 'if we are to fathom the domain of creativity' (84).

In developing tests which would measure not just the ability to discover a single correct answer, but the ability to generate multiple possibilities, Guilford formulated the concept of a structure of intelligence which involves a number of mental processes. In this model of cognition creative persons utilise divergent thinking rather than the more common convergent thinking. Convergent thinking seeks out a single response to a problem through a logical pattern, whereas divergent thinking involves a greater freedom for tangents of thought and multiple answers. This distinction is the basis for the many and influential works of Edward de Bono on 'lateral' thinking as opposed to 'vertical' or logical thinking. De Bono coined this phrase in *The Uses of Lateral Thinking*, a book which indicates the shift from scientific testing of creativity to the populist development of it. Lateral thinking is not just a cognitive means of solving problems, but a mental process which can be trained in order to generate new ideas. When de Bono says '[t]here are certain techniques and methods (of lateral thinking) which will increase the chances of creativity – partly through removing inhibiting habits of thought and partly through special settings which encourage the flow and rearrangement of ideas' ([1967] 1990: 171), he is not referring to some sort of unleashing of the inner self, but rather training oneself to consider alternatives to the generic and familiar.

Creativity is now most commonly defined as the mental capacity to produce something new and valuable. While this is similar to the concept of original genius, it is based on a democratisation of genius. Creativity is not the gift of a talented few but a latent faculty in everyone and applicable to any field of human endeavour. As early as 1917 J.E. Spingarn could write: 'Genius and taste no longer mean for us what they meant to the poets and critics of the Romantic period. Their halo, their mystery, their power are gone. By genius is now merely meant the creative faculty, the power of self-expression, which we all share in varying degrees' (137–8). More recently, Ward, Finke and Smith argue in *Creativity and the Mind: Discovering the Genius Within* that 'creativity arises from ordinary mental processes that are part of the daily cognitive repertoire of normal human beings' (1995: 7). We are being creative if we do anything from 'fasten curtains closed with a safety pin' to 'dream up different words to lampoon a familiar song' (7).

This scientific concept of a general human creativity has become the motor for economic expansion, especially in America. Rothenberg and Hausman wrote in 1976 that 'educators, educational psychologists, business executives, and government personnel concerned with manpower, are interested in creativity in an immediate and pressing way, primarily to order and identify and nurture creative talent' (5). In his recent bestselling book, *The Rise of the Creative Class*, Richard Florida adopts a pseudo-Marxist narrative to explain the connection between creativity and business in the modern global economy, although he is more interested in advising industries how to maximise productivity than in calling for revolution:

> As with other classes the defining basis of this new class is economic. Just as the feudal aristocracy derived its power and identity from its hereditary control of land and people, and the bourgeoisie from its members' roles as merchants and factory owners, the Creative Class derives its identity from its members' roles as purveyors of creativity. Because creativity is the driving

force of economic growth, in terms of influence the Creative Class has become the dominant class in society.

([2002] 2003: xv)

The Creative Class is similar to what other commentators would call the knowledge class or professional-managerial class, except Florida makes a distinction between mental labour as a commodity, and creativity as a source of economic productivity. For Florida, 'the core of the Creative Class' includes 'people in science and engineering, architecture and design, education, arts, music and entertainment, whose economic function is to create new ideas, new technology and/or new creative content' (8). Around this core there oscillates 'a broader group of *creative professionals* in business and finance, law, health care and related fields' (8).

The post-industrial discourse of creativity which animates this book enables Florida to collapse the capitalist division of labour by subsuming distinctions between work and leisure into an account of the 'lifestyle' of the Creative Class. Florida explains the collective identity of this class as an historical conflation of the protestant work ethic which informed the rise of the bourgeoisie during the industrial revolution, and the bohemian lifestyle which originally favoured individuality and creativity in opposition to bourgeois ethics. As a result, the values which comprise the ethos of the Creative Class include individuality, meritocracy, and diversity and openness. In the contemporary market-oriented university system, where student (or consumer) choice has a large influence on curricular structure and course offerings, it may be argued that the international expansion of Creative Writing in the latter part of the twentieth century has been due to its popularity as an educational environment which caters to the ethos of this Creative Class.

What does the scientific demarcation of 'creativity' mean to Creative Writing? Are writing workshops to be places where students express their creativity as a means of ethical self-formation, or places where creativity can be harnessed to produce new ideas and works? Or rather, where students can be taught to search for methods beyond the generic and the formulaic when they are writing? Perhaps the writing workshop can be seen to operate as a metaphor for the mental process of divergent thinking because it provides writers with a range of different options offered by fellow students, thus training them to internalise this process in the act of composition. There is much to be said for keeping the phrase 'Creative Writing' as the description of a subject, for, as I have said, it denotes the genres of writing which are studied and produced in writing programmes, and from the point of view of process rather than product. However, rather than seeing it as expressive writing, that which centres around the personality of the author, perhaps the connotations of divergent, lateral and problem-solving thinking would be beneficially acknowledged. Students could thus be encouraged not to tap into some mysterious source of creativity, but to consider a number of options, to explore literary possibilities on the way to producing a literary work; a work which, retrospectively, will be seen to have a logic to its composition and thus be a new and valuable contribution to literature.

2 Disciplinary origins

The common understanding that Creative Writing programmes have effected an absorption of the literary profession into universities obscures the historical origins of the discipline. Why did the writing of poetry and fiction move into the university? Was it an act of literary colonisation by the academy, or an act of cultural generosity? In order to counter the perception that Creative Writing occupies an 'anomalous' position within universities, some apologists have argued that literary apprenticeship is not new; the workshop is merely a formalisation of writers' groups or of individual mentoring relationships which have developed between famous writers. Or they have sought to construct an institutional lineage for the discipline by claiming that Creative Writing is the revival of an earlier form of writing instruction: that is, the composition of Latin and Greek verses as part of rhetorical instruction in the classical languages. The purpose of such arguments is not to provide an historical explanation for the presence of Creative Writing programmes, but to divert attention from a scrutiny of this presence, to justify Creative Writing by claiming historical precedent, no matter how tenuous the link.

In the first chapter I described a broad social interest in developing and harnessing the general human capacity for creativity which emerged in the twentieth century. Creative Writing can, to a certain extent, be located within the context of this shift from imagination to creativity. In order to understand exactly how and why writing programmes developed in universities, however, we must turn to the history of modern English Studies. Creative Writing emerged as a discipline in American universities out of the struggle between scholars and critics in the early part of the twentieth century, a struggle which saw the reformation of English Studies from largely historical and linguistic research into literature, to the teaching and practice of the criticism of literary works. Creative Writing did not simply come into being as an ally of criticism, however. The course of study which we have come to call Creative Writing is the product of four institutional trajectories – each with particular theories of literature, authorship and pedagogy that sometimes conflict and sometimes overlap. I will label these trajectories *creative self-expression, literacy, craft* and *reading from the inside.*

Creative self-expression is a technology of the self whereby language (especially through the medium of poetry) is a device for discovering and developing the expressive potential of one's own human character. The *literacy* model situates 'creative' writing within a general writing instruction which trains students for competency in a variety of compositional modes for the purposes of accurate expression and professional communication. The *craft* model involves the conjunction of formalist criticism with the concept of artistic training associated with the fine arts. *Reading from the inside* is founded on the belief that practical experience in writing literature leads to a greater knowledge and appreciation of it.

These models had separate institutional origins but eventually coalesced in the writing workshop, a pedagogical arena for the group discussion of student manuscripts. The emergence of the workshop as an independent entity, or academic specialisation, at the graduate level, leading to the award of an MFA, is the point at which Creative Writing becomes a discipline. What enabled the workshop to develop, however, was its ability to operate as an academic site for the deployment of criticism in a campaign to reform literary studies.

The four trajectories which I have outlined here are similar to those posited by D.G. Myers in *The Elephants Teach.* Myers's historical account of the rise of Creative Writing, however, is based on something akin to the creative spirit of literature manifesting itself in education as a reaction to scientific or utilitarian appropriations of literary study; a spirit which takes the form of 'constructivism' – the study and practice of literature as an art and for its own sake. For Myers the rise of Creative Writing is a story of evolution through various phases. Emerson's 'American Scholar' is the beginning of the 'case for creative writing', because it expresses a reaction to philological scholarship and posits a more creative approach to literary education (Myers 1996: 33). This argument is continued by English composition, 'a literary reformation of rhetoric', which paved the way for Creative Writing – 'but there would be a ways yet to go before it came into full view' (55). To use Myers's chapter headings, this meant negotiating 'The Problem of Writing in a Practical Age', which introduced a professional and practical approach to writing, and building on 'The Sudden Adoption of Creative Work', in which writing was taught in high schools as a means of personal growth through self-expression, before 'Criticism Takes Command'. The story thus culminates in Norman Foerster's School of Letters at the University of Iowa. This graduate school, in Myers's narrative, assumes the status of a perfect union of criticism and creative writing which quickly succumbed to the pressures of professionalisation and, hence, led to the emergence of the writing workshop as a separate entity. Despite Myers's critique of the current state of Creative Writing, his work has been employed to defend it. In a self-styled 'apology for the profession of writers who teach' (2000: 1), entitled 'Creative Writing and its Discontents', David Fenza draws heavily, by his own admission, on Myers's account to claim that 'creative writing as an academic discipline has evolved and matured over the past 120 years in order to complement literary scholarship and its pedagogy' (8).

While I do not dispute Myers's historical research, my argument here is that the various pedagogical and literary concepts which emerged with these institutional trajectories all continue to exist and clash in the workshop. This is why confusion exists over the place of Creative Writing within the academy and its relationship to English Studies. But it also demonstrates that Creative Writing is not a static discipline and can accommodate new changes to English Studies. What follows is less of an institutional history of the rise and decline (or the evolution and maturation) of a discipline than a location of various elements of contemporary Creative Writing theory and pedagogy in their original institutional contexts.

Creative self-expression

In the same way that the Romantic period saw a poetic revolution against the neatly turned epigrammatic verses and witty social observations of what Coleridge called 'Mr Pope and his followers' ([1817] 1956: 9), and what Wordsworth labelled 'poetic diction' ([1800] 1974b: 74), the strand of Creative Writing which I am calling *creative self-expression* developed as a reaction against the mechanical instruction in English composition which prevailed in American high schools. This is no idle comparison between nineteenth-century poetry and twentieth-century education, for the idea of the poetic imagination which infused the Romantic sensibility also informed the Creative Writing movement which developed within the American school system in the 1920s. The common link is not so much a belief in the social function of literature or the transformative power of art as a belief in human creative power and its origins in the natural poetic abilities of the child.

The first book of *The Prelude*, Wordsworth's autobiographical magnum opus, is entitled 'Introduction – Childhood and School-time'. Here Wordsworth provides an account of his youth – 'The simple ways in which my childhood walked' ([1850] 1950: 502) – and 'Those incidental charms which first attached / My heart to rural objects' (505). Nature becomes the source of Wordsworth's imagination and he extrapolates from his early bond with 'rural objects' a vitality of perception which is special to the child. The poetic spirit which begins first in the infant is lost to most men upon adulthood, but not to the true poet, Wordsworth himself: 'this infant sensibility, / Great birthright of our being, was in me / Augmented and sustained' (505–6). It was this infant sensibility which Wordsworth feared he had lost when he wrote his famous ode, 'Intimations of Immortality From Recollections of Early Childhood'. In his *Biographia Literaria*, Coleridge recounts the awe he experienced when first he encountered Wordsworth's poetry. He describes the quality of Wordsworth's genius thus:

> To carry on the feelings of childhood into the powers of manhood; to combine the child's sense of wonder and novelty with the appearances which every day for perhaps forty years had rendered familiar . . . this is the character and privilege of genius, and one of the marks which distinguish genius from talents.
>
> ([1817] 1956: 49)

This ability to awaken a sense of wonder at the everyday by retaining and nurturing a childhood enthusiasm for natural surroundings became one of the aims of the *Lyrical Ballads*. The question remains, how did this Romantic concept of poetic genius find its way into a school curriculum? If poetry was the means by which the special qualities of childhood were retained by the original genius, then poetry, or 'creative' writing, was the means by which a child's creative potential could be developed before, in Wordsworth's phrase, 'Shades of the prison-house begin to close / Upon the growing Boy' (1950: 460). As Coleridge noted, it was in degree rather than in kind that genius differed from the imagination of ordinary men. It was the democratisation of original genius, or the shift from imagination to creativity enabled by modern psychology and the concept of the unconscious, which provided the ground for a belief in the latent creativity in every child. The educational goal of Creative Writing in schools, however, was not a nation of literary geniuses, but a nation of children whose creative spirit had been released as a means of assisting their personal growth, via self-expression.

As I suggested earlier, this idea of creative self-expression developed as a reaction to traditional methods of teaching English composition to school children. Harold Rugg and Ann Shumaker characterised these methods as part of a regime of discipline which emphasised 'the mechanics of penmanship, correct usage of grammatical forms, punctuation, sentence structure, and paragraphing' (1928: 246). Composition was designed to train students for the need to write in adulthood, rather than to empower children to express what they wished to say. 'And then', Rugg and Shumaker trumpet, 'came *Creative Youth*' (248).

Creative Youth: Or How a School Environment Set Free the Creative Spirit was published in 1925 by the school teacher Hughes Mearns. It was an anthology of student poems resulting from a 'five year experiment in creative writing' (1925: 9) with children at the Lincoln School of Teachers' College, Columbia University. According to Myers, it was in this book that 'the phrase "creative writing" was used for the first time to refer to a course of study. It was not called creative writing until Mearns called it creative writing. And then it was rarely called anything else' (1996: 103).[1] This anthology also included a long introduction outlining the pedagogical process by which the poems were produced. The artist, Mearns insists in this introduction, is someone who 'refuses to give up his gift of seeing and thinking and feeling as a child' (1925: 70), while 'children speak naturally in a form that we adults are accustomed to call poetry; and without any searching for appropriate use of the medium' (65). What links the child and the artist is the idea that 'Literature is simply unique self-expression' (64), a practice of individuation which most adults give up when they adapt and conform to social conventions.

Mearns opens *Creative Youth* by telling us that the poems collected here have been acknowledged by critics as possessing real aesthetic merit; and the very fact that they are collected for public consumption encourages us to marvel at the creative achievements of the students. 'We are not primarily interested in making poets or even in making writers,' he nonetheless claims; 'our purpose has been simply to set up such an environment as might extend further the possibilities in creative writing of pupils of high-school age' (2). But what is the point of this? For Mearns, 'the best literary education comes with the amplest self-realization of the individual at whatever age he happens to be' (2). Writing is a device not for the practical use of communication, but for setting free the 'creative spirit' of the child. Thus employed, it is more likely to assume 'literary' form.

'Poetry, an outward expression of instinctive insight,' according to Mearns, 'must be summoned from the vasty deep of our mysterious selves. Therefore, it cannot be taught; indeed, it cannot even be summoned; it may only be permitted . . . The new education becomes simply, then, the wise guidance of enormously important native powers' (28). Such a statement requires a conviction that all children are natural poets, but it also requires a pedagogical strategy drawn not so much from the craft-based knowledge of a professional writer, or from the critical study of literature, but from a concept of the teacher-artist as an 'ethical exemplar'.[2] Mearns felt teachers must also be artists in order to understand the creative process they are encouraging in students, but it is the teacher's sensitivity and taste which is crucial to the task of drawing out creativity from the student.

The first role of the teacher, in Mearns's experiment, is to read constantly to students (79). Listening to literary works being read out loud by a sympathetic artist helps students to develop taste (81). Mearns calls this 'creative reading', for it is designed to emphasise the power of literature to put images into minds and stir emotions. The teacher must be a person of literary taste, someone able to draw out the nuances, the tone and the emotional depth of a work of literature in their oral readings, thus inspiring students to write. This 'creative reading' is not only the originary impetus for self-expression; it is a means of developing literary appreciation. 'Our final aim', Mearns asserts, 'is to acquaint this generation of children with the best English of the past, to thrill them and so transform them forever' (124).

In line with his critique of composition, no themes were assigned for students to write, and no methods of writing were set for them to follow. Instead, the teacher would continue to read out loud in class and simply wait for students to begin their own writing. The real influence of the teacher, the key to Mearns's educational strategy, was in how he or she responded to this student writing. Mearns elaborated on this pedagogical technique in his follow-up book, *Creative Power* (1929). The first step in producing creative student work is acceptance, to receive every offering, every crude creative effort, as long as it is sincere and individual. The next is approval, to always reward the original qualities in a work rather than its imitative elements. Criticism, the third step, takes place only to encourage students who are floundering due to their own frustration over a lack of technique, and 'long after the effort when all interest is being turned into a new creative venture' (1958: 245), that is, when students have moved on and the old work seems no longer their own. This criticism is to be positive rather than negative, and offered in an atmosphere of mutual trust. There is to be only indirect teaching; no reference to, or training in, principles of composition and design, although these qualities can be praised when a work displays them.

The last of 'the five teaching steps in summoning creative power' is what Mearns calls the 'miracle' (247). It is when 'the fresh original phrase appears and the strong line' (247). Thus the entire enterprise comes down to the teacher's taste, their ability to recognise genuinely creative work, their final objective endorsement of literary quality, rather than their sympathetic encouragement of original expression. 'The presumption', Mearns acknowledges, 'is that the teacher shall know what is the best work of a group' (44). It is here that the teacher is not only a fellow artist and a mentor, but a critic who is a special type of person (rather than a professional reader). Creative power becomes equated with, indeed manifested in, literary quality. The only evidence that children have 'grown' is through their work. And this work is not deemed a valid expression of the self unless it is original. In the end, it is only creative writing which the teacher deems to be of quality that marks student growth. Hence the necessity for an anthology which proves that student creative writing has literary quality, while denying that this is the goal of the classroom.

Creative Writing was a new way of teaching English. It was not simply a 'literary' movement, however. While it deployed within the education system a democratised view of Romantic authorship and its attendant theory of poetry as self-expression, the role of the teacher as an ethical exemplar was far more important to its success. This comes from a theory of education rather than a theory of literature. In *Creative Youth* Mearns explains that the environment created for his students at the Lincoln School 'is the result of a philosophy of education which . . . is not yet ready to set limits to a pupil's achievement at any stage of his growth, which believes that education is not put on like stucco on a wall, but comes primarily from within, which receives without question any sincere product, nor intrudes at every stage of growth with a too severe or too unnatural standard of perfection' (1925: 25–6). Harold Rugg and Ann Shumaker's *The Child-Centred School* acknowledges *Creative Youth* as a classic in its field, but locates Creative Writing, or self-expression in words, in a much broader context, the educational revolution undertaken by the Progressive Education Movement (1928: 63).

The 'child-centred' approach to education derives, ultimately, from Romanticism. In Rousseau's *Emile*, in line with Romantic primitivism, the child, like the noble savage, is depicted as closer to nature than civilised men, and thus uncorrupted by society. Hence the best education is to allow children to grow naturally. Furthermore, Rousseau linked this growth to individuality with his claim in his *Confessions* that 'I know my own heart' and, as a result of nature, 'I am like no-one in the whole world. I may be no better, but at least I am different' ([1781] 1953: 17). The more immediate inspiration for Progressive Education, however, came from the educational philosophy of John Dewey, who drew not upon primitivism, but upon evolutionary science for his idea of education as continual growth. According to Rugg and Shumaker, it was Dewey who 'ignited the first flame of the current educational revolution' and 'first phrased the educational philosophy of the developing American culture' (1928: 38). In 1896 Dewey established the Laboratory School at the University of Chicago, where he 'discarded the widely prevalent concepts of formal education; for example, education as preparation for the future, as the training of faculties through repeated exercise, as formation through recapitulation and retrospection. For these he substituted the simple formula of active learning and the reconstruction of experience' (41). The influence of Dewey's experiments with education, and the many publications which arose from these, led to the establishment of the Progressive Education Association in 1919.

Child-centred schools, according to Rugg and Shumaker, 'visualize the curriculum as a continuing stream of child activities, unbroken by systematic subjects, and springing from the interests and personally felt needs of the child' (36). The school thus provides a continuum of activity, rather than a set of academic disciplines, in which the child's growth can be facilitated by creative self-expression in all areas. It is not the materials with which students work that are creative, it is the expression of an individual self in these materials. 'The urge to create is one with the urge for self-expression' (227). The materials of the curriculum are thus perceived as being distributed along a scale of creative self-expression, from the acquisition of skills via verbatim repetition, to intellectual studies, to 'those activities and materials in which the essence of learning is subjective re-creation of inner experiences' (146). Creative Writing is at the end of this scale because, like the other arts, it is an activity 'especially adapted to creative effort' (151).

From 1925 onwards, the year in which *Creative Youth* was published, it is noticeable that a number of articles on Creative Writing began to appear in the *English Journal*. And in 1929 H.D. Roberts wrote two editorials describing a 'creative-writing movement' (1929a: 346) which was 'gaining a foothold in the curriculum' (1929b: 254). By 1935 the Progressive Education Association had established a Creative Writing Committee to investigate and report upon the state of this field in secondary education, and in 1937 the committee issued a book entitled *Teaching Creative Writing* which, according to the preface, was 'offered now to the teaching profession to serve both as a handbook for teachers in service and as a textbook in teacher-training classes' (Conrad 1937: ix).

The 'creative writing movement' in schools did not have a direct impact on the development of Creative Writing in universities. In a 1931 survey of Creative Writing courses in colleges and universities, Snow Longley Housh commented that the emphasis of these courses 'is normally on the finished product and the development of critical standards rather than on the enrichment of personality with which the high-school teacher is primarily concerned' (674). Nonetheless, the strategy of students looking within themselves for creative material, the perception of creative writing as a form of self-cultivation, can be seen to have influenced the concept of voice which would become prominent in writing workshops. As Mearns said, in creative writing 'the individual speaks out in his own unique voice' ([1929] 1958: 247).

Literacy

In *A History of Professional Writing Instruction in American Colleges*, Katherine Adams states that most of the graduates who are employed today for their writing skills in any industry have studied not only freshman composition, but 'advanced courses in journalism, technical writing, ad copy writing, public relations writing, business writing, creative writing, advanced composition, or writing across the curriculum' (1993: ix). Creative Writing is here characterised as one section of general writing instruction in universities, designed to provide training for the practical use of written communication in various professions.

Adams draws attention to advanced 'composite' courses in composition at Harvard University as precursors to Creative Writing because of their 'workshop' format, their collegial atmosphere, and their encouragement of students as professional writers. As universities expanded at the beginning of the twentieth century, Adams claims, a general approach to the profession of writing gave way to more

specialised training in individual genres and their professional requirements. 'Teachers thus began to approach writing mainly through its
professional manifestations, primarily as creative writing, magazine
and newspaper writing, business writing, and technical writing' (61–2).
Separate courses in versification, the short story and playwriting
emerged as specialisations of the composite course in advanced
composition, and these laid the groundwork for the development of
Creative Writing programmes.

Modern composition has its foundations in the appointment of
Adam Sherman Hill as Boylston Professor of Rhetoric at Harvard
University in 1872. The subject which Hill devised in this profes-
sorship, English composition, was designed to replace the rhetorical
reliance on the classical languages of Greek and Latin with a more
utilitarian training in effective use of the vernacular. English composition became a requirement of the entrance exam to Harvard. This
examination was based on 'literary' topics, but with an emphasis on
correct grammar, spelling and punctuation. Schools were thus obliged
to provide their students with this training, and, as we have seen, it
is against English composition that the idea of writing as creative
self-expression reacted.

Freshman composition became the only required course in the
new elective system at Harvard. According to James A. Berlin, in
Writing Instruction in Nineteenth-Century American Colleges, the oratorical
elements of rhetoric became assigned to departments of speech, and
the imaginative elements to newly formed departments of literature,
leaving composition as a general-service course which would provide
practical training in the improvement of student writing, enabling
students to enter the professional world equipped with tools of written
communication (1984: 9).

While freshman composition focused on the formal mechanics of
expository writing, elective classes in advanced composition were
instituted to provide for those students who sought further training
in genres of their own interest. The most famous advanced composition elective courses at Harvard were Hill's English 5, first offered
in 1877, and Barrett Wendell's English 12, which he taught from
1884. Their work was continued by Dean Le Baron Russell Briggs
and Charles Townsend Copeland. 'In Harvard's English 5 and 12,'
according to Adams, 'Barrett Wendell and his associates allowed
students to write poetry and short stories, giving them detailed criticism of their work and information on publishing' (1993: 70). It is
these two classes which have been seen as the beginning of a formal
apprenticeship in literary craft at universities. Furthermore, as a result

of the number of writers who attended Harvard, or universities where graduates of its composition classes taught, the teachers of English 5 and 12 were considered to have had a profound influence on the direction of American literature.

While students were allowed to submit all forms of writing in these classes, including poems and stories, the central pedagogical tool of Harvard composition was the 'daily theme'. According to Briggs, it was Wendell who 'invented the "daily theme", as the result of his own practice in training his pen' (qtd in Howe 1924: 83). 'In the courses in composition, prescribed and elective alike,' Wendell wrote in 1895, 'little importance is attached to theoretical knowledge of rhetoric as distinguished from constant practice in writing under the most minute practicable criticism' (qtd in Brereton 1995: 130). Rather than undertaking the textbook study of grammatical rules and rhetorical tropes, students were required to choose their own topics on which to write daily themes, and to write constantly about their own observations and thoughts. Furthermore, rather than being 'corrected' according to formal rules of composition, the daily themes were critiqued by tutors and fellow students alike, according to how well they seemed to express the author's ideas.

The daily theme was not just a form of professional practice for writers, but a means of self-cultivation. It was an exercise in refining written representation of the thoughts produced by experience. Rather than expressing a unique self or releasing the creative spirit within, however, composition was the expression of an individual perspective on reality, based on sensory perception. With the daily theme, according to Rollo Walter Brown, Wendell 'would have his students look squarely at some little part of the world, try to catch the color or flavor of what they saw, and then write as significantly as possible' (qtd in Brereton 1995: 32).

For Myers, English composition was the beginning of Creative Writing, not because it provided a professional apprenticeship, or even because it accepted 'creative' work for credit, but because the study and practice of writing was employed within the university for its own sake; distinguished on the one hand from the rhetorical consideration of literature as a series of determined effects upon an audience, and on the other hand from philological research into literature. 'English composition', Myers asserts, 'established an alternative method for the higher study of literature. The exact nature of this method was steady (daily) writing in which flexibility of judgement, the capacity to devise an ad hoc solution to a unique problem of literary form, was emphasized over correctness as a means of giving order to descriptive perception and first hand experience' (1996: 55). What makes this a literary conception of composition, according to Myers, is that writing was governed by 'intrinsic' demands, the students' fidelity to their own experience. Composition was thus founded 'out of a constructivist belief that the ideal end of the study of literature is the making of literature' (36).

This emphasis on the 'literary' nature of composition seems too great, however. Wendell codified his teaching principles at Harvard in his popular textbook, *English Composition*, and in this book he collapses generic distinctions between all forms of writing into the single concept of 'style'. Style, for Wendell, is 'the expression of thought or emotion in written words; it applies equally to an epic, a sermon, a love-letter, an invitation to an evening party' (1896: 4). Wendell's students were required to criticise each other's fortnightly themes according to the principles expounded in his textbook, which broke the elements of style into words, sentences, paragraphs and whole compositions, and the qualities of style into clearness, force and elegance. It seems a far stretch to see this textbook as promoting the studying and writing of literature for its own sake. Nonetheless, according to Myers, Wendell's book '*English Composition* was also creative writing's first name; and though the name was later changed, the initial conception – the original motivation behind English composition and creative writing both – belonged to Wendell' (1996: 47).

If the daily theme was the main pedagogical device of composition, and criticism of student work was based in an understanding of literature which the daily theme was designed to promulgate, advanced composition must be seen in the broader context of composition in general. Furthermore, composition as a subject has been seen as a product of the scientific method which Myers suggests it was opposed to. Andrew Levy has argued that in the same way English studies sought academic credibility through a 'scientific' approach to the study of literature, composition was motivated by 'a belief that the technical aspects of English composition could be taught with the same rigor and discipline as chemistry or mathematics' (1993: 82). For James A. Berlin, Hill and Wendell were responsible for spreading what became known as 'current-traditional rhetoric', the main form of composition teaching until the 1960s. Despite its emphasis on constant writing, Berlin argues, current-traditional rhetoric neglected a consideration of the writing process. The emphasis on sensory experience in Wendell's concept of style perpetuated 'the faculty psychology of eighteenth-century rhetoric', found in the works of Blair and Campbell, and the neglect of the effects of writing on an audience in favour of the transparency of language as a device for expository communication was 'the triumph of the scientific and technical world view' (1984: 62).

If the origins of Creative Writing lie in the individual classes on versification, the short story and play-writing, which developed as professional specialisations of advanced composition, this is because composition established the institutional validity of submitting creative work for academic credit. The pedagogy of early writing classes, however, did not draw upon the refiguration of classical rhetoric in universities which was enacted by modern composition. This is why historical accounts of composition, such as those by Berlin, do not include or double as histories of Creative Writing. Instead, Creative Writing drew upon a critical tradition, a poetics rather than a rhetoric, and thus developed out of Literary Studies rather than composition.

Craft

In *The Culture and Commerce of the American Short Story*, Andrew Levy argues that the origins of the Creative Writing workshop can be found in the explosion of handbooks on short story writing at the end of the nineteenth century which 'codified and popularized the most seminal axioms of creative writing pedagogy' (1993: 104–5). These handbooks differed from Wendell's *English Composition* in that they were concerned with providing the mastery of a guild craft rather than elaborating more general rhetorical principles which could be applied to any act of written communication. And it is in these handbooks, as I pointed out in the introduction, that the phrase *poeta nascitur non fit* takes a practical turn and becomes the question *can writing be taught?* The question was posed in a self-conscious and defensive fashion in prefatorial remarks because this is exactly what handbooks tried to do. Rather than teaching an art, however, the success of which could be determined by absolute standards of aesthetic value, these handbooks generally professed to teach the composition of commercially successful magazine fiction (while still asserting that talent or keen observation of life were the necessary and unteachable qualities of a writer). This does not necessarily mean that they were designed to teach 'hack' fiction, but that the principles and guidelines for success were derived from a 'scientific' analysis of works which had been published and acclaimed. Acceptance by magazines was the criterion for success as these were the main outlets for short fiction.

Handbooks on story writing thus emerged in response to the demand for short fiction by mass-circulation magazines, and catered to the promise of pecuniary reward, celebrity and cultural cachet which these magazines offered to writers. 'The short story writer of the early twentieth century', according to Levy, 'was a muted version of the present-day pop star' (87). In *The Development of the American Short Story*, Fred Lewis Pattee points out that the immense popularity of O. Henry had an influence on the emergence of handbooks. 'His artistry was so striking and his methods so evident that even the novice was inspired to codify his laws and imitate his devices' ([1923] 1975: 368). What handbooks drew upon, however, and helped to codify (if somewhat dogmatically) was a nascent critical movement designed not only to analyse and define the short story as a distinct genre in its own right, but to canonise it as a distinctly American genre, as a form of writing which Americans excelled at because it developed out of the conditions of American life.

The seminal publication in this regard is Brander Matthews's *The Philosophy of the Short Story*, which was first printed as an anonymous magazine article in 1884, reprinted in an expanded version the following year, and finally issued as a book in 1901. Matthews opened this work by pointing out that writers were beginning to make critical pronouncements on the principles and the practice of the art of fiction, citing Walter Besant's 1884 lecture and Henry James's now canonical response. However, what had been neglected in these recent discussions, Matthews claimed, was a consideration of the short story. This form of fiction, he asserted, in fact deserved to be seen as a distinct genre in its own right, for it differed in kind, not just in length, from the novel. Matthews distinguished the 'Short-story' (with a capital and a hyphen) from the story which is merely short, as well as from the 'novelet', the published episode from a novel or the synopsis of a novel, the tale or amplified anecdote, and the sketch. What defined the Short-story was its 'essential unity of impression' (1901: 15), its 'single effect, complete and self-contained' (17), its 'compression, originality and ingenuity' with 'a touch of fantasy' (23).

Matthews acknowledged Edgar Allen Poe and Nathaniel Hawthorne as the writers who fashioned the short story as a modern genre, and as an American genre. 'In fact,' he claimed, 'Poe and Hawthorne are as American as any one can be' (41). As a result, 'in no language are there better . . . Short-stories than in English' (29). Furthermore, he asserted the 'superiority of the American Short-story over the British', suggesting that this was due to the immense interest of American magazines in fostering the short-story, while English magazines devoted more attention to the serialised three-volume novel.

In an appendix to the 1901 edition of his book Matthews acknowledged that, while he was the first to assert this generic distinguishing of the short story from the novel, he was only codifying what had been formulated decades earlier by Poe in his review of Hawthorne's *Twice Told Tales* and in his essay 'The Philosophy of Composition'. Matthews also pointed to several books which had appeared since his original essay was published in 1884, books which contributed to the critical tradition he had begun and helped to analyse and define the genre of the short story. Several of these were handbooks on how to write the short story. As Andrew Levy points out, the short-story handbooks which proliferated from the 1890s to the 1920s were permeated by the critical insights of Poe, drawing upon his lexicon and methods of analysis in order to fashion their definitions of the story and its mode of composition, and this was due to the mediating and codifying influence of Matthews's essay (1993: 124).

'The first decade of the new century', Pattee asserts, 'was the era of the short-story handbook. The first textbook worthy of noting was that by Charles R. Barrett, whose *Short Story Writing* bears the date 1898' ([1923] 1975: 364). The subtitle of this book is 'A Practical Treatise on the Art of the Short Story', and Barrett himself claimed in the preface to the 1900 edition that 'there is no book extant which treats solely of the technique of the short story' (9). Barrett asserts that the book is 'the result of a careful study' of the work of the 'masters of the short story' and the 'critical examination of several thousands of short stories written by amateurs' (7). The 'deductions' arising from this study allow Barrett to lay down the 'rules and principles' which will 'be of practical assistance to the novice in short story writing, from the moment the tale is dimly conceived until it is completed and ready for the editor's judgement' (7). Barrett acknowledges his debt to 'the frequent fragmentary articles on the short story, many of them by successful short story writers, published in current periodicals' (9). According to Pattee and Levy these fragmentary articles, of which Matthews's would have been one, were the beginnings of short-story criticism. 'But my greatest obligation', Barrett claims, 'is to a course in "The Art of the Short Story" – the first university course ever offered in that subject – conducted at the University of Chicago in 1896 by Dr. E.H. Lewis' (9).

Handbooks can thus be seen as the product of a nascent academic and critical enterprise to study the short story. According to Pattee the proliferation and popularity of short fiction in magazines could no longer be ignored, 'even though one considered it a trivial form of literature', and 'critical journals of the 'nineties made much of the problem' ([1923] 1975: 364). This interest began with 'author-itative writers', such as William Dean Howells, who contributed 'careful papers' to the magazines (364). It was 'a shoal of lesser critics' who went to extremes such as claiming the short story as a genre naturally expressive of American life and ruled by laws as definite as the sonnet. The handbooks which followed participated in this critical enterprise by orienting these laws towards those who wished to practise the short-story form, and many were written by univer-sity or college teachers with the intention of serving as textbooks.

'By 1910,' according to Pattee, 'the short story had become a distinct subject for study in American colleges and universities' (365). A number of correspondence courses also developed to take advan-tage of the popularity of story writing. In a 1923 article for *The English Journal* Pattee criticised these courses and handbooks for reducing short-story writing to 'a trade-school matter, a handwork vocation to be acquired by mere diligence and mastery of technique' (1923: 440). Two years later H.L. Mencken blasted this entire acad-emic and commercial enterprise as 'the trade of manufacturing hack fiction for the cheap magazines' ([1925] 1991: 537), which was doing 'gross damage to the American short story' (539).

Practical guides were not the only books written about the short story, however. They co-existed with and relied upon books which recounted the history of the genre, and books which critically exam-ined its methods and techniques. Bliss Perry's *A Study of Prose Fiction* (1902), for instance, was an important critical contribution which only touched upon the question of whether the form could be taught to aspiring writers, and this in the context of how much an under-standing of the author's craft contributed to critical knowledge of the short story. Since all agreed that only technique or method could be taught, and this was arrived at by the critical study of existing stories, handbooks came to serve the double purpose of instructing writers in their craft and guiding readers in their appreciation. And many books claimed specifically *not* to be handbooks. In *The Short Story: A Technical and Literary Study*, Ethan Allen Cross claimed that his book was written for readers 'in the hope that it may be an aid to them in getting at the meaning of these stories through an understanding of their construction' (1914: vii). While asserting that it was not a manual on the writing of short stories, he pointed out that the 'analysis of the structure of the short story from the reader's point of view may be helpful to the beginner in writing' (viii). For Cross, the purpose of his book was to demonstrate that 'there is such a thing as The Technic of the Short Story' (viii).

This idea of technic is indebted, once again, to Brander Matthews. Matthews's 1905 essay, 'An Apology for Technic', can be read not only as a defence of formalist analysis, but as a description of the critical foundations of the discipline of Creative Writing. For Matthews the critic is properly concerned to approach a literary work as the result of three elements: an author's native gift, his technic and his character. Talent and character cannot be altered and can only subjectively be debated. 'Technic, however,' Matthews claims, 'can be had for the asking. Anyone can acquire it if he will but pay the price – the needful study and experiment. Any man can make himself a master of his craft, if he will but serve his apprenticeship loyally' ([1905] 1957: 217). It is this belief in the ability to acquire the skills of writing intellectually which enabled Creative Writing to develop as a discipline. Yet what Matthews is discussing is not Creative Writing, but Literary Studies. He believed that an understanding of technic was just as vital to the critic as to the writer, since both are concerned with the nature of literature. The critical study of technic, he notes, develops from the tradition of writer-critics; Dryden, Wordsworth and Poe were all concerned with discussing craft in their critical works. A critical consideration of technic, long the domain of writers, according to Matthews, is the means by which new literary conventions are developed, and the means by which knowledge of literature progresses.

According to Levy the scientific tone of handbooks, in which they systematically analysed examples of short stories and from this deduced principles of writing, paralleled the scientific approach to writing in universities. This is a valid connection if the courses these handbooks were often attached to are seen as professional specialisations of composition. However, the tone of handbooks also demonstrates the influence of a certain concept of authorship. Levy claims that Poe 'was, without question, the first creative writing teacher of the modern era' (1993: 99–100). If handbooks on writing drew on the work of Poe to construct a formalist criticism of the short story and develop a pedagogy for Creative Writing, then they also drew on Poe's 'philosophy' of composition to help develop a figure of authorship. One aspect of composition which handbooks emphasised was labour, taking pains. As Barrett wrote in the earliest handbook, the 'Heaven-sent call to write' is 'but a summons to labor – and to labor the severest and most persistent' (1900: 8). Handbooks thus participated in the promotion of a certain figure of the writer, a figure necessary for Creative Writing to emerge: that of the Modernist craftsman.

'[I]f poetry comes not as naturally as the leaves to a tree,' wrote Keats, 'it had better not come at all' ([1818] 1963: 117). In 'The Philosophy of Composition', Poe contests this Romantic belief: 'Most writers – poets in especial – prefer having it understood that they compose by a species of fine frenzy – an ecstatic intuition' ([1846] 1984: 14). Poe claimed, however, that he does not have 'the least difficulty in recalling to mind the progressive steps of any of my compositions' (14). So he set out to retrace the steps by which he wrote his popular poem, 'The Raven', concentrating on his conscious desire to produce certain effects. 'It is my design', he wrote, 'to render it manifest that no one point in its composition is referrible either to accident or intuition – that the work proceeded, step by step, to its completion with the precision and rigid consequence of a mathematical problem' (14–15).

There has been persistent conjecture that 'The Philosophy of Composition' was a deliberate parody. One person who did take Poe's essay seriously, however, was the French poet Paul Valéry. In an 1889 essay, 'On Literary Technique', Valéry describes what he calls a 'totally new and modern conception of the poet' (1985: 315). This poet 'is no longer the disheveled madman who writes a whole poem in the course of one feverish night; he is a cool scientist, almost an algebraist, in the service of a subtle dreamer' (315). According to T.S. Eliot, in his introduction to Valéry's *Art of Poetry*, Valéry 'invented, and was to impose upon his age', this 'new conception of the poet' (1958: xix). It is this figure of the author as a conscious, dedicated craftsman that ushered in the twentieth century and the writing workshop.

'The habit of long labor at poetry', Valéry wrote, 'has accustomed me to consider all speech and all writing as work in progress that can nearly always be taken up again and altered; and I consider *work itself* as having its own value, generally much superior to that which the crowd attaches only to the *product*' ([1899] 1985: 177). Work, as in industry, is important to literary craftsmen because it demonstrates their conscious control, especially important as authorship became increasingly 'professionalised' towards the end of the nineteenth century. In a Creative Writing class, likewise, students cannot wait for the leaves on the trees; they must work. For Valéry the work of writing itself is far more poetically fulfilling because it is the very practice of writing, of playing with form, that constitutes the poetic act. For the writing workshop, where exercises in form are prescribed and where something needs to be learned, the ability to demonstrate the development of a work is often more important than the final work itself. The possibility that a work can always be altered is necessary for the writing workshop, where a manuscript is approached as something which can be improved; it is work in progress.

This valorisation of artistic labour, of the work-value of literature over its use-value, has been called by Roland Barthes the 'Flaubertisation' of writing ([1953] 1968: 66). Flaubert is famous for agonising for days on end until he found exactly the right word or phrase for what he was trying to describe. He himself tutored the short-story writer Guy de Maupassant, prescribing him exercises each week, after which they would meet to discuss his work. 'The author in his book', according to Flaubert, 'must be like God in the universe, everywhere present and nowhere visible. Art being a second nature, the creator of this nature must employ analogous procedures' ([1852] 1981: 319). In the process of writing, however, Flaubert divested this creation of the spontaneous or unconscious ease with which it had been associated.

The promotion of Flaubert as a role model for young writers is obvious in the work of Paul Engle, who became the most influential director of the Iowa Writers' Workshop. In his introduction to *Midland*, a 1961 anthology of poetry and fiction from the workshops, Engle quotes Flaubert approvingly several times, especially his warning to be wary of inspiration. In his introduction to *On Creative Writing*, a 1964 'handbook' which he edited, Engle writes: '[a]ll those writers who have commented on their craft agree that a work of art is work. How could the joining of passion and idea in slippery words be anything but a labor?' (12). He goes on to describe *Madame Bovary* as the 'first really modern novel' before praising its method of composition, making explicit the link between modernity and craftsmanship (12).

Literature from the inside

In a 1931 essay in the *English Journal*, entitled 'Report on Creative Writing in Colleges', Snow Longley Housh commented on the results of a survey conducted at a number of universities and colleges. 'Of the sixty-three colleges, forty-one have some form of creative writing as part of the curriculum. Doubtless all colleges encourage creative writing as an extra-curricular activity' (672). 'But college creative writing at this time', D.G. Myers claims after referring to Housh's article, 'was a vague and aimless pursuit, one-half composition, one-half creative self-expression. Its *form* was Barrett Wendell's gift to the course, while its *content* was Hughes Mearns's' (1996: 123). The pedagogy, it might be added, was Brander Matthews's. Myers nonetheless asserts that 'creative writing as a university discipline was not instituted as the unforeseen consequence of a dozen haphazard experiments – or even three dozen – operating under nearly as many aliases. It was a deliberate effort carried out for an articulate purpose in a single place. As such it was founded by Norman Foerster' (124). This is a reference to the precursor of the Iowa Writers' Workshop: the School of Letters founded by Foerster at the University of Iowa in 1931, where Creative Writing was granted higher-degree status as part of a unified literary programme in graduate studies including criticism, and scholarly research in language and literary history.

Stephen Wilbers, in *The Iowa Writers' Workshop: Origins, Emergence, and Growth* (1980), asserts that the Creative Writing programme at Iowa has its origins in the university's support for the milieu of writers' clubs and an emerging regional midwestern literature which flourished in Iowa in the late nineteenth and early twentieth centuries. Classes in Creative Writing have been taught at the University of Iowa since 1895. From the course outlines in the University Calendar it can be seen that these classes were designed to provide students with an understanding of various literary genres (such as poetry, the short story and the play) through practice and study, thus combining writing instruction with Brander Matthews's notion of 'technic'. For instance, the outline for the first such course, Verse-making Class, read: 'Practice in metrical composition in the fixed forms of verse such as the heroic couplet, Spenserian stanza, ode, rondeau, sonnet, ballad, and song. Analysis of the best examples of these forms in English poetry. Informal discussions of artistic questions' (*University of Iowa Calendar, 1895–6*: 38). The teaching of English at Iowa at this time was organised into three groups: Composition & Rhetoric, English Literature and English Language. In the first group English was taught as a means of expression, drawing on the textbooks of Hill and Wendell, and all classes in writing were included in this category. The writing class which Edwin Ford Piper, the senior literary figure in the English department, taught from 1922 and which later became known as the 'workshop' was called Advanced Composition.

The impact of Norman Foerster's arrival in 1930 is subject to dispute, as indicated by the memory of several contemporaries. According to Wilbur Schramm, 'without Foerster there would have been no Writer's Workshop. He must have that credit, whatever else we may say about him.'[3] While Schramm indicates that Foerster provided the main impetus for an expanded writing programme, Paul Engle is more qualified in his support of Foerster when he claims that 'although he put the School of Letters rubric over all of this, already there was a tradition here for him to draw on'.[4] Janet Piper, a graduate student at Iowa when Foerster arrived, claims that her husband, Edwin Ford Piper, 'was technically in charge of "creative writing" for ten years',[5] although it was not formally organised into anything resembling a programme, before 'Norman Foerster came down / On a small Iowa town / Like a wolf on the fold.'[6] For Piper, Foerster was 'Irving Babbitt's errand-boy, with the arrogance one associates with the Toady-Come-Into-Power' (*Retrospect* 5). She describes his arrival as the imposition of a regime, as a counter-revolution against the spirit of regionalism being fostered at Iowa. The establishment of the Workshop, she argues, for which Paul Engle was 'carefully groomed' as director, was 'intended to "centralize" the creative writing programme in order to further the aims and purposes of the new regime'.[7] This regime, according to Piper, was a critical movement known as the New Humanism, which, like the Modernist revolution in poetry, was supposedly sympathetic to fascism.

What changes did this new regime make? The umbrella category of Rhetoric & Composition was dropped and the prefix 'Imaginative Writing' was added to the existing classes in Narration, the Essay, the Short Story, and Playwriting. Piper's 'workshop', Advanced Composition, became 'Imaginative Writing: Advanced'. This grouping together of certain classes according to their supposed common denominator – the imagination – indicated Foerster's desire to construct Creative Writing as a 'discipline' which could contribute to his planned reformation of English Studies. The study and practice of criticism was to be the centrepiece of this reformation, and the institutional site was to be the newly established graduate School of Letters in which a 'creative' thesis could be submitted for a higher degree. The idea of a creative thesis being submitted for a masters degree was already being promoted by Piper and Carl Seashore, although it was Foerster's wish to also implement it at the doctoral level. Foerster's target was regionalism only in so much as it hindered his deployment of Creative Writing alongside criticism against his real target – literary scholarship as it was practised in universities.

In 1937 John Crowe Ransom pointed out that the 'most important recent diversion from the orthodox course of literary studies was that taken by the New Humanists' ([1937] 1984: 96). In the 1920s and 1930s the New Humanism was part of what Gerald Graff has called a 'united critical front' opposed to the science-oriented research which took place in English departments (1987: 126).[8] Foerster described this research as linguistic philology, a study of the evolution of language as manifested in literature, and literary philology, the historical study of the sources, influences, and cultural and social context of literary works. If on the one hand, university professors produced scholarly research about literature, they also indulged in personal impressionistic appreciation of the classics. Foerster thus referred scornfully to professors of literature as 'scholar-dilettantes' (1929: 30).

Foerster, following the work of Irving Babbitt and Paul Elmer More, was a major propagandist for the New Humanism. This was a movement conceived in reaction to the twin influences of science and Romanticism on modern cultural life. For Foerster, both were founded on a concept of natural evolution which described literature in terms of organic growth (arising out of the author's vegetable genius, the evolution of genres, or the historical and social context of a specific period). This concept of literature as a natural organism led to a relativity of standards and resulted in a pedantic, fact-based literary scholarship content to describe literature in terms of its authorial sources, its literary influences and its historical environment, but refusing to enter into a critical judgement (beyond personal impressionistic responses). It also produced a literature deformed by a lack of absolute (classical) standards, conceived instead by authors and readers as individual expression or realist documentation.

Rather than being a product of nature, literature for Foerster was a human achievement to be produced, ideally, in a context of timeless values and, through its aesthetic effects, to establish ethical standards for the conduct of life. The New Humanism was devoted to the development of criticism as an attempt to establish humanistic and traditional standards for identifying universal values which can be used to judge literature, standards which would recognise the equal and interrelated functions of aesthetics and ethics in a literary work.

The role of Creative Writing which Foerster envisaged was as an aid to criticism, providing a practical insight into the workings of literature. As a by-product it was also a means of providing a humanistic education for aspiring writers by exposing them to other areas of scholarship in the School of Letters before undertaking their creative thesis. This latter goal was influenced by Foerster's Arnoldian view of the relationship between literature and criticism. 'Before a new order of creative literature can arrive,' Foerster wrote in *American Criticism*, 'the way must be prepared by criticism' ([1928] 1962: 256). This means that criticism creates a base of humanist knowledge for writers and readers to draw upon, rather than helping authors to write. Criticism will keep writers in touch with 'the permanent and the universal' in literature, so that they are not slaves to their own individualism, and will provide an audience capable of judging literature according to the standards of value founded in tradition.

In 1931 Foerster delivered a paper at the opening of the School of Letters, which was reprinted as the opening essay in *Literary Scholarship: Its Aims and Methods*, a manifesto of the School of Letters. Entitled 'The Study of Letters', this essay reviews most of Foerster's arguments from earlier books. For Foerster, the idea of research was too narrowly associated with scientific method and he argued for a more traditional and humanistic understanding of scholarship to replace the research model. The School of Letters was a way of reviving the rounded Renaissance scholar and repairing a split between writers and critics on the one hand, and researchers and historians on the other (1941: 12). The underlying ideal of the School of Letters, then, was to resolve the struggle between scholars and critics by merging the characteristics of both in a vision of the 'American scholar' as a man of letters steeped in a humanist tradition and able to contribute to a variety of literary fields. The practical aim was '[t]o restore a vital relationship between scholarship and letters by preparing scholars for careers as teachers (collegiate as well as graduate), as critics, or as writers' (21). A liberal education would reproduce this ideal figure of the humanist scholar in the teacher, and provide the necessary background for those who would specialise in various areas of 'scholarship', whether they be literary or critical.

Foerster recognised the importance of scientific research into language and literary history, but argued that 'today a new need in the history of scholarship has again arisen, the need of a scholarship more closely affiliated with the creative and critical interests of letters, and more concerned with the values which the humanities have to offer a world threatened with a barbarism expertly scientific in war and peace' (20). His school would 'encourage a common intellectual life among students of letters', where letters was integrated with history, fine arts, philosophy and religion. Students would be provided with a background in the other humanities before being offered 'a rigorous discipline in the specialized types of literary activity – the study of language, the study of literary history, the theory and practice of literary criticism, and the art of imaginative writing' (20).

Of these disciplines, Foerster explains, 'both language and literary history are background subjects, ancillary to the main enterprise, which is the interpretation and evaluation of imaginative literature, of the poem, the play, the novel. Finally arrived at literature itself, how are we to deal with it? How are we to come to understand it, in the fullest sense?' (24). The answer, he suggests, is learning how to read, and by this he means learning the art of literary criticism. Referring to the French *explication de textes*, Foerster advocated 'practice in close analysis of concrete literary works or passages' as well as the more abstract study of literary theory to aid in this reading (25). One more method of aiding critical interpretation and evaluation was the practice of writing:

> The scholar, being primarily a reader, must learn to read well. He must also learn to write well, within the limits of his talent. One of the best ways of understanding imaginative literature is to write it, since the act of writing – the selection of materials, the shaping of them, the recasting and revising – enables the student to repeat what the makers of literature have done, to see the processes and the problems of authorship from the inside. The time he spends in writing poems, stories, or plays, if he has any talent whatever, will not be lost; pen, paper, and wastebasket are the apparatus of a laboratory second only in importance to the central laboratory of the literary scholar – the library. If he accomplishes nothing more, he will acquire the habit of writing about literature in a language tolerably fresh, alert, and apt.
>
> (26)

This is what I call *reading from the inside*: the practice of writing as a means of developing literary appreciation and critical skills. It is obvious that the classes offered to both undergraduates and graduates in the department of English with the prefix 'Imaginative Writing' were perceived by Foerster as fulfilling this function of reading from the inside. Imaginative Writing was also one of the four disciplines which graduate students could specialise in after they had developed a 'general literary culture' and 'passed a searching general examination' (27). If the student's ability, Foerster explained, 'lies in imaginative writing, he will seek both to discipline his vision and to master his medium', and the result would be 'a work of imaginative literature, the standard . . . being equivalence to the quality of the books issued by the best American publishers' (27). For Foerster the discipline of Creative Writing operated in classes as a practical aid to the comprehension of literature, which would be useful to critics, and in graduate theses as a specialisation within a broad course of study which provided aspiring writers with a liberal education.

In his contribution on 'Literary Criticism' to *Literary Scholarship*, Austin Warren diverges from Foerster's emphasis on ethical standards, leaning towards a description of aesthetic criticism when he discusses the role of Creative Writing. 'If the proper reading of poetry begins with the reconstruction of the poet's meaning, then it is important to be able to experience poetry as the poet experiences it. If, furthermore, the total meaning of poetry cannot be disengaged from its technical devices, then to write verses oneself is a chief help to the comprehension of other men's' (1941: 172). Warren discusses not only the practice of writing, but a particular type of criticism which derives from a writer's perspective. 'It follows that, for the aesthetic criticism of literature, some proficiency in the writing of its forms (the poem, the play, the novel) is highly salutary. One reads in a new way, with a fresh attention, when he studies the craft of a writer in the hope that it will aid his own; and that practical concentration leaves a permanent perceptiveness of how a writer sees and how he translates what he sees into words' (172). So as well as promoting the practice of writing as an aid to criticism, Creative Writing promotes a type of reading similar to Brander Matthews's notion of technic. This is Warren's justification for 'imaginative writing' alongside philosophy, linguistics and literary history as 'disciplines requisite to criticism' (172).

What characterises Creative Writing as a discipline in its own right? The aim of Creative Writing itself is provided by Wilbur Schramm in his chapter on 'Imaginative Writing'. Schramm's first move is to assert that, if the split between scholars and writers effected by the emphasis on scientific research in universities is to be repaired, imaginative writing must be considered an 'honorable discipline' alongside language, history and criticism in the graduate school. To prove this he argues that the 'creative process involves both hard thinking and imaginative insight', thus emphasising the rigour and labour involved (1941: 182). He also suggests that 'modern psychology' has demonstrated that 'the process of creating art is essentially the same as the process of creating a new formula, a new philosophic synthesis, or any other new birth in the world of ideas' (183). As proof of this shared process he cites Graham Wallas's influential book, *The Art of Thought*, with its four stages of 'Preparation, Incubation, Illumination, and Verification'. In other words, Schramm is appealing to the twentieth-century view of creativity as the source of all human endeavour, which I outlined in the first chapter, as a justification for Creative Writing.

Schramm then endeavours to answer the question, 'What has imaginative writing to contribute to other advanced disciplines?' (191). He asserts that 'writing as a scholarly discipline would tend to raise the level of *all* writing done by scholars' (191). Creative Writing is also said to provide insight into art. Schramm is not talking about Foerster's practice of writing in this instance, but Warren's emphasis on a particular practice of reading. 'The imaginative and critical discipline of reading a poem as though writing it would be salutary for the scholar who tends to treat literature as a piece of history . . . and encourage studies of literature as an *art*' (194). Schramm also asserts that 'the study of writing should make for better teachers' (195–6), which is the goal of graduate study. The ideal, again, is Foerster's man of letters. 'After all, is not the ideal professor of literature, as we envisage him, a combination of the attributes of scholar, critic, and writer?' (196).

Schramm turns, then, to what help can be offered the actual writer. He argues, firstly, that not every writer can profit from university training, but that the university offers 'vocational training' (200). Since most writers cannot support themselves by writing they turn to journalism or hack work which, for Schramm, 'is patently less desirable than any of the supplementary vocations the literary graduate school has to offer, of which the chief are teaching, editing, and professional criticism' (201). He briefly touches on the idea of patronage: that having undertaken graduate study and been able to return as teachers, writers 'have found a profession which offers unrivalled opportunities of leisure and contemplation' (202). Schramm also brings up the concept of apprenticeship, first likening Creative Writing to Renaissance art schools, then seeing the university as a substitute for informal gatherings of writers:

> But most of all the university offers stimulation: living in the company of young persons who want to write, working in an atmosphere where good poetry, fiction, criticism, are constantly being written and published, cooperating in authorship by discussing and criticizing manuscripts. How well this system of group apprenticeship can work was shown brilliantly by the writers who gathered in the nineteen twenties around John Crowe Ransom at Vanderbilt.
>
> (205)

Schramm points out how many of these writers were now editors and teachers as well as writers, arguing that 'many universities can reproduce or approximate the conditions under which the Vanderbilt group flourished' (205). Finally he turns to the 'practical' question: 'How is writing to be taught – insofar as it can be taught?' (209). Here he fudges, asserting that 'the essentials are the master, the apprentice, the group, and around them the intellectual wealth of the university' (210). The master is a writer who is also adept at a particular type of criticism, at reading 'with an artist's eyes' (210), the apprentice is the graduate student and aspiring writer, the group is the workshop of fellow writers designed to approximate the gatherings of the Vanderbilt poets, and the intellectual wealth of the university that which provides a liberal education. 'Advanced students will produce poems, plays, stories, novels, some of them very good. The students who are graduated from the university, whether or not they have published good writing, will have a chance to see much *in* literature, as well as learn much *about* it' (211).

If anything can be gathered from the School of Letters it is that Creative Writing was only one element in an attempt to establish criticism as the central discipline of the humanistic study of letters, and that in order for Creative Writing to operate as a discipline it depended upon the operation of criticism as a pedagogical device. The sort of criticism which would become operationalised in the writing workshop, however, was not Foerster's ethically oriented and tradition-bound New Humanism, but the craft-oriented aesthetic criticism hinted at by Warren and Schramm. Foerster's vision of reading from the inside was only a vague concept that the practice of *writing* could serve as a preliminary aid to critical understanding by providing an 'inner comprehension of art' (1929: 60). Responding to claims that the New Humanism neglected the aesthetic qualities of literature, Foerster suggested that his 'sponsoring' of Creative Writing in the graduate school at Iowa indicates a sympathy for the New Critics ([1941] 1966: 58). Indeed, it was the practice of critical *reading* as an aid to writing, which developed from handbooks and courses on short-story writing and was reformed by the New Critics, that enabled the pedagogical development of the workshop.

The crucial transition period from 'Imaginative Writing' as a disciplinary element of the graduate School of Letters to the Writers' Workshop as an independent programme leading to the award of an MFA was from 1939 to 1942; a period from the death of Edwin Ford Piper to the appointment of Paul Engle as the director of the Workshop. These years are coincident with the rise of the New Criticism. 'It is possible', Gerald Graff has claimed, 'to fix 1937–41 as the turning point for the consolidation of criticism in the university' (1987: 152). 1937 was the year in which John Crowe Ransom's seminal essay, 'Criticism Inc.', appeared, and this was followed by books such as *Understanding Poetry* (1938), *Modern Poetry and the Tradition* (1939) and *The New Criticism* (1941). Furthermore, the journals founded or taken over during this period, such as *Southern Review* and *Kenyon Review*, espoused the principles of a movement which, from 1941, was being called the New Criticism (see Muller).

'The New Criticism', Jonathan Culler concisely argues, 'originates as an argument about the nature of poetry in T.S. Eliot's *The Sacred Wood*, and as a conservative Southern resistance to values associated with science, industrialization and urbanization' (1988: 9). Eliot's influence can be found in his (early) insistence that poetry be treated as poetry, in his theory of the impersonality of poetry, in his authority as a poet-critic, and in his refiguration of the poetic tradition which downgraded Romantic and Victorian poetry and drew a line of more 'intellectual' poetry from the Metaphysical poets, via French Symbolism, to Modernism. The group of poets at Vanderbilt University who established the journal *The Fugitive* in 1921, and who formed the basis of the Agrarian movement, publishing *I'll Take My Stand* in 1930, also wrote this self-consciously Modernist poetry, the sort of poetry they wished to canonise when they moved into the academy as teachers and critics. While the New Criticism is thus vitally linked to Modernist literature, it nonetheless owes a debt of lineage to Romanticism. Not only did the early Agrarian sentiments of poets such as Ransom and Tate link them to Romantic anti-indus-trialism, but the New Critics shared Coleridge's opposition of poetry to science, and his view of poetry as the symbolic reconciliation of discordant opposites. Frank Kermode comprehensively traces this relationship in *Romantic Image* (1957).

Despite the differences of the critics usually grouped under this title, the New Criticism came to denote a common interest in the evaluative judgement and non-reductive analysis of individual literary works: in order to establish how they create an organic unity out of conflicting elements within the verbal structure, realised in terms such as irony, tension and paradox. As the New Criticism became estab-lished as a pedagogical device in universities (mainly through the influence of the textbook *Understanding Poetry*) with its emphasis on close reading or practical criticism, its principles became inscribed in prohibitive terms such as the Intentional Fallacy, the Affective Fallacy, the Didactic Heresy and the Heresy of Paraphrase. These terms indicate how the New Criticism defined itself in opposition to 'extrinsic' approaches to literature (to use Wellek and Warren's phrase). The construction of the autonomous aesthetic function of literature is further indicated by the titles of books such as the *Well-wrought Urn* and *The Verbal Icon*.

What is the connection between Creative Writing and the New Criticism? The New Criticism was successful in gaining acceptance into English departments over other competing critical movements, including the New Humanism, for three reasons: (1) unlike other movements it relied upon the literary authority of critics who were also poets. According to Gerald Graff, 'many of the first critics to achieve a foothold in the university did so on the strength of their poetry rather than their criticism. It is worth pondering the probability that the critical movement would not have succeeded in the university had it not been tied to creative writing, from which it was soon to part company' (1987: 153); (2) it devised an operational pedagogy – practical criticism – to promote its views of literature; (3) practical criticism was designed to analyse and interpret 'difficult' Modernist poetry, such as *The Waste Land*, hence providing the grounds for its institutional canonisation.

While Foerster provided a rationale for the place of Creative Writing in Literary Studies, the workshop developed and became the dominant mode of teaching writing because of the influence of the New Criticism. Creative Writing became an institutional site for the literary authority of writers, the close scrutiny of individual student manuscripts relied upon practical criticism, and Creative Writing was itself concerned with the production of contemporary literature.

'Practical criticism,' according to Hugh Bredin, 'as a teaching device, means the close and attentive reading of literary texts, usually poetry, usually by a small group, under the guidance of a tutor' (1986: 27). This could easily describe the writing workshop, where criticism is applied to student manuscripts as well as literary texts. D.G. Myers has even claimed that 'the method that came to be known as "practical criticism" or "close reading" was founded upon the sort of technical discussion of poetic problems that would occur among a group of poets', in particular the Fugitive group at Vanderbilt (1996: 131). It will be remembered that Schramm envisaged the workshop as an approximation of the conditions of the Fugitive group and praised the members of this group who went on to forge teaching or editing careers. And of course it was Fugitive poets such as Ransom, Tate and Robert Penn Warren who became major figures of the New Criticism. Cleanth Brooks suggests that his ideas on the necessity of tension and unity between individual words in the whole poem were gained from the Fugitives' poetry before I.A. Richards's *Practical Criticism* displayed this concept in critical commentary (Brooks 1981: 589). Indeed, R.P. Blackmur, who at least one commentator has claimed was responsible for the 'invention' of New Criticism, 'earned his keep' teaching Creative Writing with Allen Tate at Princeton University's Creative Arts Programme (Fraser 1981: 540).

In 1940 Allen Tate wrote a short article, entitled 'We Read as Writers', for *Princeton Alumni Weekly*, describing his first year of teaching Creative Writing in the Creative Arts Programme. Tate begins by defining literature 'in the ordinary sense of the word – fiction, poetry, literary criticism; and it is these kinds of literature that people cannot be taught to write' (505). While writing cannot be taught, however, he argues that it is possible to form a 'Creative Writing group' (505). Such a group provides an authorised place for writers in the university and gives them a 'current of fresh ideas', Tate says, recalling Matthew Arnold's concept of criticism with this phrase. At Princeton this group took place in freshman year, rather than at the graduate level. 'Occasionally such groups have formed spontaneously,' Tate points out. 'I was a member of one in a southern university in 1921' (505). This was the group of poets who founded *The Fugitive*, and 'of the original seven members, three became professional men of letters' (505). Tate's plan was to approximate the conditions for such a group at Princeton, which, if it did not produce any writers, would at least provide for students a 'knowledge of the conditions under which literature is written' (505).

In his Creative Writing group at Princeton, Tate pursued a policy of non-intervention; no grades were awarded, and readings and exercises were voluntary. He discussed student manuscripts in individual meetings, but in group gatherings 'we are groups of readers, not writers, for the moment; but we read as writers' (506). Since writing cannot be taught, his aim was to prepare students to teach themselves to write by a particular practice of reading. Tate describes this reading practice by establishing an analogy with architecture; one can trace the historical origins of the architectural style of various buildings, or one can study how the building was actually constructed. This knowledge of construction is vital for those who wish to 'put up buildings ourselves' (506). Tate then goes on to argue that '[w]e study literature today from various historical points of view – as if nobody ever again intended to write any more of it . . . The official academic point of view is that all the literature has been written, and is now a branch of history' (506). This is precisely the sort of argument employed to promote criticism and the study of contemporary literature in the university. The 'Creative Writing group . . . is a group of intensive readers . . . in so far as it is possible we try to read a certain poem as if we were writing it. It becomes a practical problem, which is the first kind of problem that confronts the imaginative writer' (506).

This short article by Tate is an important document in the history of English Studies. For a start, it had an obvious influence on contributors to *Literary Scholarship*, which was published in the following year. Wilbur Schramm made the same argument that the workshop could approximate the conditions which produced the Fugitive group at Vanderbilt. He also quoted this article directly in his attempt to justify the emphasis of Creative Writing on the reading of literature. Tate's idea of reading as a writer, of studying how a literary work is put together by its writer, became the dominant pedagogical mode of the workshop, as we will see in the next chapter.

Tate's article, however, was also used to justify the presence of *criticism* in the university. Austin Warren displays its influence in his discussion of aesthetic criticism in *Literary Scholarship*. And in a 1940 editorial in *Kenyon Review*, entitled 'Mr. Tate and the Professors', John Crowe Ransom – who had himself taught Creative Writing at Vanderbilt (see K. Adams 1993: 94) – drew attention to Tate's article. Ransom points out that Tate 'is not the ordinary university professor. He has generally had his own vocation as an actual creative writer and critic, and only very occasionally the kind of official connection with literature that goes with teaching in a university' (1940: 348). This is a means of establishing Tate's credibility, but Ransom reiterates Tate's argument that he cannot teach students how to write, that he can only 'teach them how to read, and thereby, and only indirectly, how to write' (348). He then draws attention to how Tate's reading differs from that offered by professors who provide historical readings of literature. It is reading which is concerned with the structure of works of art.

Ransom reminds us that Tate 'defines the project of creative writing indifferently under three heads: as fiction, as verse, and as literary criticism' (349), before arguing that the 'most powerful impeachment of the official policy of the professors, if it deserves making at all, would have to do with their failure to teach the act of criticism, rather than their failure to teach the making of fiction or verse, which they might have some ground for regarding as a vocational activity' (349–50). So Ransom twists Tate's argument for Creative Writing (which includes criticism) into an argument purely for criticism. Ransom goes on to argue that 'the observations made in Mr. Tate's short article have helped to crystallize some editorial intentions' (350) to the extent that he organised a symposium to be held in both the *Kenyon Review* and the *Southern Review*. Cleanth Brooks's contribution to this symposium, 'Literary History vs. Criticism', also draws upon Tate's article to defend the role of criticism, while ignoring the role of Creative Writing in the university.

Tate's view of reading as a writer was also deployed by Cleanth Brooks and Robert Penn Warren in *Understanding Fiction* (1943), the companion to their highly successful *Understanding Poetry*. For Brooks and Warren a work of fiction is an organic unity comprised of an ironic tension between conflicting elements. The theme or idea of that work is not expressed mechanically by the fictional structure, but is one structural element in organic relationship with other more formal elements such as plot, style, tone and character. In effect, this textbook applies New Critical views of poetry to fiction. It also promotes Henry James's view of fiction (and they quote James approvingly) over Walter Besant's, who can be seen as the progenitor of handbooks.

This meant that commercial magazine fiction was not to be considered literature because, rather than constituting an organic unity, such stories were written to elicit a 'stock response' from readers. As a result, the view of composition as a 'bag of tricks', as 'the mechanical manipulation of characters and scenes according to a set formula' (Brookes and Warren 1943: 569) designed to produce this stock response, was rejected in favour of a more organic and unified view of the creative process. This is obviously an attack on handbooks and the short-story courses which supported them. 'A good writer', Brookes and Warren assert, 'knows that the technique of fiction involves not the mere exploiting of a bag of tricks, but the careful study of the possible relationships among the numerous elements which go to make up a piece of fiction' (570). An appendix of these elements is provided, designed to serve 'a double function, a function for the student reader of fiction and for the student writer of fiction' (xii). Rather than outlining isolated devices for mechanical manipulation, however, this appendix describes formal elements which supposedly can only be understood when examined in organic tension with each other in individual works. The 'careful study of the possible relationships' between these elements, which constitutes the technique of fiction and provides an understanding of the compositional process, is thus to be attained by a process of critical reading.

Furthermore, in line with Mearns, students are encouraged to look within themselves for material, rather than producing stock responses through the manipulation of rhetorical devices.

> The imitation of particular effects distracts the student from the candid exploration of his own feelings and attitudes; the imitation in terms of principles should give him the instruments by which he can explore his own feelings and attitudes and realize them in form. This is only one way of saying that the only way to teach something about writing may be through a discipline in critical reading.
> (xiii)

Hence *Understanding Fiction* is an argument that the New Criticism provides a pedagogy for literary study *and* for Creative Writing. Creative Writing was yet another arena for criticism to establish itself in the university, and thus provided a credible institutional alternative to the handbook or the extension or correspondence course in short-story writing.

The influence of the New Criticism can be seen in R.V. Cassill's 1962 handbook, *Writing Fiction*. Whereas *Understanding Fiction* stressed that only the practice of criticism could teach something about writing, Cassill's idea of 'reading as a writer' emphasises the notion of the organic unity of the text as a key to understanding the creative process itself. He thus draws attention to the writer's task, rather than the critic's. 'No choice of character, action, language, names, or anything else is an isolated one. Each successive choice made as the writing progresses has to be made with respect for what has already been established. This is a respect for what I will call the overall unity of fiction' (9–10). In other words, the organic unity of a work is a result of conscious aesthetic decisions, and the author is guided by a need to impose unity on the chaos of experience. 'You will find that as you write, and as you consciously try to heighten the general effect of unity, one unifying device will conflict with another . . . With these inherent conflicts every writer does the best he can . . . Constant compromise, constant adjustment is the very essence of the creative process' (217).

Emergence of the workshop

We have seen that various attempts to 'teach' writing were implemented not on the basis of providing patronage and apprenticeship for writers, but as the basis for studying literature. Advanced composition was part of a general programme to rebuild the classical discipline of rhetoric in order to improve students' skills in written communication; short-story courses exploited the demand for vocational training in magazine fiction, but were part of a broader critical and nationalist movement to define and analyse the short story as a genre, itself part of a movement to raise fiction to the status of high art; Creative Writing in schools was part of the Progressive Education movement and was designed to facilitate the self-expression and personal growth of children by the reading of literature and the writing of original verse and prose. Finally, Creative Writing developed in universities as an adjunct to criticism, helping students to study literature as an art. It is with the establishment of the workshop

as a community of writers that literary training for potential publication came to be seen as the main aim of Creative Writing.

The original meaning of the word 'workshop' was a building in
which manual labour took place. When used figuratively it denoted
the labour or scheming that took place in the mind. By 1900 this
had been extended to a metaphor for the compositional process of
an author, such as when a visiting playwright at Harvard invited
students 'to step into a little dramatic workshop' and 'see a humble
workman in the craft',[9] or when William Ker commented that
Dryden, in his essays, 'cannot explain the secrets of the dramatic
workshop with the same confidence and intimate knowledge as
Corneille' (1900: xxi). Note the air of demystification about these
statements. In 1932 Laurence D'Orsay attempted to distance his
book, *Stories You Can Sell*, from the numerous short-story handbooks
which already existed, by claiming in the introduction that 'For the
first time in literary history, writer-readers are taken into the workshop of a professional author and, so far as possible, into his mind;
shown step by step just how he plans and writes his stories, from the
first glimmer of a vague but suggestive plot idea to the finished
product' ([1932] 1942: vii).

With the official naming of the Iowa Writers' Workshop this
figurative space of authorial work, this Modernist metaphor for the
creative process, had become a literal place. Rather than a solitary
garret, however, the workshop was a communal gathering of writers.
Stephen Wilbers points out that the term was used unofficially to
describe Edwin Ford Piper's graduate writing seminar, entitled
'Imaginative Writing: Advanced', and its summer extension (1980:
51). When Wilbur Schramm took over this seminar after Piper's death
in 1939, he officially renamed the course 'Writers' Workshop'. The
phrase first appeared in print to denote a course (English 101s) being
offered for the summer session of 1939. In the programme for this
summer session, entitled *Creative Writing in the University of Iowa*, it is
stated that 'opportunities will be offered to writers, teachers of writing, and all other persons who want to learn more about the art from
its successful practitioners' (Iowa University 1939: 1). Once again there
is the suggestion of a revelation of professional secrets here.

The Writers' Workshop was described in the 1939–40 catalogue
as 'Group conferences and individual conferences' (213). By this time
the word 'workshop' had also acquired its modern meaning as a
meeting to discuss ideas and work through problems. In 1913 the
'47 Workshop' was established at Harvard University. This was a
'trying-out place' for plays written in George Pierce Baker's dramatic

composition classes, and its purpose was to help playwrights develop their scripts and to experiment with new methods of staging (see Kinne 1968). A national meeting of teachers at Sarah Lawrence College in 1937 to discuss strategies in Progressive Education was also referred to as a workshop. This was a sufficiently new usage for the *New York Times*, in its coverage of the event, to print the word in tentative quotation marks (Barnard 1937: 5).

Creative Writing, we have seen, was at the vanguard of the Progressive Education movement, and the writing workshop in which students meet to experiment and discuss their work is a product of modern democratic education. By 1940 Marie Drennan was able to caricature the concept of the workshop in this way: '[t]he true workshop, according to educational extremists, is a course planned and executed by the students themselves, with no more guidance from the teacher than a lifted eyebrow or a wagging finger. It is supposed to be vital because it encourages self-expression' (532). Drennan suggests that her work in Freshman English at Ohio Wesleyan University is a 'modified workshop for composition courses' (532). The classroom, for Drennan, is 'the atelier of the craftsman whose apprentices work and learn with him' (532).

The idea of craftsmanship, I have shown, is the necessary precondition for the workshop. For, in keeping with its original meaning of a place of labour, the workshop was also in part a challenge to the Romantic poet for whom ease of composition, and spontaneous excitement rather than voluntary will, was the mark of genius. Creative Writing emphasises the Modernist labour of writing, but rather than the idea of art as impersonality, which you would find in Flaubert or Eliot, it is also (through the influence of Mearns) based on the Romantic notion of art as self-expression. The workshop does not give students guidelines for writing successful stories, as turn-of-the-century handbooks based on the lexicon and methods of Poe had done. But rather than invoking the Modernist search for new literary forms, it is more likely to resist any impositions on students' 'creativity' and simply provide them with the craft skills to narrativise their individual experience and express their personal 'voice'. 'The process of writing a short story begins,' Wilbur Schramm advised in *The Story Workshop*, 'not with a handbook nor with a search for distant and unusual material, but with yourself. You must know your mind before you know others. What interests *you*? What sense impressions have *you* received in a given situation? What stories are in *your* life?' (1938: 5).

In the discipline of Creative Writing, then, criticism helps the writer develop craft or technique, this craft is honed in order to express the creative spirit or the individual voice of the writer, and the workshop provides professional training, or literacy, in a specialised area of written communication. The workshop not only approximates writers' groups, but is a product of modern democratic education centred around the individual needs of the students.

The term 'workshop' was soon applied to the whole programme in writing at Iowa. When Paul Engle took over in 1942 it came to signify the institutional site of literary apprenticeship. In 1964 Engle edited a book called *On Creative Writing*. He argued that one of the major themes of the twentieth century was the alienation of the writer from society and that the role of Creative Writing courses was to counter this by providing a space for 'an international community of writers' (vii). This space was the workshop, where the community could literally gather. 'The older poet has often advised the younger, even if not asked,' Engle claimed in a 1973 conference. 'Teaching creative writing is simply advice organized, regularly available, with a name and number' (Conference on Teaching 1974: 27). According to Wilbers:

> Paul Engle's argument in support of the Program in Creative Writing was an extension of Norman Foerster's and Wilbur Schramm's line of thinking. Although the emphasis of the program under Engle's direction changed from treating creative writing as part of a broader scholarly discipline to viewing scholarship as an activity beneficial to the writer, at base the premise was the same: the creation of literature is academically as respectable and important as the study of literature.
>
> (1980: 83)

Wilbers here is trying to gloss a profound difference. It is not the premise that is the same, it is the justification. The premise under Engle did not explain how Creative Writing related to Literary Studies: it became an apprenticeship in literary art by the good grace of its patron, the university. What makes the development of the workshop under Engle significant is that classes in Creative Writing had previously been offered within undergraduate courses in English, and therefore alongside other subjects. When it became a postgraduate degree it was still part of the School of Letters. But with the workshop it became a separate entity for a separate degree, the MFA. Classes in Literary Studies were required, but only to make students better writers.

One cannot place the blame for a division between literature and criticism solely on a professionalisation of Creative Writing, however, because from the 1940s criticism too was becoming professionalised.

According to Alan Golding, 'professional academic criticism was started by critics who were poets first, professors second' (1995: 78). The New Criticism relied on the authority of poet-critics, and on a tension between amateurism and professionalism. Golding suggests, however, that as criticism became more professionalised its initial emphasis on evaluation diminished and it became concerned with mere explication. 'The early New Critic had hoped to be a man (and they were all men) of letters in the university, a kind of amateur professional ... But in the course of the New Criticism's institutionalization, the split between poet and critic that its first practitioners hoped to avoid did indeed occur' (86). For Golding the emergence of the Iowa Writers' Workshop at the same time as the textbook *Understanding Poetry* is symbolic of this split, and later writing programmes 'have their origins in poets' desire to preserve poetry from an increasingly arid and routine criticism', of which Theory is only the latest manifestation (86). In other words, rather than the workshop becoming professionalised, it can be seen as an attempt to retain the amateurism of evaluation. I would suggest it also attempted to retain the authority of the writer in the academy.

Wimsatt and Beardsley's 'Intentional Fallacy' (1946), for instance, which claims that knowledge of authorial intention is unnecessary for critical analysis, also precludes the need for a writer's knowledge. The separation between literature and criticism articulated by Rene Wellek and Austin Warren in their influential book, *Theory of Literature*, a virtual codification of New Critical aesthetics and practice, is not only a theoretical one, but one designed to establish the academic credentials of criticism. 'We must first make a distinction between literature and literary study,' they argue. 'The two are distinct activities: one is creative, an art; the other, if not precisely a science, is a species of knowledge, or of learning' ([1949] 1963: 15). Wellek and Warren reject educational attempts to 'obliterate this distinction', such as arguments that 'one cannot understand literature unless one writes it' (15). It may be recalled that Warren himself had asserted the benefit of Creative Writing to criticism some years earlier in *Literary Scholarship*. Reminiscing in 1979, however, Wellek reveals that 'Austin Warren and I felt that we had sailed under false colours when we contributed to a book edited by Norman Foerster. We formed the project of writing a book, *Theory of Literature*, which would combine the new critical outlook of Austin Warren with my knowledge of continental developments' (1982: 155).

If he was a champion of the New Criticism, Wellek also acknowledged its inevitable eclipse. In an article entitled 'American Criticism of the Sixties' he asserted that '[u]ndoubtedly the most successful and widespread movement in American Criticism since the New Criticism has been Myth Criticism, most influentially codified in Northrop Frye's *Anatomy of Criticism* (1957)' (1982: 108). In *After the New Criticism* (1980), Frank Lentricchia positioned Frye's book as a turning point in English Studies. Published a year after Murray Krieger's *The New Apologists for Poetry* had asserted the exhaustion of New Criticism, *Anatomy* shifted attention from the individual text to the archetypes or mythic topoi which underlay all literature. While it was indebted to a post-Kantian lineage of the symbol which continued through to the New Criticism, Lentricchia claimed, *Anatomy* also prefigured the importation of structuralism into Literary Studies.

Anatomy was concerned with staking out the disciplinary identity of criticism by eschewing the conceptual frameworks of neighbouring disciplines, such as history or philosophy. It can also be described as the continuation of a project of liberating criticism from its parasitical dependence upon art. For Frye this meant challenging the authority of the writer. 'The axiom of criticism must be, not that the poet does not know what he is talking about, but that he cannot talk about what he knows' ([1957] 1971: 5). Furthermore, he argues, 'the poet speaking as critic produces, not criticism, but documents to be examined by critics' (6). This diminishes the authority of a centuries-old tradition of the poet-critic. It also implies that poets by definition would not be able to teach Literary Studies.

The workshop, then, becomes the only place within the university for writers to assert their literary authority as writers. However, this authority has been directed towards the narrow goal of training other writers, rather than a more general contribution to the academic study of literature. For Myers, the 'alliance with criticism' represented by Foerster's School of Letters 'lasted only long enough for creative writing to get on its feet' (1996: 145). Where originally 'creative writing was the perfection of one tendency in the history of criticism . . . knowledge *how* conceived as both the only means of access to and somehow the equivalent of knowledge *that*' (147), it became in following decades a professionalised programme which reproduced itself by training students to become writers in order for them to return as teachers of writing. Myers's argument is that as a result of institutional pressures the original *motivation* for Creative Writing changed, but he is not clear on how the *pedagogy* changed. He claims that the practice of *reading as a writer* elaborated by Cassill 'is clearly a vocational concept of knowledge, embedded in a highly organized discipline of work', yet Creative Writing still remained a discipline of criticism, of 'constructive knowledge' (159). Even though Creative Writing became professionalised (and it is worth asking why this always seems to be a dirty word, connoting a fall from grace) it remained an institutional site for the deployment of criticism. To understand how Creative Writing developed as an independent discipline it is not enough to assert that its original aim was obscured. Instead we must examine the operation of the workshop itself and its theoretical relationship to English Studies.

3 Workshop poetics

> For the sake of proceeding let us define instruction in creative writing as the performance of practical criticism, by an instructor and members of a class, upon original poems and stories submitted by members of the class. All who participate in this instruction are, therefore, literary critics.
>
> (Dave Smith 1985: 218)

What distinguishes the Creative Writing workshop from the class in Literary Studies? The obvious answer is that students in the former produce 'creative' or literary works for assessment, while students in the latter produce essays in literary theory or criticism. Hence a distinction can be made between the writing and reading of literature. This leads, however, to an unconvincing division between supposedly original and primary creative writing and the mere secondary commentary of critical writing (which is only a form of reading). If we examine what actually goes on in a writing workshop we quickly realise that, like the class in Literary Studies, it is a discussion of texts. Some practical exercises in form or observation or automatic writing may be conducted in the workshop, but the actual work which will be submitted for assessment is written outside class and read inside class. Because of the emphasis on workshopping one might even claim that there is more actual reading in a Creative Writing class than in a Literary Studies class. The objects of discussion in the latter tend to be works of literature and their critical commentaries, as well as general theoretical works. In Creative Writing the objects of discussion may include general accounts of the creative process, handbooks of writing, perhaps even some critical commentaries, but tend to be either exemplary texts (by which I mean published works of literature deemed to be worthy of analysis and emulation, and sometimes imitation) or student manuscripts. So because the Creative Writing class consists primarily of literary objects of discussion, because it is seen as a *writing* workshop, the critical principles which underpin and allow discussion (reading) tend to remain invisible and undertheorised.

The question here is, are there critical principles specific to the writing workshop? Is the pedagogical process merely guided by the idiosyncracies of the teacher, the practising writer able to pass on knowledge by virtue of his or her innate talent and secret knowledge of the craft? Or is there a more systematic approach to the study of exemplary texts and student manuscripts, one based not so much on the first-hand knowledge of writers, but on a certain type of criticism? If so, does this differ from the critical approach provided in Literary Studies? Or, to speak more abstractly, since the range of approaches in a Literary Studies class is far more heterogenous than a writing workshop, is there a writer's theory of literature which is different from a critic's theory of literature? Is there something specific to Creative Writing classes, some quality of the creative imagination which does not derive from criticism? Is there a poetics of Creative Writing?

In order to answer this question we must first define the context in which the term 'poetics' is being used. I have argued that while a writing workshop differs from a class in literary studies in the sense that assessable submissions are fictive rather than critical-theoretical, the pedagogical practice of the workshop is fundamentally one of critical reading. In other words, what enables the writing workshop to function is not a theory of writing, but a theory of reading (because while the workshop may seek to discourage the Romantic myth of spontaneous, untutored genius in favour of the Modernist craftsman, a student may still, *in principle*, produce work in an unanalysable flash of inspiration, without conscious knowledge of the tools of composition, and submit it unchanged by suggestions provided in the workshop). How a work is *composed* by the student is not as important as how it can be *read* in terms of the critical approach of Creative Writing. What sort of reading, then, or critical study, is usually denoted by the term 'poetics'?

In its simplest definition poetics is a theory of poetry. The name is associated most readily with Aristotle's treatise (or lecture notes) on epic poetry and tragedy. Aristotle introduces this work by proposing 'to speak not only of poetry in general but also of its species and their respective capacities; of the structure of plot required for a good poem; of the number and nature of the constituent parts of a poem; and likewise of any other matters in the same line of inquiry' (1984: 2316). The *Princeton Encyclopaedia of Poetry and Poetics*, first published in 1965, employs this broad use of the term, with entries on all matters of theoretical concern regarding poetry. The term need not be restricted to poetry, however. For instance, in *The Novelist at the Crossroads* (1971) David Lodge includes an essay entitled 'Towards a Poetics of Fiction: An Approach through Language'.

The use of the word which I am interested in here, is in relation to what Jonathan Culler called 'structuralist poetics' in his 1975 book of the same name. In this book Culler was concerned with revitalising Literary Studies, which he described as existing in a state of crisis due to the inability of the New Criticism to adequately defend itself as a form of knowledge (vii–viii). As a result he turned to a study of French structuralism in the hope that it might provide the basis for a new approach to Literary Studies. 'Rather than a criticism which discovers or assigns meanings,' Culler says, this new form of study 'would be a poetics which strives to define the conditions of meaning . . . The study of literature, as opposed to the perusal and discussion of individual works, would become an attempt to understand the conventions which make literature possible' (viii).

In his *Introduction to Poetics*, Tzvetan Todorov divides the study of literature into two attitudes. The first he labels interpretation, which is concerned with describing or excavating the meaning of specific texts. The second attitude, which investigates the conditions under which all texts are produced, is denoted as science. Poetics, he claims, breaks down the opposition between these two attitudes: 'it does not seek to name meaning, but aims at a knowledge of the general laws that preside over the birth of each work' (1981: 6). Unlike the scientific attitude, however, which is derived from discourses such as psychology, philosophy and sociology, it seeks these laws 'within literature itself' (6). Poetics and interpretation, therefore, are complementary, for without analysis of actual works the poetic structure, the 'list of literary possibilities', will be invalid. Poetics, for Todorov, is a combination of the practice of reading and a theory of literature, but rather than coming to an evaluative conclusion about particular works, it seeks to explore the relationship of the structural quality of individual works to an overarching structure of literature in general.

Gérard Genette also discusses this problem in *Narrative Discourse*, which is both a study of Proust's *Remembrance of Things Past* and the construction of a method of analysis. The paradox of poetics, Genette claims, is that 'there are no objects except particular ones and no science except of the general' (1980: 23). While structuralist poetics is an attempt to apply the model of Saussurean linguistics to the study of literature and so arrive at a scientific knowledge of a totality of structure in the literary system, it nonetheless draws upon and contributes to the tradition of Anglo-American narratology which derives from Henry James's meditations upon the novelist's craft.[1] It thus can be utilised for the purposes of interpretation.

Poetics in this sense is obviously formalist in nature. In a recent special issue of the journal *New Literary History* devoted to 'Poetry and Poetics', the editors claimed that, due to the influence of Cultural Studies and New Historicism throughout the 1990s, too much scholarly attention had been paid to the context of literary works, hence concentrating on their content, and that a revived poetics was required (1999: 1). It should be noted, however, that Stephen Greenblatt describes New Historicism as a 'cultural poetics', a study of the social energies or material conditions which enable the production and reception of particular works of art (Greenblatt 1989). Poetics of any kind, then, attempts to devise general principles of criticism and theories of reading rather than evaluative critiques of individual works. In asking if there is a poetics of Creative Writing, I mean a general theory of literature (fiction, poetry, drama) – but literature as creative writing, that is, as process rather than product, something which has been written rather than something which is to be read; and a general theory of literature which enables the analysis of specific texts, in particular, the student manuscript. Is there a pedagogical practice of criticism which is writerly rather than readerly?

The aim of this chapter is to outline the pedagogical processes of the writing workshop and explore their theoretical underpinnings. Since the teaching of Creative Writing *is* undertheorised and idiosyncratic the best way to determine this is to analyse some of the common principles and assumptions which inform the workshop. These can be grouped under three phrases which circulate within pedagogical discussion relating to Creative Writing: *reading as a writer*; *show, don't tell*; and *discovering a voice*. In what follows I will trace the origins of these strategies in relation to Literary Studies, and examine how they contribute to a poetics of Creative Writing.

Reading as a writer

The best way to learn how to write, according to most teachers of Creative Writing, is to read. In *Creative Writing in America: Theory and Pedagogy*, a 'book for high school and college teachers who are interested in how creative writing can be taught effectively' (1989: xi), the editor, Joseph Moxley, points out that the 'need for writers to be active readers is stressed more than any other recommendation' by the majority of contributors (xvi). In Kate Grenville's *The Writing Book*, a bestselling handbook which has served as a textbook in many Australian writing programmes, the final point is that '[t]he more you read, the better you'll write' (1990: 190). There must be more than this to Creative Writing, however, or it would be no more than an institutionalised book club. There must be a particular method of reading which is taught. And there is. Students of Creative Writing are encouraged to read not merely for literary appreciation, but in order to aid their writing. This is what we understand by the term *reading as a writer*, reading with the aim of discovering ways to improve one's own writing. Is this different from a critical understanding of literature which might be imparted in a class on Literary Studies, however? In order to ascertain this we must undertake an historical analysis of this type of reading as a pedagogy and a form of criticism.

The method of reading as a writer seems to have its origins in advice delivered to literary aspirants by that nineteenth-century doyen of professional authors, Walter Besant. In his 1884 essay, 'The Art of Fiction', Besant advises that an aspirant 'should with the greatest care and attention analyze and examine the construction of certain works, which are acknowledged to be of the first rank in fiction' (29). The aim is not only to come to an appreciation of these works, but to determine how they were made. 'He must not sit down to read them "for the story", as uncritical people say: he must read them slowly and carefully, perhaps backwards, so as to discover for himself how the author built up the novel, and from what original germ or conception it sprang' (29).

Besant reprinted sections of this essay in *The Pen and the Book*. Besant's discussion of poetry in this broad-ranging book contains little concrete advice. When it comes to novels, however, Besant argues that they 'should be read in moderation or for the purpose of analysis. And the use of analysis is to find out how the story is worked out – how it is planned: and how it is told' (1899: 99). He then outlines a process for this analysis. First, the 'student' should 'read it through uncritically' (100). He should allow himself to be 'quite carried away by the story' as this is proof of an imagination (100). The student 'should then read it again, this time critically' (100). Following this he should 'take pen and paper, and write down the leading idea of the story' (100). He should examine how this idea is located in a particular place, with a particular set of characters, then analyse the role of each character, and the function of 'scenery and surroundings . . . In other words, he might pull the story to pieces and then reconstruct it himself' (100).

Besant does not suggest that general laws can be extracted from this analysis and then applied by writers. In fact, while he recommends reading the 'masters', he warns against too great a consumption of contemporary writers, as this may hinder the development of an individual style. Besant's advice is vague because at this stage in history no formal critical methods for studying the novel had been devised. He has no tradition of analysis to draw upon, and in fact relies upon a discussion of his own work. Hence, when he advises young writers to read 'critically' he distinguishes this as work from mere enjoyment of a book. Criticism is defined as a professional approach, where the writer is an apprentice craftsman.

The phrase, 'reading as a writer', was first used in 1934 by Dorothea Brande, a teacher of Creative Writing, and her description of its method bears striking similarities to Besant's advice. In her bestselling book, *Becoming a Writer*, which dedicates a chapter to the subject, Brande advises that 'to read effectively it is necessary to learn to consider a book in the light of what it can teach you about the improvement of your own work' ([1934] 1983: 99). This means overcoming a natural distaste for 'dissecting a book' (99), or putting one's 'favourite author under a microscope' (100), and reading critically. Reading critically here means reading a book not purely for appreciation but 'for style, or for construction, or to see how its author has handled his problems' (99–100). The first step in this process is to read 'rapidly and uncritically', purely for enjoyment (100). The next is for the reader to register a response in writing via a synopsis, followed by asking what they liked and disliked about the book and trying to answer these questions. One must then reread the book, noting not so much what the author is writing about, but how he or she is writing it; that is, paying attention to the structure, dialogue, point of view, etc. When this 'critical attention' (103) becomes habit, according to Brande, one can read 'for enjoyment and for criticism simultaneously' (104). What Brande means by 'reading as a writer', then, is obviously the utilisation of criticism. Criticism is not defined beyond analytical scrutiny as opposed to idle enjoyment. Elsewhere in the book Brande uses 'criticism' to denote the secondary act of revision of a first draft which has been worked up from the unconscious; the use of the faculty in the writer equivalent to the neo-classical notion of judgement, and what psychologists might today call the left brain.

It is another bestselling fiction handbook, *Writing Fiction*, published in 1962 by R.V. Cassill, which gives the phrase 'reading as a writer' its distinctiveness. The opening chapter of the book's first section, 'The Mechanics of Fiction', is entitled 'Reading as a writer'. 'Good writers', according to Cassill, 'are your real teachers of how to write fiction, and their novels and stories are the means by which they teach' (6). He warns against mining fiction purely for selfish purposes, however. 'There is a fine line to be drawn between emulation, on the one hand, and mechanical borrowing or stealing on the other' (6). The point of reading is 'to reveal and explain principles that are common to all good fiction, principles everyone is obliged to observe as soon as he learns how to do so' (6). Cassill is at pains to distinguish this analytical scrutiny from other forms of reading in a way which Brande never did. This could be because Creative Writing had, by the 1960s, become 'professionalised' as D.G. Myers puts it, and therefore required a disciplinary identity. It is Cassill, in fact, who founded the Associated Writing Programs in 1967, thus establishing a legitimate professional organisation for teachers of Creative Writing.

The 'ordinary, intelligent non-professional', according to Cassill, reads mimetically, that is, expecting an illusion of life so that he or she can identify with certain characters or values. There is a sort of hermeneutic search for meaning. This, for Cassill, 'is the primary justification for fiction' (7). The critic, however, 'generally wants to determine where to place this particular story' (7). This differs from general reading in that it seeks a context for the work. Here Cassill mentions the work's location in a particular genre, how it compares to the work of other writers, its relationship to psychology, its literary influences, the adequacy of its form in serving its meaning. 'The critic's way of reading fiction', Cassill claims, 'is a good way too, and a very valuable approach for a writer' (7). It is obviously not essential, however, for Cassill suggests that if a young writer has 'time and opportunity' he could 'supplement his writing program with classes in the analysis of contemporary fiction' (7). We can only assume that the sort of reading which writers must undertake is not covered by the term 'criticism' or the work of the critic. What a 'writer wants to note', according to Cassill, 'beyond anything that concerns even the critic, is how the story, its language, and all its parts have been joined together' (7–8).

This does not seem an alien motivation for literary critics, but Cassill claims that the sort of reading which Creative Writing teaches is distinct. For a start, it consists of a very compressed sort of analysis. He quotes the opening sentences of a Chekov story and discusses in detail how they set up the narrative, noting irony, concrete description of setting and dramatic quality. Is this any different from the 'close reading' practised by the American New Critics? For Cassill, the writer who reads 'must, above anything else, be aware that the story might have opened otherwise' (8). That is, rather than trying to understand a finished work as critical observers, students must attempt to recreate the process of composition as if they were the writer. 'A writer reading must be forever aware that the story exists as it does because the author chose his form from among other possibilities' (9). An author attempts to convince those who read for pleasure that his or her work could not be written with any other arrangement of language; a writer reading must analyse how this seemingly natural match arose out of a number of choices, and hence derive an understanding of the process of craft. This writer, for Cassill, must read with 'close concentration' (11), but he does not call this criticism. A dichotomy is established, then, between the reading practices of the writing workshop and the reading practices of the class in Literary Studies, one which consolidates the split between writers and critics.

Cassill's distinction has since become a commonplace in Creative Writing. Because the motto of the Iowa Writers' Workshop, that writing cannot be taught but talent can be nurtured, is still largely prevalent, and because writing teachers stress that constant reading is the most important thing students can do, alongside constant writing, the notion of reading as a writer is important for Creative Writing to retain its disciplinary distinction. Joseph Moxley points out that almost every contributor to *Creative Writing in America* asserts that

> we need to teach students to read like writers. Yet, this doesn't mean we should teach literature courses for writers in the same way that we teach literature courses for literature students. After all, the student writer's focus should not be on theme or principles of literary criticism, but on the choices authors considered when composing. Writing students need to become active readers – to study the point of view, the tone, the plotting and other techniques that the authors employ.
>
> (1989: 259)

In one of the articles in this collection, David Jauss asserts that 'reading won't help you much unless you learn how to read like a writer. You must look at a book the way a carpenter looks at a house someone else built, examining the details in order to see how it was made. A scholar reads the product; a writer, the process' (1989: 64). Again we can see that while 'creative writing' is a synonym for liter-ature, it is also one which emphasises the literary work as a process to be examined rather than a product which can be contextualised, or from which meaning can be extracted.

By 1993, in Nancy Walker's essay, 'The Student Writer as Reader', this distinction seems to have become almost naturalised, rather than one which is taught. Walker claims that 'students who are also writers and students who are not writers read literature differently. I do not remember precisely what I was teaching when I first understood this; I do, however, remember wondering why it had taken me so long to see what should have been obvious' (35). The distinction which Walker uses is that 'writers read from the inside out rather than the reverse' (35). Walker echoes the definition of Cassill when she writes:

> The student who is a writer, even an inexperienced one, perceives more readily than others do that a novel, story, poem, or play is the result of a process in which certain choices have been made along the way – one word instead of another, a decisions to interrupt chronology, a particular metrical pattern. This student has made such choices and knows they are part of the creation of literature.
>
> (36)

Walker does not state that students who have taken Creative Writing classes have been taught to read as writers; she suggests that the practice of writing has provided them with some sort of intuitive inside understanding of the mechanics of literature. This sort of understanding, that a work 'could have been better or worse than it is had the author made different choices', Walker claims, 'may, in turn, empower the student to move from being a reader to being a critic' (36). The inference is that Creative Writing does not involve criticism, but that it could lead to it.

We have seen here an attempt to distinguish Creative Writing from Literary Studies by virtue not of the work students produce, but of the manner in which they read literature. It is a difficult distinction, however, based on a difference of motivation (to learn how to write rather than how to appreciate literature), and presum-ably of expertise (the writer drawing upon his or her first-hand experience of the craft rather than a training in literary study). 'Most teachers of creative writing', according to Ron McFarland, 'try to examine work in the genre from a writer's point of view, as opposed to literary critic's or scholar's, though the extent to which they succeed in differentiating is probably debatable. Often I find myself slipping back into the voice and perspective of my classes in literature' (1993: 35). It is obvious that the terminology employed in the writing workshop, such as plot, structure, point of view, dialogue and character, is formalist in orientation. And it is also obvious that this sort of reading of literature wishes to concentrate on the craft of writing: how a work of literature is made, rather than extra-literary concerns. The claim, however, that 'reading as a writer' is somehow not criticism, based on a writer's point of view rather than a critic's, cannot be validated. The origins of the sort of criticism known as 'reading as a writer' is in the Anglo-American tradition of narratology which takes its cue from the New York prefaces of Henry James (writing as a critic of his own work) and finds articulation in the pioneer work of Percy Lubbock, *The Craft of Fiction*, long before the phrase comes into use. It is in fact no different from what Lubbock terms 'creative reading'.

Lubbbock's enterprise in this book is to establish a new methodology for the criticism of fiction. He wishes to somehow grasp 'the shadowy and fantasmal form of a book' in its entirety; not the critic's memory of certain scenes, his 'cluster of impressions', and any thematic extrapolations from these, but the book itself ([1921] 1954: 1). When reading and discussing a work of fiction, Lubbock claims, we take content, subject matter or thematic concerns from the work, we remember their impression upon us and compare these impressions to our knowledge of what the book is purporting to represent, but we pay little attention to the form in which they reside, and hence have no knowledge of how the novel was made. Whereas Cassill distinguishes between the ordinary reader and the critic, for Lubbock criticism tends to be a more rigorous understanding of the impression a literary work gives anyone upon an ordinary reading, but it differs by degree rather than kind and fails to deliver to us an understanding of the work itself.

In order to move beyond this, Lubbock claims, in the same fashion as Brande and Cassill after him, a certain distance from one's impression of the events and characters in the book must be obtained: 'far from losing ourselves in the world of the novel, we must hold it away from us, see it all in detachment, and use the whole of it to make the image we seek, the book itself' (6). To achieve this we must pay attention to the form of the book, its structure, how it was made. This critical activity, this ability to take the impressions of life which a novel affords and shape them into a single form which can be called the book itself, according to Lubbock, 'is a kind of "creative reading" (the phrase is Emerson's) which comes instinctively to few of us' (16). The author observes life, selects elements from it, and reworks them with his imagination. He then orders 'all this life that is now so much more intensely living than before' (18) with the skill of his art. Life is liberated, distilled, unified in a single design. The critic works with this material to build the book, and 'must therefore become, for his part, a novelist, never permitting himself to suppose that the creation of the book is solely the affair of the author' (17).

The methods of storytelling are what Lubbock is interested in. 'Let us very carefully follow the methods of the novelists whose effects are incontestable,' he exhorts, 'noticing exactly the manner in which the scenes and figures in their books are presented' (20–1). Lubbock articulates the same fear which Brande discusses: a fear of dissecting a novel. Understanding how a novel is made, however, means that there is more to do than 'to watch receptively and passively' the 'march of experience' (16). It entails an active collusion in the creative process.

How a novelist finds his subject is beyond us, Lubbock claims, but how this subject is treated is the beginning of an understanding of the book (23). Here is another similarity with the workshop. Students are not prescribed subjects, although they are often encouraged to write from what they know. Nor are books chosen as exemplary texts based on their content. It is how a text is made that comes under scrutiny. For Lubbock, the point at which we begin to study an author's craft is where 'the critical question, strictly so called, begins. Is this proceeding of the author the right one, the best for the subject? Is it possible to conceive and to name a better? The hours of the author's labour are lived again by the reader, the pleasure of creation is renewed' (24). Here is where we see the crucial similarities between his work and, not only the concept of 'reading as a writer', but also the workshop process itself. Lubbock here is demonstrating that a writer chooses one method of presentation over another, the same as when Cassill discusses the choices of the writer. Furthermore, asking whether it is possible 'to conceive and name' a better proceeding in method is precisely the sort of critical scrutiny that a student manuscript is subjected to. And this occurs because of training in 'reading as a writer', or, as Lubbock would have it, 'creative reading'. In discussing what he sees as various flaws in Tolstoy's *War and Peace*, Lubbock asks: 'How would he have treated the story, supposing that he had kept hold of his original reason throughout? Are we prepared to improve upon his method, to re-write his book as we think it ought to have been written?' (57). The qualms that Lubbock experiences in the face of a canonised text are not felt when his method is transferred to the student manuscript. For workshopping does not just ask how a finished work might have been improved, but how a work in progress might be coaxed towards becoming a finished piece.

'The practice of this method', Lubbock says about his study of fiction, 'appears to me at this time of day, I confess, the only interest of the criticism of fiction' (273). Lubbock's final comments make it clear that the formalist approach to the study of fiction is the same as the approach taken up as a pedagogical tool in Creative Writing classes and 'naturalized' as a writer's perspective in opposition to a critic's: 'The author of the book was a craftsman, the critic must overtake him at his work and see how the book was made' (274). This is exactly what students do in workshops when they read as writers, when they examine how exemplary texts are made. What distinguishes the writing workshop from this type of 'creative reading' is that it also applies this critical method to student manuscripts.

From the examples presented here one must ask the question, why does the poetics of Creative Writing seem to be a poetics of fiction? Most handbooks of writing are guides to writing fiction. This can be seen as a renovation of the tradition of short-story handbooks which existed before the establishment of Creative Writing, although these were based on Poe's reading of his poem 'The Raven'. Creative Writing developed in universities at the same time that fiction became accepted as a form amenable to study. Furthermore, the fact that free verse became the dominant poetic form of the twentieth century makes it more difficult to teach 'techniques' or the craft of poetry. Various dictionaries of poetic devices and metrical forms tend to fulfil this technical function. To answer the question of whether a poetics of Creative Writing largely derived from the study of fiction also embraces poetry and drama we need to examine what critical judgements are made, what advice is offered, when one reads both exemplary texts and student manuscripts as a writer.

Show, don't tell

The most common piece of advice in Creative Writing classes, and hence the critical statement most often applied in workshop readings of student manuscripts, is *show, don't tell*. This phrase was already common when R.V. Cassill wrote his 1962 handbook. 'An experienced writer, criticizing the work of any apprentice,' Cassill writes, 'is apt to say repeatedly, "Don't tell us what your character or scene is like. Show us"' (5). This is generally an exhortation for more concrete description which will allow a reader to 'see' a scene, to be convinced of its verisimilitude rather than having to rely upon a sketchy report. For instance, if a sentence read, 'She could barely restrain her anger at this comment', a teacher (and experienced students) might ask to be shown the anger, rather than simply being told that there was anger. The sentence might then be rewritten as: 'She smiled tightly in response while underneath the table her knuckles creaked as her fingers twisted the cloth serviette into tight little knots.' (This might then be pared to read: 'She smiled in response and her knuckles creaked under the table as she twisted the serviette into tight little knots.') Or if a room is described as cluttered, a teacher might suggest that the scene be 'fleshed out' by more description of what is actually in the room. John D. MacDonald, in 'Guidelines and Exercises for Teaching Creative Writing', advises:

> Do not let them tell you about their characters. Do not let them say, 'She was a nervous and troubled woman.' Make them show you the woman sitting there, sweaty, wringing her hands, rattling her spoon on her coffee cup, pinching her under lip. Don't let them say, 'He was a fool.' Make them show you the fellow doing a fool thing.
>
> (1989: 86).

Ron McFarland claims that '[t]he advice to "show" rather than "tell" qualifies as universal. This comes down to the use of concrete detail in writing, especially imagery' (1993: 34). McFarland's account of how he worked with a student to improve her poems demonstrates how this advice applies equally to poetry as to fiction. Such advice can indeed be said to derive from Imagist manifestos of poetry. Ezra Pound's 1913 'A Few Don'ts by an Imagiste' advises that an Imagist poet must '(u)se no superfluous word, no adjective, which does not reveal something' (1972: 131). An Imagist will also eschew abstract expression of ideas in favour of the concrete image, the symbolism of the natural object. It is better, Pound suggests, to present an image – 'that which presents an intellectual and emotional complex in an instant of time' (130) – than to describe a scene in the way a painter would depict it. In his introduction to his edition *Literary Essays of Ezra Pound*, T.S. Eliot claimed that 'Pound's criticism is always addressed, implicitly, first of all, to his fellow craftsmen' (1954: xii), and that no other poet-critic was 'so consistently concerned with teaching others how to write' (xiii). It is not Imagist poetry which survives in the workshop, however, but a watered-down version of Pound's statements in the form of pedagogical advice. 'Unfortunately,' a 1918 review in *Poetry* of an Imagist anthology claimed, 'Imagism has now come to mean almost any kind of poetry written in unrhymed irregular verse, and "the image" – referred solely to the visual sense – is taken to mean some sort of pictorial impression' (qtd in P. Jones 1972: 23). This is a handy description of the sort of poetry which will arise when 'show, don't tell' is taken literally.

In *The Writing Book*, Kate Grenville sets an exercise in description for aspiring writers and then suggests that they rewrite the piece without adjectives or adverbs. 'This will force you to be very specific, and to "show" rather than "tell" . . . Without adjectives and adverbs, you're driven back to verbs as a means of expression and you might find yourself describing the character in terms of actions: body language, gestures, posture, activities' (1990: 138).

So the advice to show rather than tell generally applies as a sort of critique which urges students to make their events and descriptions more 'concrete', appealing to as many of the senses as possible to more fully realise the events and characters they are describing. In essence, students are being encouraged to make a scene more 'dramatic' (and the word 'scene' is already a dramatic term). 'Go through your story and find places where you've "told" rather than "shown",' Grenville advises. 'Consider whether the story would be more interesting if it were re-written so that information was acted out rather than summed up' (183). Cassill in fact suggests that '[f]or economy and deftness in giving information to the reader – for learning how to show him instead of telling him what he has to know – we can find worthwhile examples in many plays' (1962: 12). This advice can be seen as an effort to restrict lazy writing. It involves, however, not just a distinction between 'flabby' and 'concrete' writing, but an implicit assumption that a literary work will be more effective if we do not have to rely upon a narrator (even a first-person narrator) to do anything except show us what is happening. Is this the advice of writers who have an indepth understanding of their craft, or is it the prescription of a certain type of critical opinion regarding the function of narrative?

The distinction between showing and telling is as old as the distinction between dramatic and narrative poetry. In Book III of *The Republic* Plato makes a distinction between dramatic poetry, which literally shows the action of a story on stage, lyric poetry, in which the poet tells his story, and epic poetry, which combines both because a poet tells a story as well as making use of dramatic poetry by reciting the speeches of his characters (1961: 639). In the *Poetics* Aristotle retains Plato's distinctions when he claims that a poet 'may either speak at one moment in narrative and at another in an assumed character, as Homer does; or one may remain the same throughout, without any such change; or the imitators may represent the whole story dramatically, as though they were actually doing the things described' (1984: 2317).

Plato argues that in an ideal state 'the poet should conceal himself nowhere' (1961: 638) because it is not possible to mimic all types of men and women, but more importantly because it is only good men doing and saying good things who should be imitated; anything else would adversely influence an audience. This means Homer would have to tell his tale completely by narration and without imitation (in the restricted sense of representing characters). This is, in fact, a compliment to Homer and all poets. For a poet is to be banished from the republic only because he would be worshipped as 'a holy and wondrous and delightful creature' (642). In his comments on epic poetry, 'the poetry which narrates, or imitates by means of versified language' (1984: 2335), which are concerned with what makes effective poetry, Aristotle praises Homer for speaking as little in his own person as possible, that is, for effacing himself as the narrator in favour of providing as much action and dialogue as possible and imitating characters (2336).

In praising Homer, Pope writes in the preface to his translation of the *Iliad* that 'everything is acted or spoken. It is hardly credible in a work of such length how small a number of lines are employed in narration' ([1715] 1965: 112). Comparing the success of this to the *Aeneid*, Pope writes: 'We oftener think of the author himself when we read Virgil than when we are engaged in Homer' (113). In *Biographia Literaria* Coleridge praises Shakespeare for the fact that in his plays '[y]ou seem to be told nothing, but to see and hear everything' ([1817] 1956: 177). There is a tradition in all forms of narrative art to aspire to an effacement of the condition of narrative, that is, to mask the narrator. This is why critics such as Ian Watt in *The Rise of the Novel*, F.R. Leavis in *The Great Tradition* and Walter Allen in *The English Novel* claim that the historical origins of the novel lie in the drama, rather than in epic poetry or earlier forms of prose fiction such as the romance.

This historical argument has its corollary in an aesthetic prescription. From Flaubert onwards the trajectory of the novel is often regarded as the development of techniques to impersonalise the narrator in order to efface the presence of the implied author, and dramatise as much of the action as possible. According to Wayne Booth in *The Rhetoric of Fiction*:

> Since Flaubert, many authors and critics have been convinced that 'objective' or 'impersonal' or 'dramatic' modes of narration are naturally superior to any mode that allows for direct appearances by the author or his reliable spokesperson. Sometimes . . . the complex issues involved in this shift have been reduced to a convenient distinction between 'showing,' which is artistic, and 'telling,' which is inartistic.
>
> ([1961] 1983: 8)

Henry James was probably most responsible for the dissemination of the idea of 'showing' or 'rendering' as a criterion of evaluation, for his crucial work on point of view was systematised by Percy Lubbock. For Lubbock the historical 'progression' of novelistic craft was one towards its dramatisation, and James signalled the high point of this achievement, locating the 'centre' of action in a character's point of view so that narration itself was enacted in a dramatisation of his or her consciousness. In discussing *Madame Bovary*, Lubbock asserts:

> I speak of his 'telling' the story, but of course he has no idea of doing that and no more; the art of fiction does not begin until the novelist thinks of his story as a matter to be shown, to be so exhibited that it will tell itself. To hand over to the reader the facts of the story merely as so much information – this is no more than to state the 'argument' of the book, the groundwork upon which the novelist proceeds to create.
>
> ([1921] 1954: 62)

According to Booth, it is Lubbock who 'taught us' to believe that the art of fiction does not begin until a novelist shows rathers than tells ([1961] 1983: 8). This observation, Booth argues, this championing of the aesthetic achievements of modern fiction, soon solidified into a rule for both composition and evaluation as it was taken up by both commercial handbooks on fiction writing and scholarly and critical work (26–7). Booth demonstrates how this is a flawed and restrictive principle for evaluation, but it is nonetheless the principle on which a major critical tool of the writing workshop is based. R.V. Cassill claimed that Flaubert 'taught most of the good writers of the past century – all those who "read as writers" when they looked into *Madame Bovary*' (1962: 6). Studying Flaubert's writing, according to Cassill, is a way of learning how to show a story, to make it concrete.

The appeal to convincing and authentic depiction of sensory experience which this advice relies upon can work to perpetuate Lubbock's implicit favouring of the genre of realism and the mimetic philosophy behind it. And indeed, as I pointed out in the introduction, American writing workshops have been criticised for their contribution to the prominence of minimalism or dirty realism. In Australia as recently as 1998 Dean Kiley wrote (in a story which provides an account of a 'real' writers' festival, but employs email transcripts and an anecdotal narrator rather than scenic description): 'At least three generations of Creative Writing students have grown up with the legacy, passed down from interview to interview, of the official Garner naturalistic narrative realism method' (802). This method is supported by the phrase, *show, don't tell*, advice which, Antoni Jach claimed in a recent handbook, is limiting and prescriptive because it encourages 'scene-setting followed by dialogue' (2002: 62).

The critical tradition I have sketched out favours a historical view of the novel progressing towards an invisible narrator who will simply present events (or experience) without commentary or evaluation. Transformed into a teaching device in the writing workshop, *show, don't tell* may be exemplified by this mode of narration, but it is ultimately an injunction to efface the presence of the author's craft – making the aesthetic choices an author has made seem like the only possible ones – rather than a desire to disguise the fact that an author has constructed rather than reflected reality. 'Perhaps the last thing you need to find out, reading as a writer,' R.V. Cassill writes, 'is how an author has managed to disguise his own presence, how he has kept the curtain always between himself and the reader' (1962: 11).

As such, advice to disguise the presence of the author's *craft* can easily apply to an anti-realist mode of writing such as metafiction. A work such as John Fowles's *The French Lieutenant's Woman* exposes the conventions of realism in order to draw attention to its own fictional status, but it does not necessarily draw attention to how the work itself was actually put together. The 'intrusions' upon the narrative draw attention to the role of the *narrator* and *implied author*, rather than that of the author. It is because the advice to show rather than tell is operationalised at the syntactic level rather than the structural, especially in relation to description, that it is so pervasive. One can imagine a writing tutor encouraging Fowles to *show* us this intrusive narrator sitting at his desk, toying with his characters as he contemplates the writing of fiction in the age of Barthes and Robbe-Grillet.

Show, don't tell also arises from anti-didacticism, an evaluative ethos which asserts that overt morality in literature is to be equated with aesthetic failure. While the Horatian formula of poetry as instruction and delight held sway up until the neo-classical period, the romantics tried to break the link between literature and didactic morality. 'In the romantic tradition', according to Ken Ruthven, 'a good writer is one who shows rather than tells' (1979: 188). This tradition culminates in Poe's condemnation of 'the heresy of the Didactic' ([1848] 1968: 158). Discussing Wordsworth's Intimations ode in *The Well Wrought Urn*, Cleanth Brooks argues that the second part of the poem, the attempt to come to terms with the loss of childhood vision, is lacking because 'I must confess that I feel the solution is asserted rather than dramatized' ([1947] 1968: 121).

The most famous example of an injunction to show rather than tell is F.R. Leavis's censuring of Joseph Conrad in *The Great Tradition*. Leavis points out that '*Heart of Darkness* is, by common consent, one of Conrad's best things' ([1948] 1972: 201) and that it 'achieves its overpowering evocation of atmosphere' by concrete physical descriptions which 'carry specificities of emotion and suggestion with them' (202). As proof he quotes liberally from the book, choosing descriptions of the gunboat shelling the wilderness, and of the grove of death. 'By means of this art of vivid essential record,' Leavis claims, 'in terms of things seen and incidents experienced by a main agent in the narrative, and particular contacts and exchanges with other human agents, the overwhelming sinister and fantastic "atmosphere" is engendered' (204). We can see in this comment an application of Eliot's 'objective correlative' to the art of fiction, but we can also see praise for the fact that Conrad's effect is achieved by 'showing' the action. In these passages, Leavis tells us, the 'author's comment' on the insanity which the wilderness produces in Europeans is not separable from the descriptive content. 'There are, however, places in *Heart of Darkness* where we become aware of comment as an interposition, and worse, as an intrusion, at times an exasperating one' (204).

Here Leavis is articulating the idea stemming from Romanticism that literature ought not to be didactic in its commentary, as well as the idea of showing rather than telling, of letting the story tell itself through concrete description rather than authorial assertion (in this case, via Marlow's framed narrative voice). And here Leavis links 'telling' to a particular style of writing, what he calls Conrad's 'adjectival insistence', with an onerous recurrence of abstract nouns such as inscrutable, inconceivable and unspeakable. The sentence of Conrad's which he reserves for the greatest condemnation is: 'It was the stillness of an implacable force brooding over an inscrutable intention.' Leavis writes:

> The same vocabulary, the same adjectival insistence upon inexpressible and incomprehensible mystery, is applied to the evocation of human profundities and spiritual horrors; to magnifying a thrilled sense of the unspeakable potentialities of the human soul. The actual effect is not to magnify but rather to muffle.
>
> (204–5)

For Leavis, this adjectival insistence rather than concrete description ruins the effect of the novel, and he blames this strategy on Conrad borrowing techniques of short magazine fiction established by Edgar Allan Poe. The scene in which Marlow meets Kurtz's Intended is particularly criticised, a scene which more than any other in the book echoes the Gothic qualities of Poe's fiction. 'If he cannot', Leavis thunders, 'through the concrete presentment of incident, setting and image invest the words with the terrific something that, by themselves they fail to convey, then no amount of adjectival and ejaculatory emphasis will do it' (208).

Leavis is railing against Conrad's attempt to render the profundity of the 'human condition' in obscure statements rather than concrete scenes. Translated into the pedagogy of the writing workshop this sort of criticism of canonical literature is likely to have far more modest applications. For instance, in a 2002 writing handbook, Deborah Westbury describes the practice of 'showing' as almost an act of courtesy, an endeavour to share an experience with readers: 'The best writing is generous. To show the readers what you saw, felt, touched, tasted, smelled is to enable them to enter into your original experience. To simply "tell" them leaves the reader on the outside of your experience. It is not generous or interesting' (150).

The pedagogical injunction to show rather than tell, then, is not only practical advice about craft based on the guild knowledge of writers, but the dissemination in the workshop of a long-standing critical opinion on the aesthetic development of both poetry and the novel towards a dramatisation or 'showing' of the material. This opinion is realised in the microscopic attention paid to sentence construction, where the advice to show rather than tell is a convenient pedagogical tool for commenting on student manuscripts, encouraging the pruning of excess language or the fleshing out of a scene with more description. Because this practical advice has evolved from critical debates about narrative technique it bears a relationship to the murky concept of voice and its connotations of unmediated speech.

Discovering a voice

In their critique of 'orthodox creative writing classrooms', Joe Amato and Kassia Fleisher argue that the teaching of craft has 'the aim of capturing highly individuated experience', employing the term 'voice' as its 'intellectually fuzzy co-conspirator' (2001: 9). The origins of the concept of a writer's voice can be related to the distinction between dramatic and lyric poetry which I outlined above. A poet speaks either in the voice of a character, or in his or her own voice. Hence voice originally referred to a poet's choice of genre. It is important here to understand the development of the relationship between voice and style. In the classical rhetoric of Cicero and Quintillan, *elocutio* was the selection and arrangement of words, following *inventio* (finding of the topic) and *dispositio* (organisation of material), and preceding *memoria* (memorising the oration) and *actio* (delivery). Style is descended from rhetorical 'elocution', and the rhetorical treatment of poetry was prominent throughout the Renaissance, with the idea of style as an ornament to the poet's material. For instance, George Puttenham's *The Arte of English Poesie* (1589) outlines a number of figures of speech designed to create a particular 'style' – high, mean or low.

With the increasing influence of organic theories of poetry in the late eighteenth century, however, where form and content cannot be so easily dissociated, style came to designate an intrinsic quality of a work and the sign of an author's individual genius. Wordsworth addresses this in his 1800 Preface to the *Lyrical Ballads*. Here he tries to reconcile his aim of imitating or adopting the 'language really used by men' (1974b: 71) with his idea that 'poetry is the spontaneous overflow of powerful feelings' (72). He achieves this by making the poet a representative of all men, able to speak for all while speaking from his own self. That is, he colours the language of men with the imagination of a poet, who is endowed with a more lively sensibility and a greater ability to recall and experience passion than other men.

Wordsworth's adoption of language used in 'low' and 'rustic' life was designed to return poetry to its origins in 'passion excited by real events' (90) and avoid what he called poetic diction, especially the 'personification of abstract ideas' which was only a 'mechanical device of style' (74). In his long refutation of Wordsworth's preface, Coleridge claimed that a person of any taste who had studied Shakespeare's principal plays would be able to recognise an unattributed quote from any of his other plays as undeniably Shakespearian. 'A similar peculiarity, though in a less degree,' Coleridge continues, 'attends Mr. Wordsworth's style whenever he speaks in his own person; or whenever, though under a feigned name, it is clear that he himself is still speaking' ([1817] 1956: 229).

So when a poet 'speaks' from natural passion rather than adopting mechanical devices (and Coleridge even condemned the 'language of men' as a flawed and artificial device) it is manifested in an individual style. This is what leads to the concept of a poet's voice. In a 1938 issue of *Scrutiny*, James Smith analyses the poem 'Michael', claiming that 'Wordsworth, who was so often an imitator, here speaks with his own voice' (1968: 154). There is a value judgement here that the poet's own voice is more authentic than an imitated one.

As we have seen, Romantic theories of creativity are democratised in Creative Writing pedagogy, where students are encouraged to develop an individual style by the process of finding a voice. In her handbook Dorothea Brande warns against the danger of a contagious style, of writing after the fashion of admired authors. 'The important matter', she asserts, 'is to find your own style, your own subjects, your own rhythm, so that every element in your nature can contribute to the work of making a writer of you' ([1934] 1983: 139). Brande's advice for achieving this was to tap into one's own unique and individual unconscious via a series of writing exercises, thus drawing out original material. In an article entitled 'Calling up the Spirits', Glenda Adams printed extracts from the letters of a friend, praising the 'clear, idiosyncratic, lovely' voice which permeated them (1991: 26). After advising the friend to write a book she received the opening chapters in the mail, only to be disappointed. The charming and authentic voice of the letters had gone, Adams suggests, because her friend 'had developed a plan and had set out to Write a Book' (26). For Adams all writers must deal with the fear of 'that loss of voice, or worse, never finding it, regardless of the persistence and effort given to the work' (26).

One reason why students are encouraged to write about what they have experienced, or about what they know, is that this will supposedly ensure that they write in their own 'voice', and the work they produce will be 'authentic'. An effect of this, according to Cassill, who constantly urged students to return to what they know in the choosing of subject matter, is that by drawing upon individual experience 'the writer will discover who he really is. His own identity will be clarified as his ability to write of his own experience increases' (1962: 23). This benefit is enough, Cassill claims, 'to entitle writing fiction to a place in the curriculum of the liberal arts' (23).

Discussing the teaching of poetry, John Koethe has argued that, contrary to popular opinion, writing programmes do not 'instill a formulaic approach to writing verse' (1991: 70). There are no prescriptions based on a theory of poetry, as one might find in a movement or school, such as the Black Mountain poets. Instead there is a freedom and tolerance – but this is the flaw of writing workshops. 'In the absence of explicitly articulated theoretical principles regarding the nature and purpose of poetry, they inculcate, by default, a poetics of the "individual voice" that valorizes authenticity and fidelity to its origins in prepoetic experience or emotion' (70).

The most damning critique of Creative Writing from the perspective of postmodern theory can be found in an article by Donald Morton and Mas'ud Zavarzadeh, entitled 'The Cultural Politics of the Fiction Workshop', and this critique centres on the concept of voice supposedly perpetuated by writing workshops. Morton and Zavarzadeh describe Creative Writing as the last bastion of traditional humanist literary criticism against the onslaught of postmodern critical theory, and argue that the 'main cultural purpose' of the workshop is 'to teach the student how to discover the "self"' (1988–9: 161). The result of this discovery is a person who considers him or herself to be a free, self-constituted subject within society, and it is this idea of the autonomous subject 'that assures the continuation of patriarchal capitalism' (161). In the workshop, the discovery of a free and true self is a mark of creativity and this is registered as voice: 'The mark of the arrival of the creative person at the domain of the translucent experience of truth is called "voice." To find and develop one's "voice" is the unquestionable sign of creativity, which in turn is – as we have argued – itself a sign of irreplaceable "selfhood"' (163).

This is condemned, by reference to Derrida, as logocentric. Voice is 'taken to be the sign that the writer has achieved transparency of self . . . the immediate access of self to its inner truths which are void of difference and identical with themselves' (164). Voice is related to the notion of 'presence', which valorises speech over writing. 'By regarding "voice" as the mark of the true writer, the creative writing workshop becomes the accomplice of the metaphysics of presence, of logocentrism and its accompanying phonocentrism, which is the underlying theory of sense-making in patriarchy and in capitalism' (165). This relationship between logocentrism and capitalism is asserted rather than proved, by an argument that the 'free' self is an ideological construct, but there is no indication of how its relation-ship to patriarchy might be argued (except by implicit reference, one assumes, to Derrida's notion of phallogocentrism). 'The visible and external mark of the unique "voice" of the singular writer is his or her "style"' (166). They suggest that while style 'is the materiality of writing' the workshop attempts to eliminate this materiality with its theory of style as invisible; the idea that no marks of craftsmanship should be visible in writing. Furthermore, the voice encouraged by the workshop, they argue, is in fact a realist, minimalist style which dominates the publishing industry. This demonstrates that voice is a construct. It is the voice of the 'entrepreneur' and perpetuates political and economic repression (173).

Morton and Zavarzadeh's critique of voice relates to the *creative self-expression* model of Creative Writing. This model tends to be most overt in adult education and community writing classes, where it often operates as a therapeutic technology of the self, although such a con-cept of voice and selfhood also exists for many writers and teachers of writing at the university level. 'Creative writing', Dave Smith claims, 'is one of the few formal opportunities in education for self-discovery and self-creation' (1985: 224). In his article, 'Writing in the Cold', Ted Solotaroff describes the efforts of several graduates of writing programmes to publish their work. They eventually accepted rejec-tion, he suggests, because they realised that their manuscripts did not deserve publication: 'they were mainly part of a protracted effort to find a voice, a more or less individual and stable style that best uncov-ers and delivers the writer's material' (1985: 269). There is an implicit understanding here that the origin of a writer's voice is in their pre-linguistic self, which needs to be unearthed, discovered. However, while this discovery takes place through the process of writing, its goal is the development not of the self, but of an individual style, that is, a particular mode of selecting and arranging words. It is here, in the interrelationship of voice and style, that the concept of 'voice' and its relation to authorship becomes complicated. For as well as a term relevant to expressive theories of poetry, voice is a narratological con-cept. In this sense voice does not indicate the inner self of the writer, it indicates the speaking position of the text itself.

To explain this concept I shall turn to Genette's *Narrative Discourse*. For Genette, 'narrative perspective' is 'a mode of regulating informa-tion, arising from the choice (or not) of a restrictive "point of view"', and 'of all the questions having to do with narrative technique' is 'the one that has been most frequently studied since the end of the nineteenth century' ([1972] 1980: 185–6). Here he cites Lubbock's *Craft of Fiction* as one of the exemplary studies. However, most of the works on this subject, according to Genette, 'suffer from a regrettable confusion between what I call here *mood* and *voice*, a confusion between the question *who is the character whose point of view orients the narrative perspective?* and the very different question *who is the narrator?* – or, more simply, the question *who sees?* and the question *who speaks?*' (186). Voice, in this formulation, has nothing to do with an authorial selfhood, but is the narrating instance which structures a literary work. For another confusion which Genette points out is to 'identify the narrating instance with the instance of "writing," the narrator with the author, and the recipient of the narrative with the reader of the work' (213). The voice of a work in this instance is not that of the author, but of the narrator.

The application of this narratological understanding of voice complicates the neo-Romantic expressivist concept of the authorial voice which Morton and Zavarzadeh criticise. In his article, 'How a Writer Reads', Stephen Minot argues that while in literary studies attention is paid to theme and characterisation, writers require a different focus, and so he draws attention to techniques such as 'the means of perception' (or point of view), scene construction and voice. For Minot, voice 'is in a sense the flavor of the means of perception' (1989: 92). This is a question of who the narrator is and the role of this figure in the narrative. 'While the passive reader is flipping ahead,' Minot asserts, 'impatient to get a rush from a dramatic plot, the writer is savoring those subtle distinctions of voice right from the beginning' (92).

The two concepts of voice do not necessarily operate independently, however. Kate Grenville's *The Writing Book* demonstrates the conflation of the expressivist and the narratological concepts of voice in Creative Writing pedagogy. This handbook has chapters on character, point of view, dialogue, description and voice, each with a description of the particular categories, followed by examples of their operation in extracts from published work, and a set of exercises for developing competence in the use of these categories as narrative devices. 'You can't have a story without a voice,' Grenville argues. 'As soon as you use words, you're making a series of decisions about how you'll put them together, and those decisions reflect the writer's subjective judgement as to which words sound best' (1990: 80). So for Grenville a particular arrangement of words is the product of a writer's individuality. 'Voice could also be called "style": but style sounds like a polish applied at the end whereas voice is an integral part of the whole story. Voice isn't just a few tricks of language but part of the texture of the story' (80). For Grenville there is no such thing as good or bad style; rather, what needs to be considered is the appropriateness of the style to the material. 'Every story has its own voice, just as every person does' (80). So the guarantee of a story's originality is its style, or arrangement of words, and as these are chosen by the author, it is the author's voice which provides the originality. Following Genette, however, Grenville argues that voice is the complement of point of view. She then distinguishes between the writer's natural voice, presumably what they might write a letter in, and voices the writer borrows to fit the point of view, to match the story at hand:

> The voice of a story can be the natural voice of the writer. That natural voice has inbuilt strengths – it usually flows easily, it's consistent, it has the energy of real life and it sounds convincing . . . But the decision you make about point of view might mean that you have to contrive a voice that's appropriate for the point of view, which might not be your own voice. So the challenge for a writer is to find a way of keeping the energy and authenticity of your own voice, while adapting it to meet the needs of different points of view.
>
> (81)

She then recommends that writers be assured of their own voice before adapting it.

We have, then, an oscillation between the expressivist notion of voice as the authorial guarantee of a work, evident in its style, and the narratological notion of voice as a structural element of narrative, translated in the workshop as a technical device for writers. So Creative Writing draws not only on an expressivist view of literature but on a tradition of Anglo-American formalism and structuralist narratology in order to construct a method of teaching. The identification of structural elements in exemplary texts is translated into a set of narrative conventions, an understanding of which can be honed through practical exercises, and made available as a series of aesthetic choices which an author must make when composing and revising a narrative. It could be argued here that this does not answer the charge of Morton and Zavarzadeh that the writing workshop operates with an unreconstructed Romantic idea of authorship. If 'voice' is just another device which the author can utilise, it is collapsed into the idea of craft, which is only the technical means by which an author discovers and expresses their voice. It is necessary, then, to consider how the notion of authorship is operationalised in the workshop.

Authorship

Morton and Zavarzadeh contend that Creative Writing perpetuates a model of textual commentary as a secondary reading concerned with 'the re-discovery of original meanings' and complemented by a concept of writing 'as the immediate act of intuiting reality' (1988–9: 158). In their view, the text being read is a 'full text' and the 'function of the reader in the dominant fiction workshop is therefore also predetermined: to recover the meaning that is located in the text by its originary agent, the author' (158). In other words, they characterise reading in the workshop as a hermeneutics, an interpretive search for meaning, which is anchored in the selfhood of the author. This is nothing more than a caricature of Creative Writing pedagogy. In fact, the opposite takes place: the reader provides a response to the text independently of the writer's intention, a response which is framed as advice which the writer may or may not take into consideration when redrafting. Morton and Zavarzadeh never actually analyse the workshop, content instead to describe its ostensible underpinnings in abstract terms. The assumption of individual talent, which they contend is an ideological construct, may exist, but to what extent does it influence the actual workshopping process? What is the function of the author in the poetics of Creative Writing?

The workshop proceeds, in David Lodge's words, 'by a special application of formalist criticism' (1996: 175–6). An important distinction to be made here is that between work done on the published text embodying an exemplary standard and work done on the student manuscript which aspires to or must meet this standard. By what criteria are texts selected to embody an exemplary standard? Obviously it is not their innate or supposed innate qualities because there are no set texts comprising an overarching canon across Creative Writing programmes as in traditional English literature (although some exemplary texts may be taken from the canon). There has never been a self-evident canon, unproblematically there. On the whole, texts are determined by individual teachers, and these are often those which seem teachable. The work of Hemingway and Carver has traditionally assumed something akin to canonical status, because it embodies the objective, minimalist sort of writing which is promoted by the advice to show rather than tell. Some texts may be selected for the way they use specific conventions, like the second-person narrator for instance. Or because they break with certain conventions, or pose interesting questions about narrative structures. And so on.

The object of analysis in Creative Writing is the craft of writing apprehended by a critical apparatus directed at the compositional techniques evident in the exemplary text. If this is the case there is little interest in what can be revealed, in what resides beneath the text. There is no attempt to draw out a meaning or a plurality of meanings. No one asks what does this mean, what does this say about an author or a historical period or a tradition? No one attempts to analyse the workings of narrative in order to uncover a truth. In short, there is no depth model of hermeneutic analysis in Creative Writing. A text does not work because of the rich nuances of meaning it displays, because of its innate aesthetic quality, because of its ability to represent something else, something extra-textual. It works because it suggests an accomplished use of convention. The exemplary text is examined according to how its conventions operate to construct narrative representation. What the exemplary text represents, then, is its own narrative devices, its own craft. Or, rather, craft as determined by practices of reading derived from formalist literary criticism and operationalised in the discipline of Creative Writing. The workshop explores the artifice of fiction, how verisimilitude is constructed or challenged, rather than a concept of writing as the 'immediate intuition of reality' as Morton and Zavarzadeh claim (1988–9: 158).

Morton and Zavarzadeh suggest that writing workshops need to take account of the postmodern idea that all reading is writing and all writing is reading. 'The creative writing student who knows theory', they argue, 'and who has read Marx, Lacan, Foucault, Lenin, Kristeva, Derrida, Gramsci, Heidegger, Cixous, Deleuze, Althusser, Luxemburg, Adorno will not approach the workshop with the same naïveté or accept its orthodoxies as will the student who has read the traditional syllabus of the literature department, which is entirely composed of poems, novels and stories' (169–70). Instead of 'resisting' theory, Morton and Zavarzadeh contend, the workshop should be a 'pedagogical space' where 'the construction of what is represented as "reality"' is made intelligible' (173). Unfortunately there is no indication of what this pedagogical space might look like, other than a class in theory. There is no indication of what sort of work should be produced.

One would assume that Morton and Zavarzadeh might encourage the reading and production of postmodern metafiction which, in *The Mythopoeic Reality*, Zavarzadeh had asserted was a 'narrational metatheorem' (1976: 39) that revealed 'the absurdity of the contemporary totalizing novel's claim to a metaphysics of experience' (224). Metafiction has been characterised as fiction which contains within itself a critique of its own status as fiction, hence operating as the fictional accomplice to postmodern theory in its critique of realism.[2] What a novel such as Fowles's *The French Lieutenant's Woman* does, however, is draw attention to the *conscious choices* of the author (by dramatising this process through the self-conscious intrusions of the narrator). The authorial intrusions in this novel are less (postmodern) criticisms (or anticipations of criticism) of the work by Fowles himself, than the product of an aesthetic choice based on the point of view of the narrator and *implied author*; a choice in making the novel's own fictionality, its structure, an integral and active component of the plot. The long history of reflexivity in fiction (which can be traced to the 'first' novel, *Don Quixote*) makes it difficult to defend metafiction as a specifically postmodern genre, and hence many critics have argued that in fact reflexivity is an inherent function in all fiction. The very name 'fiction' denotes the fact that the novel is not historical reportage. Wenche Ommundsen suggests, then, that 'metafiction is the product of a certain practice of *reading*, a particular kind of attention brought to bear on the fictional text' (1993: 29). This practice of reading which makes the conventions of literary artifce the burden of any text, realist or otherwise, is a practice which also operates in Creative Writing pedagogy.

Hence when Cassill claims that *Madame Bovary* has taught all those who read as writers how to efface their presence in the text, how to show rather than tell, he means that this realist novel has been laid bare by a practice of reading (1962: 6). As Leo Bersani has pointed out, Flaubert's agonised attempts to find the perfect match between word and object in fact draw attention to his craftsmanship. The irony of *Madame Bovary*, for Bersani, is 'that the care with which Flaubert sought to make language transparent to reality consecrates the very opaqueness of language which he dreaded' (1981: xviii). The novel draws attention to its constructed nature even as it attempts to disguise it. It 'is an early, only half-explicit, not yet fashionable attempt to locate the drama of fiction in an investigation of the impulse to invent fictions rather than in any psychologically, morally, or socially significant "content"' (x). Thus *Madame Bovary* can be seen as the beginning of the modern novel's self-reflexive investigation of its own relationship to the reality it purports to represent, via formal experimentation, an investigation which culminates in postmodern metafictional novels of the late twentieth century.

Authorship exists in the workshop as an implicit assumption, in the sense that an exemplary text is attributed to an agent who has consciously employed techniques of writing. 'Reading as a writer' operates by approaching the text as a series of artistic choices made by the author. That agent is anonymous, however. The author is named, obviously, and thus performs a classificatory function, perhaps the author's life is even discussed, but there is no attempt to surmise about or discover through the text what the author intended to say or what sort of person the author is. The canonised text works to embody an exemplary standard not because it expresses the creativity of an empirical being but because of its dexterous formation of compositional techniques. And while these techniques are implicitly attributed to a conscious organising agent, that agent is only the anonymous embodiment of the compositional techniques themselves.

The same critical modes of reading used to identify exemplary texts are applied to student manuscripts. However, in the workshop environment these manuscripts are presented as incomplete work. The critical strategy in this instance is not to find an exemplary standard but to apply practices of reading to the manuscript for didactic or remedial purposes. Hence, as well as identifying compositional techniques in the work, there occur suggestions for alterations or a reconsideration of narrative structure. There are affirmations of quality, queries about the direction of the work, and all this commentary is directed towards the writer. The writer is the origin of the piece, the owner and the one responsible for its development towards an exemplary standard. The writer may be consulted for clarification and subsequently put forward a motivation, an intent, which was not apprehended or indeed was misinterpreted by readers. Hence the writer comes to embody that conscious organising agent implicitly acknowledged in readings of the exemplary text. This agency is certainly the product of an author-function, but it cannot be described as the focal point of an unreconstructed authorial criticism.

The object of analysis for intellectual work performed on student manuscripts is not the reconstruction of the writer's intention; there is no desire to latch on to a single wordless meaning and enable its expression. In this critical environment the writer speaks not from the position of an author with a preconceived essence of selfhood that needs to be expressed, a vision of society that must be relayed; the writer is that student who has internalised a set of theoretical principles, thus organising a response according to the same critical strategies adopted to identify exemplary texts. This is not to say that students do not perceive themselves as creative beings using writing as a medium for their ideas. The student manuscript is undoubtedly an authored work but it is not critically apprehended or evaluated within the discipline according to a paradigm of authorial criticism derived from Romanticism. Furthermore, the reading practices which enable Creative Writing to operate as a discipline are not reifications of the writer's consciousness. They are derived from formalist literary criticism.

This begs the question, are students rewarded for their talent, or their ability to perform intellectual work in the worskshop? We have seen by examining the role of formalist criticism in the workshop that Creative Writing is one site within the academy for intellectual work in Literary Studies (whether students are desirous of pursuing careers as writers, critics, academics or otherwise is immaterial to the work they actually do in class). This work is not formalised in an essay, however, but discharged in class discussion and manuscript revision. Upon receiving a pass for a class, or for a whole degree, students have an institutional accreditation conferred on them, no different from students who write essays for classes in literary or cultural studies. In other words, they are granted a form of cultural capital.

Students are ultimately evaluated, however, on the 'quality' of the creative work they submit. The criteria for this quality differ in undergraduate and postgraduate courses. The grounds for evaluation at the undergraduate level are less to do with a manuscript's artistic/commodity potential than its ability to somehow demonstrate an understanding of 'what works' according to a mode of reading organised by a set of theoretical principles. Thus, evaluation can be guided by the extent to which students have considered the critical comments of peers and tutors in their redrafting of workshop material for final submission. Hence proficiency or talent need not be displayed, good writing need not be achieved, but intellectual work must be done. Already the grounds for academic evaluation are distinguished from artistic or commodity potential and are more firmly established in terms of specific reading practices.

At the postgraduate level, which operates as a professional training for writers (or a teaching qualification for already established writers), a creative thesis is required to be of 'publishable quality'. Hence the grounds for conferring postgraduate qualifications may seem to be based less in the ability for academic scholarship than in the potential for work to be transformed into a commodity for the publishing industry. However, not only is the notion of 'publishable quality' lifted from criteria for standard academic theses, it is really a rhetorical strategy because there are obviously no strictly determinable guidelines for *success* in literary publishing. Rather, the texts produced in postgraduate writing programmes are eventually appraised and accredited according to their ability to circulate within the discipline and its institutionally determined practices of reading. That is, the postgraduate manuscript must eventually be able to sustain the sort of critical scrutiny which is applied to published texts that are circulated within the discipline as examples of good writing.

I use the term 'published texts' as a deliberate strategy for outlining definitional problems. The examples of writing which are upheld in undergraduate and postgraduate writing courses serve different purposes. In undergraduate courses they symbolise a level of ability which students should aspire to and hopefully meet. In postgraduate work the creative thesis must meet this standard. It must eventually become a first-order text capable of transcending its existence as intellectual work and aligning itself with 'canonised' ones in the discipline. The fact that these canonised texts, these exemplars of fiction, are published works is, of course, not the issue. The point of concern is not even what resides in the exemplary text. It is the specific critical operations which can be performed on the exemplary text. Thus the creative thesis, or the ability of its producer, is not evaluated on its potential to be circulated outside the university as a publishable commodity; it is evaluated according to its potential to sustain critical scrutiny, to be approved by specific practices of reading. Hence the essential nub of Creative Writing is the theories which inform it as a body of knowledge, the critical procedures which enable work in the discipline to be read in a certain way.

I have argued that students are evaluated in terms of how they internalise a set of critical principles in the workshop. This internalisation functions not only as a demonstration of intellectual labour, manifested in the redrafting of a manuscript before submission, but as the pedagogical inculcation of a specifically Modernist view of the compositional process. The institutionalisation of the ideal of the Modernist craftsman in Creative Writing pedagogy is a byproduct of the accompanying institutionalisation of the New Criticism. The key figure here is the most influential poet and critic of the Modernist era: T.S. Eliot.

In his 1956 essay, 'The Frontiers of Criticism', Eliot claimed that his best critical work could be described as 'workshop criticism' (1957: 107), or, as he describes it, criticism which is 'a by-product of my own private poetry-workshop; or a prolongation of the thinking that went into the formation of my own verse' (106). This means, not that his criticism took the form of practical advice to writers, but that it was centred on the authority of the poet. Throughout Eliot's first and most influential collection of criticism, *The Sacred Wood*, we find claims that poets make the best critics, or that poets are compelled to engage in criticism, the goal of which is to facilitate solutions to the present problems of art. This is why he claimed that criticism should focus its attention on poetry rather than the poet. His famous reworking of tradition, from a static list of books consecrated by time, to a dynamic order where all works exists simultaneously, an order which is retrospectively refigured by the introduction of each new work, is not only a description of how a critic should approach literature, but a defence of the modern poet. When Eliot writes that 'the historical sense compels a man to write not merely with his own generation in his bones' ([1920] 1960: 49), but with a feeling that the whole history of literature has a simultaneous existence, he is describing a practice he would take up with *The Waste Land*.

In 'The Function of Criticism' Eliot recalls his comments on tradition and affirms that the genuine artist surrenders himself to this simultaneous order of the whole of literature. He then asserts that the critic must also pursue the same endeavour. Eliot characterises the end of criticism as the 'elucidation of works of art and the correction of taste' ([1923] 1964: 13). Like artists, the critic 'must discipline his personal prejudices and cranks' in favour of the 'common pursuit of true judgement' (14). He goes on to condemn impressionistic critics who prefer to listen to their 'Inner Voice' rather than contribute to this collective enterprise, or 'Outer Authority'. He then turns to reworking the relationship between the creative and the critical which Matthew Arnold had established. For Eliot, criticism is an essential part of the creative process. 'Probably, indeed,' Eliot writes, 'the larger part of the labour of an author in composing his work is critical labour; the labour of sifting, combining, constructing, expunging, correcting, testing: this frightful toil is as much critical as creative' (18). While he reaffirms his ideas about the superiority of criticism by writers, he goes further in arguing that '[t]he critical activity finds its highest, its true fulfilment in a kind of union with creation in the labour of the artist' (19). This is a different conception from that forwarded in *The Sacred Wood*, because the criticism of the poet is contained *within* the creative process, and any formal criticism which the poet may write is a spillover from this original work.

In talking of 'correcting', 'testing', 'expunging', Eliot sees criticism in this sense as a secondary revision of the work in progress. Eliot's emphasis on the role of criticism in the creative process bears a relationship to the neo-classical duo of imagination and judgement.

However, criticism is not a vague censor, as it was in this earlier conception, but an interactive mode of reading, a progressive critical revision. Since Eliot does not describe what form this critical labour might take, the connection which must be made is that the creative process internalises the criticism which he had previously described. As a poet writes he is concerned with a constant elucidation of the work and correction of his own taste (which revives the aesthetic view of taste as the guarantee of original genius), which is part of a pursuit of true judgement, a surrendering to Outer Authority, or Tradition.

Eliot's influence on Anglo-American criticism is well known. But his idea of the interrelationship of criticism and creativity from the point of view of a poet-critic also had an impact on the way criticism was employed in the writing workshop. The workshop is concerned with elucidating the student manuscript, correcting taste (which means the taste of the writer), and the common pursuit (that of the classroom) towards an outer standard (that which leads to a pass and/or publication). This communal critical process is then taken as a guide for revision which the student internalises when redrafting. 'Remember,' Paul Engle wrote in 1964, 'criticism is not simply a fiendish attack on a book, but a constant part of the writer's job, beginning with his rejection of one concept in favour of another, one image, one phrase, rather than others' (xi).

The critical principles which the student internalises, as I have shown, are to be found in the practice of reading as a writer, and in the advice to show rather than tell. The origins for this process can be found, once again, in Dorothea Brande's *Becoming a Writer*. Brande includes a chapter entitled 'The Critic at Work on Himself', in which she encourages aspirants to read over the material which they have generated from their unconscious. In order to benefit from this 'corrective reading', Brande advises, it is necessary to 'learn to read as a writer' ([1934] 1983: 99). The implementation of this process in the workshop can be seen in Wilbur Schramm's contribution to *Literary Scholarship*:

> The writer must therefore be a critic before he can be a good writer, even as the critic must be an artist before he can be a good critic ... He need not put into public circulation his opinions of other men's works. But he must learn to look at art with an artist's eyes. He must read other men's work with the intelligent understanding of a fellow craftsman, in order to see how others have met the common problems of the craft and to

estimate the effectiveness of their solution. Above all, he must learn to read his own work with uncompromising severity. *He teaches himself to write by a process of constant self-criticism.*

(1941: 195; emphasis added)

The poetics of Creative Writing, then, consists of a critical study of exemplary texts which is no different from the formalist criticism we have traced from Percy Lubbock through to elements of structuralist narratology. The end of this study is not so much a critical evaluation of these texts (it is enough that they possess canonical status, or are innovative in form, or represent contemporary movements in literature), nor a structuralist account of the linguistic codes which underlie all narrative, nor even a stockpiling of narrative methods and devices which may be of use to the writer, but the development of a method of 'reading as a writer'. This same method of criticism is then deployed in the analysis of student manuscripts, of works in progress, with the intention not of passing final evaluative judgement, but of aiding its progress to a completed form, and with the secondary intention of encouraging the aspiring writer to internalise this form of criticism as a method of revision and editing and an integral part of the 'creative' process. Hence the poetics of Creative Writing is not a bridge between the criticism or interpretation of individual texts and a science of literary structure, but both criticism, a formalist examination of the methods by which a literary work is made, and a 'making', a form of reading which participates in the drafting process.

4 Creative Writing in Australia

'The 1960s', according to Stephen Wilbers, 'was the decade in which creative writing programs or "writers' workshops" became common-place in universities and colleges across the country. Many of these programs were founded, directed, and staffed by Iowa Workshop graduates' (1980: 105). It was a teacher from the university of Iowa, R.V. Cassill, who established the Associated Writing Programs in 1967, and this, according to D.G. Myers, marked the 'professional-isation' of Creative Writing. While founded with thirteen member institutions, the AWP's website now lists over three hundred.

What were the reasons for this rapid proliferation? For James Ragan, the rise of audio-visual technology, or what he calls the 'New Mediaism', in the 1960s, was responsible for a decline in public literacy. Disenchantment with these social changes supposedly prompted a 'mass movement' of writers into the university, who then contributed to the subsequent proliferation of writing programmes (1989: 165). 'The boom years of the Associated Writing Programs as a growth industry were the 1970s,' Jed Rasula asserts, 'a decade notable for the rise of the self-help publishing market' (1996: 421). The link, for Rasula, is that 'the workshops took self-development as a seemingly unschooled or "natural" incentive for writing' (422). In other words, the valuation of authentic experience and emotion in the workshop is designed to cater to the self-help market, and self-expression is part of 'a more pervasive process of social inscription and subjectification' which reproduces the capitalist consumer market (424). At the same time, it should be noted, current-traditional rhetoric in composition was replaced by more expressivist theories, thus drawing from and contributing to the popularity of Creative Writing programmes (see Bishop 1990: xv).

What also needs to be considered, however, is what happened in English Studies during this period. In the decades of Creative

Writing's expansion English Studies underwent a series of disciplinary upheavals known as the 'crisis' in English Studies. A crisis occurs when there is a breakdown of consensus regarding the goals of research and teaching in a discipline, when an object of study can no longer be taken for granted. As early as 1964 Graham Hough's 'Crisis in Literary Education' described a growing discontent with the failure of the Leavisite enterprise in England. The famous conference on 'The Languages of Criticism and the Sciences of Man' at Johns Hopkins University in 1966 was convened in response to a supposed crisis in the human sciences brought about by Continental structuralist enterprises (see Macksey and Donato 1972), and in 1970 Paul de Man's 'Criticism and Crisis' outlined the effects of this on Literary Studies.

The loss of faith in the cultural and educational authority of English was centred on the exhaustion of Anglo-American 'practical criticism', and was accompanied by the rise of what has become known as Theory. 'Theory' is a frustratingly imprecise but generally accepted umbrella term for a mode of anti-humanist, anti-foundationalist, and counter-intuitive textual enquiry derived from a collocation of extra-literary disciplines and employed to critique the assumptions underpinning traditional literary criticism. If, in the early part of the twentieth century, a united critical front was opposed to historical and philological scholarship in universities, in the latter part of the century a united 'theoretical' front was opposed to the hegemony of criticism in the university. In which case, the emergence of various strands of feminism and Marxism, of semiotics, structuralism, deconstruction, poststructuralism, postmodernism, reader-response theory, psychoanalysis, sociology, the New Historicism and cultural materialism all had in common a critique of English Studies as it was organised around a particular understanding of literature arrived at by practical criticism.

Reginald Gibbons offers two, perhaps contradictory, accounts of the expansion of writing programmes in relation to the rise of Theory. The transformation of criticism by Theory, Gibbons argues, was caused by the drive to professionalise Literary Studies in the university. This professionalisation was also responsible for the expansion and consolidation of Creative Writing programmes in the university. At the same time, however, Creative Writing emerged to 'fill the gap' created by the devaluation of the human value of literature – a necessary victim of the shift from critical evaluation to theoretical analysis. The 'activity of reading' was thus replaced by 'the activity of writing' as a means of maintaining the value of literary experience in the university (1985: 31). 'That is to say,' Gibbons asserts, 'the proliferation of the writing programs is as much a negative reaction to the teaching of literature and the practice of criticism as it is a development in the situation of contemporary writing' (31).

George Garrett concludes that, as a result of the rise of Theory, 'creative writing courses and programs have become the forlorn hope for traditional literary criticism and even scholarship' (1992: 671). This is the basis for Morton and Zavarzadeh's critique of Creative Writing, for they claim that, in the face of radical postmodern critical theory, 'humanist scholars and critics are embracing creative writing programs as bastions of the inviolable human imagination' (1988–9: 160). Whether or not there was any direct correlation between the rise of Theory and the expansion of Creative Writing programmes, these programmes, in general, consciously positioned themselves in opposition to Theory.

By 1986 Marjorie Perloff could describe English Studies as a discipline divided between the A Team of the Creative Writing Workshop and the B Team of the Graduate Seminar in Theory (45). Both Garrett and Gibbons contend that this division between Creative Writing and Literary Studies is due to the fact that Theory has no relevance to the needs of contemporary writers. As a result, one might surmise, Theory failed to have the same impact on the graduate workshop as it did on the graduate seminar because it could not be adapted to the pedagogy of the workshop. In 'From Work to Text' ([1971] 1977) Roland Barthes announced that the interdisciplinary work of Marxism, Freudianism and structuralism had necessitated a conceptual and methodological shift within Literary Studies, such that the object of study was no longer a discrete set of 'works', embodied in books, but an infinite number of 'texts', all linguistically interrelated. This word, 'text', has since become ubiquitous in Literary Studies, even if not used in the same context as the one in which Barthes used it. David Fenza, executive director of the AWP, claimed in 2000 that 'creative writing classes have always esteemed, not *texts*, but literary *works*, which writers willed into being because they needed to name an experience or idea their culture had not yet named' (13). In a Creative Writing class 'students create worlds of their own making', and this 'will to make art' is an 'exalting' experience (13). Such an experience cannot be provided in 'a class tempered by recent literary theories' because, in ignoring the creative will of individual authors in favour of a variety of social contexts, 'professors of literary theory often deprive writers of their humanity' (13).

One way of understanding the popularity of structuralism and poststructuralism in the academy is to see these theoretical movements as a continuation of the push for independence from the authority of writers which I outlined at the end of Chapter 2. In 'Literary Commentary as Literature' Geoffrey Hartman drew attention to the 'school of Derrida' (1980: 189) which is influencing a 'creative criticism' (191) liberated from its role as mere commentary. Using Derrida's work as an example of the contamination of 'source text and secondary text' (206) in poststructuralist writing, the difficulty of separating the commentator's discourse from the author's, Hartman writes that 'literary commentary today is creating texts – a literature – of its own' (212). Jonathan Culler, in turn, was able to claim in 1988 that contemporary criticism and theory now perform within universities the avant-garde role which used to be performed by literature (38–40).

In his widely known and well-regarded book, *Cultural Capital* (1993), John Guillory claims that debates over the curricular content of the canon are symptomatic of a crisis of cultural capital in the university. Moves to 'open up' the canon by studying the literary representation of marginalised identities do not necessarily provide those groups with political representation. The more important factor is the institutional conditions which unevenly distribute cultural capital throughout society by regulating the access of minorities to literacy. Guillory argues that the canon debate is based on the assumption that literature is the dominant form of cultural capital in the humanities. This is a false debate, however, because literature, as the cultural capital of the bourgeoisie, has been superseded and replaced within the technobureaucratic organisation of the university by Theory, which is the cultural capital of the new professional-managerial class. The failure of Theory to provide a new rationale for the humanities is what, in fact, underlies the canon debate. What Guillory is attempting here is to shift the focus of the canon debate away from an examination of the responsibility and agency of authors (as representative members of a constituency), and towards the institutional conditions regulating access to cultural capital, a capital manifested in the graduate school 'Theory canon'. If one accepts his argument then it is obvious that contemporary English Studies has little need for literature, let alone writers. Guillory's book is both an examination and an example of the impact of Theory.

From its inception modern English Studies has attempted to shore up its professional disciplinary status within the university, and this has involved an increasingly sophisticated arrogation of the literary authority of the writer. There has thus been no space within the disciplinary organisation of contemporary English Studies for the authority of the writer *as* writer. Because the writer has been divested of authority within the academy there is no space for the literary work to contribute to Literary Studies, except dumbly. Discussion of literature takes place *within* the workshop, but this is a silent discourse not only because it is seen as 'practical' advice, but because it does not produce critical treatises (except handbooks on writing). Hence Creative Writing can only be *commented upon*. This commentary, of course, assumes the form of the double question: can writing be taught, and should it be?

The supposition that the expansion of Creative Writing may have been a conservative reaction to the rise of Theory has now become a justification for its continued existence and a reason for its growing popularity. In a 2002 posting on *Electronic Book Review*, Marjorie Perloff claims that Creative Writing programmes fill 'a need that English simply refuses to satisfy. I am talking about literary study, increasingly neglected as beside the point by the so-called Englit department in deference to the heady new world of Cultural Studies' (1). That said, Perloff is dismissive of the 'anti-intellectual and separatist paradigm' of writing programmes where the main goal 'seems to be to train its students to publish short stories and poems in The New Yorker as well as novels with Doubleday or Simon and Schuster' (2). For Perloff, the 'wave of the future' for Creative Writing is no longer the MFA, but the PhD based on the Buffalo Poetics Program, in which the workshop is 'subordinate' to the teaching of literature of the past, literatures of foreign languages, and poetic theory (2).

Despite these recent innovations, publications and annual conferences for the AWP continue to demonstrate a lack of interest in the relationship between Creative Writing and other disciplines within the academy, and to be narrowly concerned with the teaching of craft. The discipline of Creative Writing relies on the assumption that its allegiance is to 'literature' and literary culture, rather than to any form of intellectual enquiry, and that its contribution to the academy is in fostering literary appreciation. For Fenza, Creative Writing and literary studies are, or ought to be, complementary because together they contribute to 'both conservation of past works and the innovation of future works' (2000: 13).

By comparison, conferences for the Australian Association of Writing Programs, which have been held annually since 1996, suggest that Creative Writing in Australia has a far more pluralist and interdisciplinary nature. In a sense, AAWP conferences are always interdisciplinary because writing programmes are housed in a range of different faculties and schools: English and Cultural Studies, the

Creative Arts, Media and Communication Studies, and Professional Writing. Furthermore, while the terminal degree for aspiring writers in the United States is the Master of Fine Arts, there are a range of masters and doctoral degrees in Australia, most of which require an accompanying critical essay.

What is the reason for this difference? Unlike the North American disciplinary history which I outlined in Chapter 2, the development of Creative Writing in Australia has been much more piecemeal, without any homogeneous purpose, and without any one institution or individual being of seminal importance. Furthermore, it emerged in the late 1960s *alongside* the rise of Theory in Australian universities and colleges, as a challenge to traditional literary education, rather than as a defence of it. It is this history, and the relative newness of the discipline, which has placed Australian Creative Writing programmes in a more flexible and interdisciplinary position than those in America. It is not my intention to describe an ideal model of Creative Writing which exists in Australia and which, if transported to American universities, could solve whatever problems exist there. For a start, despite their differences, the workshop model is the dominant mode of Creative Writing pedagogy in Australia as much as it is in America. I plan, however, to take advantage of the historical fact that Creative Writing developed in Australia out of a different 'crisis' from that in America, precisely in order to investigate whether these conditions have contributed anything to the discipline. This history is important not only because it has not been written before, but because it is somewhat at odds with the common understanding of the discipline's origins. It is generally accepted that Creative Writing developed in vocational colleges as a practical training in the literary craft, before being absorbed into the university system via a wave of amalgamations in the 1990s. I will argue, instead, that Creative Writing developed in both colleges of advanced education and universities as a series of local pedagogical responses to the international crisis in English Studies which accompanied the rise of Theory. As a result the emergence of Creative Writing in Australia is emblematic of its emergence around the world as the disciplinary and imperial coherence of English Studies fractured.

As the case studies which I will present below demonstrate, Creative Writing developed in Australian tertiary institutions in three main forms: as a 'practical' approach to the study of literature in departments of English and Literary Studies; as the teaching of written communication alongside other genres such as journalism or advertising in new degrees in Professional Writing and Communication;

and as the teaching of an art form alongside other artistic media such as painting or music in schools for the Creative Arts. Creative Writing only developed in this disparate and interdisciplinary fashion, however, when the discipline of English had its academic hegemony over literature challenged by the advent of Theory, the nationalist push for Australian Literary Studies, and the expansion of tertiary education. These challenges opened up the possibility for Creative Writing to emerge as an alternative means of literary education.

The common factor in the various courses, majors and programmes in Creative Writing which emerged was the workshop, which has its origins, of course, in the discipline of Creative Writing in America. Furthermore, by virtue of being concerned with the study and practice of literature, Creative Writing cannot be conceptually dissociated from Literary Studies. The very phrase 'creative writing' is a synonym for literature. In a very real sense Creative Writing arose in opposition to the academic study of literature in *departments* of English because it demonstrated that literature could be deployed within universities in different professional and pedagogical ways than it had traditionally been; indeed, it could be deployed in other disciplines. Nonetheless, it cannot be conceived as operating outside the *discipline* of English which is now so heterogenous and capacious as a result of the very crisis which precipitated the emergence of Creative Writing.

English Studies in Australia

In 1945 John Ewers published a survey of Australian literature called *Creative Writing in Australia*. The term 'creative writing' obviously operated as a synonym for literature, for published works of fiction and poetry. Even when a revised edition was reissued in 1962 there was no self-consciousness about the phrase; in fact 'creative writing' is never used in the body of the text. One reason why the discipline of Creative Writing has developed relatively recently in Australia is the strong ties Australian universities have enjoyed with British literary education. While Creative Writing has recently become a huge growth area in the United Kingdom, this growth has had to contend with the endemic scepticism produced by English Studies.

In the 1967 Clark Lectures, F.R. Leavis found universities neither qualified nor appropriate for the education of writers. He disliked the American tradition of 'the creative writer on campus' – and indeed the word 'campus' (1979: 63). 'Further,' he stated, 'I don't at all think that candidates for Honours should be encouraged to believe that by submitting original poems, novels or plays to the examiners, they may improve their claim to a good class' (63). These comments cannot be dismissed as the curmudgeonly mutterings of a single Englishman, for, as Rene Wellek points out, Leavis was 'the most influential practical critic of the century in England' (1982: 54). His influence on English Studies was the result not only of the force of his criticism, but of the fact that this criticism was the product of an educational mission closely connected with his efforts to establish an ideal English school as a central discipline within the university. While the term 'practical criticism' has often been used to refer to the dominant mode of English Studies in both British and American universities in the mid-twentieth century, Creative Writing enjoyed a connection with American New Criticism which it could not enjoy in the Leavisite project.

In 1963 two lecturers from the University of Western Australia wrote in the American journal, *College English*, that Leavis and I.A. Richards 'have had an enormous effect on the teaching of English literature in universities in the British Commonwealth', including Australia (Gibbons and Gibbons 1963–4: 368). John Docker argued in his 1984 book, *In a Critical Condition*, that the wide influence of Leavisite and New Critical textual analysis in Australian universities had created a 'metaphysical ascendancy' where cultural elitism, the autonomy of literary works and the moral force of literature were upheld (83–109). Whether or not one agrees with what Brenton Doecke has called 'Docker's mythic struggle between radical nationalists and the metaphysical ascendancy' (1997: 71), it is obvious that Creative Writing was not an issue of importance. When interviewed by Richard Freadman in 1983, Leonie Kramer and S.L. Goldberg, both of whom Docker would characterise as members of this 'metaphysical ascendancy', expressed a distaste for the development of Creative Writing in Australian universities (Freadman 1983: 14–15).

It is due to this state of affairs in Australian universities that Nigel Krauth and Tess Brady argue that when Creative Writing courses began to emerge in tertiary institutions in the 1970s they 'carried with them the stigma of being an American (or anti-British) idea' (1997: 47). Krauth and Brady argue that before the introduction of tertiary writing courses in Australia, 'there was little concern for the process of producing the literary text; the focus of English Departments was the received text and the reading process' (47). The writing process, they assert, was ignored because of 'the illogical consideration that the act of writing was somehow beneath the dignity of tertiary study' (47). This is a somewhat specious argument. The act of poetic creation had been an object of serious study since the Romantic period. Rather, the production within the academy of writing which purported to be literature was looked down upon as improper and presumptuous.

In an article entitled 'The Universities and Creative Writing', which appeared in *Drylight*, the journal of the Sydney Teachers' College, in 1960, S.E. Lee listed with admiration the number of important poets and novelists who have graduated from English universities. 'And this is how it should be,' he declared, 'a university education should so inform and broaden that the writer approaches his chosen career better equipped to use the intellect and creative imagination with which he has been naturally endowed' (33). This argument is very similar to those which accompanied the establishment of the Iowa School of Letters. Lee was quick to follow this up, however, with a disclaimer:

> On the other hand, I don't think it is the function of a university to teach play-writing and story-making in the same way as business institutes teach advertising techniques – as is done in certain American universities. Faulkner and Steinbeck – both non-graduates – did take some university courses, but not in learning *how* to write.
>
> (33)

Two years later Lee penned a brief preface for an article by A.D. Hope entitled 'Creative Writing', in which he welcomed Hope back to *Drylight*, 'the magazine he did so much for by fostering creative writing during the years he was with us' (Hope 1962: 3). Hope had served as a lecturer in English and Education from 1937 to 1945. In this article he talks of a visit he paid to the United States and Canada in 1958 and his observation of Creative Writing programmes. While he reveals a scepticism about the possibility of teaching writing based on this observation, he also discusses a course he devised as an 'experiment' (5) or 'trial run' (6) in Creative Writing at Sydney Teachers' College in the 1940s. Hope claims that he 'was interested in what I had heard of creative writing courses in universities overseas', and also felt that it would be beneficial for teachers to 'have some first-hand experience of writing', since creative work was being encouraged in schools in order to 'extend and vary the ordinary drill in classroom composition' (5). Hope commented that the course was 'reasonably successful' (6) before concluding that Creative Writing is better suited as an extra-curricular activity. This, no doubt, was the first Creative Writing course in a tertiary institution in Australia.

There is no doubt, either, that Hope's visit to America doused any sympathy he may have felt towards Creative Writing in universities. Upon his return he delivered a paper to the Fellowship of Australian Writers in 1959, a later version of which was published in *The Cave and the Spring* under the title 'Literature versus the Universities'. The civility with which he discussed the topic in the *Drylight* article is missing in this caustic essay. Referring to the century-old struggle to establish English as a valid discipline beyond the shadow of the Classics, he suggests that, considering the influence that the university study of literature has had on the production of new writing, it might have been better if Classics had won out (1965: 165). While research and criticism in literature was originally carried out for its own sake, with no organised relations between writers and scholars, Hope suggests that, due to the massive bulge in student numbers and the subsequent rise of postgraduate work since the war, 'English, from a new and not very utilitarian subject, has become a high-pressure industry' (166). A generation ago, 'research in the field of literature was undertaken in the interests of literature', but now 'the purpose of nine-tenths of the research and criticism that goes on is to help the researcher to qualify in the great rat race' (167). The need to find fresh material for original research has seen the work of forgotten, second-rate writers exhumed from their literary graves and subjected to serious critical study. This endeavour has now moved on to living writers. 'No sooner does a modern writer achieve some fame in the United States,' Hope complains, 'than his books are prescribed in university courses, his work becomes the subject of dozens of research theses and critical theses, and he himself is invited to write and lecture on his own creative processes' (169).

According to Hope, all modern writers now write 'in an atmosphere of critical inspection' (169). Rather than following and developing a tradition of writing, contemporary authors write in the shadow of the latest literary theories, so that 'literary criticism which had once been the handmaid of literature was fast becoming the mistress' (170). This finds its ultimate realisation, Hope argues, in the developing industry and profession of Creative Writing. The poet who is trained in a university and returns to teach there is influenced to write in illustration of critical theories, thus reversing the 'proper order of nature' (172). Because universities require more and more works of serious literature to analyse, they are 'taking over literature and breeding their own writers and standardizing their own supply' (173). The situation is so dire, according to Hope, 'that it will not be long perhaps before there are no wild writers left anymore' (171).

Comparing the impact of American writing programmes to that of Marxism on the Russian writers who became embroiled with the aims of the Soviet government, he concludes in portentous fashion: 'Don't think that it can only happen in Russia and the United States. The same economic forces are at work in the United Kingdom, in Australia, and indeed in the whole world' (173).

These sentiments towards Creative Writing were not noted or addressed in contemporaneous reviews of *The Cave and the Spring*. In *Meanjin* Chris Wallace-Crabbe (a poet-professor who would later display an interest in Creative Writing) found this 'ruthless' piece amusing in light of the fact that Hope is often regarded as an 'academic poet' (1966: 115). And in *Southerly* Vivian Smith saw the essay, amongst others, as a demonstration that 'Hope's criticism and his poetry arise from the same centres of concern' (1965: 284). If anything, these reviews demonstrate that discussing Creative Writing was of no great concern. At the time Hope's essay appeared, writing programmes did not exist in Australian universities. History would prove that his warning was not heeded by the 'wild' writers themselves. The proclamation which another writer, the novelist William Dick, made in the *Australian Author* in 1974, after visiting the Stanford Creative Writing Center, demonstrates a growing interest *outside* the academy:

> A further question I'm asked is, 'Do you think we should have creative writing courses in Australia?' 'Definitely,' I answer. Every one of our universities and colleges of advanced education should have one. It should be autonomous and not part of the English department. It should be run by writers for writers. It should work in with the English department and should be funded adequately. I'd like to see the Literature Board get behind a project to set up writing centres in our universities. The classes should be available to anyone in the community and students should be chosen on the basis of talent, not academic qualifications just because it's a university. (33)

The obvious response to this demand is, why? The only reason Dick proffers is that, '[t]here are many people who want to write' (34). Writing programmes have proliferated in universities because they are immensely popular. Hence one way to understand their emergence is to examine the conditions for student demand. The origins for this can be found in the links between education and what Dorothy Green has called 'the modern cult of "creativity", equated with "self-expression"' (1991: 47).

Creative English

The democratisation of creativity which enabled the *creative self-expression* model of Creative Writing to develop in American high schools in the 1920s also motivated the 'creative writing' movement which rose in English and Australian schools in the 1960s as part of a shift towards a new educational paradigm variously called the 'New English' or 'Creative English' or 'Personal Growth'. Thus the main impetus for the development of Creative Writing in schools was not literary, but pedagogical. It was less concerned with either understanding literature (although that was a byproduct) or producing writers, than with the personal development of individual students via their own writing. And it evolved out of a reaction against traditional methods of teaching English composition; 'the failure of the textbook' as Geoffrey Summerfield puts it (1968: 26). Lessons in grammar, drills in spelling and punctuation, and an emphasis on the correct use of language came to be questioned as the most effective means of producing literacy, and were considered a hindrance to the development of self-knowledge and active language use in children.

This new approach to English was enabled by the conjunction of modern genetic psychology and educational theory, what Jean Piaget calls the 'new methods' (Piaget 1971). These are based on the premise that children are not small adults, with similarly functioning minds. They cannot be seen as *tabula rasae* able to receive knowledge ready-made for absorption; their interest must be engaged. While this central idea is centuries old, and can be traced from Rousseau through to Dewey, it is only in the twentieth century that an educational science developed around it as a result of the findings of psychological studies of child intelligence. According to Piaget, the 'traditional school imposes his work on the student: it "makes him work" . . . The new school, on the contrary, appeals to real activity, to spontaneous work based upon personal need and interest' (152).

We have already seen in Hope's reflections on his work at the Sydney Teachers' College that Australian school teachers were experimenting with alternatives to traditional modes of composition in the 1940s. In *Towards a New English Curriculum*, L.E.W. Smith points out that the publication of Marjorie Hourd's *The Education of the Poetic Spirit* in 1949 saw many British primary schools 'engaged in "child-centred creative writing"' throughout the 1950s, although 'it was not until the 1960s that the movement spread to the secondary sector' (1972: 7). This period, according to R.D. Walshe, was the beginning of a world-wide explosion of interest in creativity (1971: 7).

The Anglo-American Seminar on the Teaching of English, held in 1966 and known as the Dartmouth Seminar, marks the point at which curricular experiments took shape as an educational theory and solidified into a movement. In *Growth Through English*, his 1967 book based on the Dartmouth Seminar, John Dixon claimed that the 'cultural heritage' model of English, which we would associate with the tradition of Arnold to Leavis and the idea that 'culture' resides in the canon of English literature, was being replaced by a 'personal growth' model which focuses on the child and his or her active use of language as a means of self-knowledge. By 1970 L.E.W. Smith was able to proclaim that 'there now seems no doubt that there is a "New English"' (4). 'Parsing and clause analysis, filling in blanks in sentences, writing for an undefined audience in an artificial way with the aim of avoiding mistakes, all the old English is out: and "creative" English is in' (4).

The Dartmouth Seminar also brought home the difference between English and American views of writing in the school system. In his book *Writing Matters*, Peter Moss describes the two broad approaches to writing during this period: the American rhetorical tradition, concerned with a functional approach to language as a practical tool for communication; and the British tradition, concerned with the process of writing as a means of self-expression. Here there was less interest in correcting the product which a student hands in, and a greater concern with how the process of writing facilitated a personal response to some external experience or stimuli (1981: 4–25). That it was the American participants who warned against the dangers of too great a faith in the self-expression of the child, as Dixon points out (1969: 12), and who showed greater interest in a functional model of communication, can be explained by the fact that America had already been through this in the Progressive Education movement of the 1920s.

Creative Writing developed in Australian schools as a direct result of the influence of British 'personal writing'. A perusal of *English in Australia*, the journal of the Australian Association for the Teaching of English (founded in 1965, with A.D. Hope as president), reveals that Creative Writing was established as a pedagogical device in schools long before it reached universities. In a 1968 issue Joan Woodberry observes that '[c]reative writing in English teaching has been with us for a long time now' and 'shows signs of becoming a gimmick' (29).

If students were to be encouraged to write 'creatively' in schools, it was necessary to develop in teachers an ability to foster this creativity. Thus Creative Writing first entered the tertiary education sector as part of the curriculum in teachers' colleges. In a 1966 article in *English in Australia*, Glen Phillips described a 'poetry workshop at Grayland's Teachers' College' which 'aimed to help student teachers to see the value of poetry writing as a genuine activity' (41). One of the first colleges of advanced education to offer classes in Creative Writing was the Mitchell CAE (originally Bathurst Teachers' College and now Charles Sturt University). Here the New Zealand poet, Louis Johnson, taught classes in the Department of English and Modern Languages from 1969. However, Creative Writing was 'part of the College's overall aim to provide a sound educational background to future teachers in the related subjects of literature and self/written expression, reading and writing' (*Mitchell CAE Calendar 1974*: 38).

In 1984 Pam Gilbert wrote that '"Creative Writing" appears to have won itself a secure and valued foothold in school English curriculum programs' (4). Creative Writing is today still firmly established in the school curriculum from primary to upper secondary levels, although the self-expression model has been modified by the development of socio-linguistics and the subsequent introduction of transactional writing (which was concerned with the need for competency across a wider range of language usage, and geared towards engaging an audience in social contexts beyond the classroom) and process writing (which sharply identified the various stages of writing from generative techniques through to drafting, redrafting, editing and revision). Interested students will thus be keen to pursue it into their university studies and establish an educational continuum. While personal development through strategies of creative self-expression may not be a professed educational goal of university writing programmes, the workshop model nonetheless caters for student desires in this area. Kevin Brophy attributes the attraction of Creative Writing to the entry of pleasure into the academy, describing workshops as a site for the modern technology of the confessional (1998: 235–43).

Brophy also suggests that Creative Writing can be the site of a 'minor literature', an alternative literary phenomenon running alongside mainstream publications (37–47). Most students, however, wish to carry their minor literary works into the professional arena, which is why promotional material for writing programmes draws attention to the number of students who publish work and win literary prizes. Here is the other great source of student demand for Creative Writing courses. The desire to write, catered for by a 'cult of creativity', is inevitably entangled with the desire to be read.

The 'new' Australian writing

The crucial factor for the wide-scale attraction of writing programmes is a cultural environment in which it seems possible and attractive to become a published author. In a 1996 interview Gerald Murnane, senior lecturer in fiction writing at Deakin University, reminisced that in 1959, when the campus was Toorak Teachers' College and he was a student, 'no-one in their right mind would have wanted to be a writer in Australia' (Braun-Bau 1996: 44). That year *Meanjin* published an article by Vincent Buckley entitled 'Towards an Australian Literature'. In this article Buckley pointed to the continuing debate over whether there was even a body of work which could deservedly be called Australian literature. He side-stepped this question and instead proposed 'some questions about the possibility, and the pro-priety, of having Australian literature as a subject of formal teaching and discussion in a university' ([1959] 1967: 75). In the 1962 edition of *Creative Writing in Australia*, Ewers stated that Australian literature was only just beginning to be recognised as a valid area of study in universities. He also claimed that there 'have never been sufficient Australian publishers for the needs of all Australian writers', forcing many to seek first publication overseas (12). Pretensions of teaching Creative Writing in Australian universities could only find purchase if there was a tradition of Australian writing. The gradual legitimisa-tion and canonisation of Australian literature as a cultural form via formal study in the academy, and the development of a stronger local publishing industry, contributed to this.

While poet-professors such as Hope, Buckley and James McAuley were contributing to the institutionalisation of Australian Literary Studies as part of a desire to establish a national canon, and thus to the fostering of a literary culture, Australian writing underwent signifi-cant changes. The 'new' writing which developed in the late 1960s and throughout the 1970s was, firstly, a generational shift. Many of today's 'established' writers emerged at this time, in the shadow of the Vietnam War and the 1960s 'counter-culture'. They emerged, however, in reaction to established traditions of Australian writing: against the classicism and formal prosody of 'academic' poets such as Hope and McAuley; and against realist fiction, especially the 'bush' story exemplified by Henry Lawson and associated with the *Bulletin* magazine. In fact there was a shift away from a sense of a *national* literature, with writers turning overseas for inspiration. In poetry this revolution could be seen as a belated shift towards Modernism (in its European and American variants), but also as an embracing of postmodern American poetry, especially the New York School and the Black Mountain poets (the link between Modernism and postmodernism is an awareness, and self-conscious exploration, of language as non-representational, and an avant-garde commitment to experiment, especially with free verse). Fiction writers were influenced by the postmodern fabulism and metafiction of North and South America.

This generational shift and move towards a literary internationalism was accompanied by a challenge to traditional means of publication, made possible by technological changes. Rejected from mainstream or establishment journals and publishing houses, young writers employed type-setting typewriters, roneo copiers and cheap off-set printing to establish an alternative network of 'underground' magazines and small independent presses. They also gained wider audiences through public readings in both poetry and prose. By 1977 *Australian Literary Studies* had devoted an entire issue to the 'New Writing in Australia', containing not academic assessments, but essays and statements by the writers and editors involved. It is worth briefly tracing the emergence of this new writing because it occurred at the same time that Creative Writing classes began to develop in tertiary institutions.

In 1968 Rodney Hall and Tom Shapcott published *New Impulses in Australian Poetry*, an anthology designed, they wrote in the introduction, 'to clarify the accomplishments of Australian poetry in breaking fresh ground during the past decade, particularly since 1960 . . . This is the first time such a wide selection of this new poetry has been brought together in one volume which includes no poems by the accepted hierarchy' (1). The contemporaneity of this collection, however, was soon overshadowed by the new wave of poetry by slightly younger writers which emerged from 1967 to 1970 in cheap or free 'underground' magazines and at public readings. When editorship of *Poetry Magazine*, the official journal of the Poetry Society of Australia, was taken over by Robert Adamson, who renamed it *New Poetry* in 1970, the experimental work of those which John Tranter later called 'the Generation of '68' was given a more prominent arena for publication (see Tranter 1978). In the same year the established journal, *Meanjin Quarterly*, published an energetic and elliptical article by Kris Hemensley (who, along with Tranter, was the most prominent spokesperson of this movement) entitled 'First Look at "The New Australian Poetry"', hence giving a name to this movement.

This was also the year in which Shapcott published another anthology, *Australian Poetry Now*, which attempted to include examples of all the directions Australian poetry had taken over the past decade. Shapcott wrote in his introduction:

> For the first time since the early to mid-forties, when *Angry Penguins* and *Barjai* made youthful sorties upon middle-age-minded conservatism, young poets are rejecting and rediscovering, making loud claims for themselves and their ideas. Their presence already troubles the weekend calm of the established journals (who give them a pat of apparent recognition which they hope will keep them in order), and, in the areas of their own activities they spawn innumerable broadsheets, 'underground' pamphlets, mini-mags collated with love, hope, energy and amateur duplicators.
>
> (1970: ix)

For Shapcott this new generation of poets were 'inheritors of post-war affluence and admass Techniculture' (ix). The most important distinction he makes in this anthology, however, is between academic or university poets and 'underground' poets. While representatives of both were included in this collection of sixty-four poets, it is clear that the dynamism of youthful contemporaneity is associated with the 'underground' poets. In a 1974 issue of *New Poetry* John Tranter argued that there was a polarisation in the publishing scene between the big publishing houses and the smaller independent presses. He referred to the latter as 'the area which has shown most growth since 1967, and which, intentionally or otherwise, is laying the foundation for the next generation of "Aust. Lit."' (43).

At the same time that the 'new' poetry was being established, a similar generational shift took place in Australian fiction. More than just a passing of the guard, however, this generation was seen to have revived the flagging art of the short story. According to Michael Wilding, 'something happened in Australian writing around 1968–69' (1977: 117). Reaction to the Vietnam War, he argues, was manifested in the form not only of political protest, but of cultural change, opening up Australia to international literary influences and the social energies of the 1960s counter-culture. At this time Wilding and Frank Moorhouse were publishing stories in soft-porn 'girlie' magazines to avoid censorship restrictions. 'But no less censoring,' according to Wilding, 'even if much less recognised, were the limitations imposed by the very nature of the formal, overground media: by the traditional literary editors for publishers and for magazines, what their taste could understand, or tolerate' (115).

What enabled new forms of Australian fiction to emerge into the public arena was, like the new poetry, changes in the modes of production, the means of publication. For instance, in 1972 Wilding, Moorhouse and Carmel Kelly established *Tabloid Story*, a magazine devoted to publishing new and experimental fiction and distributed, ingeniously, as a free supplement to host publications with wide circulation (including *The Bulletin* and many university newspapers). With the publication in 1977 by Angus & Robertson of *The Most Beautiful Lies*, edited by Brian Kiernan, Wilding, Moorhouse, Peter Carey, Murray Bail and Morris Lurie were brought together as representatives of a new generation of fiction writers in Australia.

Perhaps the most important contribution to the consolidation of the new writing in Australia was the establishment of the Literature Board of the Australia Council in 1973 (replacing the old Commonwealth Literature Fund), following the election of the Whitlam Labor government in the previous year. This government funding body began providing grants to individual writers, to magazines and to publishers. This was considered by some to be the end of the poetry revolution of the late 1960s precisely because it allowed 'underground' literary enterprises to become financially viable and institutionally acknowledged, and thus part of the mainstream. One agenda of the Literature Board, however, was to remedy what it saw as the moribund state of Australian fiction. According to Ken Gelder and Paul Salzman, the 'Literature Board's early policy was to correct a perceived neglect of the novel in Australia, and in fact the novel now has become the dominant literary genre' (1989: 3). An injection of funds quickly produced what Carl Harrison-Ford called, in 1975, 'a boom in Australian fiction' (4). According to Barry Oakley, in the late 1960s Penguin Books, under its general manager, John Michie, and publisher, John Hooker, began to focus strongly on producing Australian literature. But it was not until Brian Johns took over as publishing director in 1979 that this became a priority: 'the final effect was like the discharging of a large blunderbuss – out came Australian titles of an extraordinary range and variety' (1995: 4).

What did this explosion in literary activity have to do with the rise of Creative Writing? For a start there are chronological links. At the same time that the new Australian writing was developing, workshops in Creative Writing were proliferating. In 1969, Joan Clarke observed in *The Australian Author* that 'in recent years there has been a strong trend towards the "teaching" of creative writing' and that in 'Australia we have summer schools, evening classes, workshops and seminars which are never short of enthusiastic participants' (38).

In 1973, and in the same magazine, Michael Dugan remarked that despite the truth of the 'common saying that "writers are made, not taught"' this 'does not appear to deter the large number of writers' schools that operate in most Western countries' (23). He felt compelled to list some points of advice for aspirants, including the need to be suspicious of schools with only a post-office box address.

At this stage writing programmes were also beginning to develop in tertiary institutions. Their impact was felt by 1983 when Frank Moorhouse edited the short-story anthology, *The State of the Art*. In the introduction Moorhouse claimed that ten years earlier he had not found an abundance of riches to choose from for the annual *Coast to Coast* anthology which he was asked to edit, but that this time he did. In an issue of *Australian Literary Studies* the following year he noted that 37 per cent of contributors to *The State of the Art* had done (or taught in) writing courses. 'I once believed', Moorhouse wrote, 'that writers should run away to sea rather than do writing courses but as my friend Don Anderson said, now young writers – and not so young writers – run away to Cee-A-Es. I'd probably say that they should run away to sea and then do a course or vice versa' (494). For Brian Kiernan, Moorhouse's selection for the traditionally stodgy *Coast to Coast* anthology in 1973 demonstrated that 'a new generation had arrived' (1977: xiii). Moorhouse's 1983 selection demonstrates not only that writing courses were beginning to contribute to Australian writing, but that the new generation had inspired younger writers to undertake writing courses.

What I am suggesting is that the new Australian writing, which developed out of cheap or free magazines and was accompanied by public readings, helped to open up for many people the possibility of authorship in Australia. It is impossible to know whether more people actually started writing in this period, but it can be surmised that more people entertained the possibility of publishing their work. Kris Hemensley wrote in 1970 that '[t]he emergence of the little mags – *Crosscurrents/Our Glass/The Great Auk/Free Poetry/Flagstones/Mok* & the others – dented the status of the Published Poet. First it was important to print as many poets as possible' (120). John Tranter wrote in 1974 that '[a]fter the brief flourish of little magazines and presses around 1967 and 1968, a second and stronger wave of books, booklets, magazines and anthologies has washed over the bookshops leaving a tang of freshness in the air and a crop of young talents budding on the beach head. It has never before been so easy for a young poet to be published' (43). Michael Wilding noted in 1978 that after 'each issue of *Tabloid Story* a different batch of new contributions arrives' (316). Many of these were from unpublished and unknown contributors. Given that *Tabloid Story* circulated widely in universities, it can be surmised that these stories came from students. In a 1985 anthology of performance poetry entitled *Off the Record*, the poet PiO wrote that the small magazine explosion of the late 1960s was an attempt to bypass a stranglehold which 'academic' poets such as Hope and Buckley had 'on the production and distribution of poetry in Australia' (3). Coupled with the revolutionary fervour of the 1960s, he argues, this ground-level interest in poetry promoted a belief that everyone could be a poet. 'For a generation of Australians used to the born-with-it arguments adopted by English Departments this idea was refreshing if not downright revolutionary' (4).

If 'underground' writers created a greater enthusiasm for writing, then it is obvious that writing workshops would begin to flourish, for they are themselves another form of public reading and underground publishing (a 'minor' literature, as Brophy says). Another, perhaps more important, point to make, however, is that alongside this flourishing of small-press publication, writers came more and more to assume positions in universities as the tertiary sector expanded throughout the 1960s. Hall and Shapcott address this in their 1968 anthology when they note that

> a far greater proportion of our poets are on university staffs than in the past . . . As to the enormous increase in university poets, this is indicative of the general change in the social significance of universities, which are far larger and more influential than they were twenty years ago. As is common with an ascendant social group, the universities have taken upon themselves the function of patronage. The reason more poets are on university staffs now than before is that this kind of work leaves them most freedom to practice their art.
>
> (10)

Shapcott and Hall are accepting of this change, although nonetheless wary of the self-consciousness which can affect university poets. What must be remembered is that these poets all taught literature, not Creative Writing. It meant though that, as Australian literature became accepted as an object of study, and the possibility of teaching Creative Writing gradually emerged as even more challenges to traditional English Studies developed, there would be a large number of writers already working in universities who would be able to teach it. In fact, the presence of practising writers in universities was the necessary precondition for the development of Creative Writing, not only because they were able to teach it, but because they generally instigated it. Shapcott's history of the Literature Board of the Australia Council points out that one of its major projects was to provide funds for writer-in-residence schemes at tertiary institutions (Shapcott 1988). This began in 1974 and over the next decade virtually every university and CAE took advantage of the project, hosting a range of local and over-seas writers, many of whom conducted writing workshops during their residence. Shapcott, who has since become Australia's first Professor of Creative Writing at the University of Adelaide, quotes David Malouf's claim that one benefit of the writer-in-residence project was that it would 'allow practitioners to see how our literature is being treated in the universities and to offer their own suggestions about how this could be improved or made more relevant' (Shapcott 1988: 123).

One more connection between the expansion of Creative Writing in tertiary institutions and the development of the Australian publishing industry is the impact of youth and authorial celebrity on readership and marketing practices in more recent years. In a 1993 review article entitled 'The Cult of the Author', Susan Lever argued that 'the market for Australian fiction is so strained that the promotion of individual writers is an essential part of its survival. The "star" system ensures some media attention and sales for writers, and literary criticism must ride on the backs of "star" authors' (230). 'We live in an autobiographical age,' Luke Slattery observes in an article on the Adelaide Writers' Festival, 'in which the writer's personality is deeply enmeshed with the reception of his or her work' (1996: 1). The Adelaide Writers' Festival was established in 1960, but literary festivals have become increasingly numerous and popular since the mid-1980s (when Melbourne, Newcastle and Sydney were established), and are major venues for the literal embodiment of authors as the origin of their work. According to Ivor Indyk:

> The marketing of Australian writing has gone hand in hand with the proliferation in creative writing classes, and the two phenomena are intimately connected. The cult of the author is obviously a powerful incentive for those who harbour the desire to write, and even for those who don't . . . Anecdotal evidence would seem to suggest that a large part of the audience at literary festivals is made up of such would-be writers, writers whose aspiration towards a personal literary authority finds some satisfaction in a vicarious identification with the author celebrated on the stage.
>
> (1997: 39)

Increased opportunities for publication, or, more importantly, the perception of an increase, along with the cult of authorial celebrity, have coincided with the thirst for self-expression through writing. In 1980 the Vogel awards were established, increasing the opportunities for publication of writers under thirty-five. An early winner was Tim Winton, a product of the Western Australian Institute of Technology's writing programme. Lucy Sussex has noted that the proliferation of writing programmes has coincided with vast increases to entries in literary competitions (1997: 66). In his article, 'Literary Awards and Creative Writing Schools', Nigel Krauth writes that it 'seems that every tertiary-level school wants to produce a Vogel winner' in order to 'lay claim to a particular expertise and superiority' (1999: 2).

A preoccupation with discovering and publishing (although not necessarily nurturing) young writers, which Marion Halligan has condemned as 'literary pederasty' (1997: 38), is something which Creative Writing programmes feed off and feed into. This is no more explicitly manifested than in the recent phenomenon of 'grunge-lit'. Regardless of the motivations of individual writers, their works were marketed and received as virtually diaristic vehicles for the celebrity of the authors as representatives of 'Generation X'. Grunge literature was also seen to be influenced by American 'dirty realism', which is a dirty name for new minimalism; the product of a generation of writers influenced by Raymond Carver (such as Bobbie Ann Mason, Bret Easton Ellis and Jay McInerney) and spawned by Creative Writing programmes (see Dawson 1997).

The increasing popularity of writing courses as a possible gateway to authorship (where self-expression and celebrity are merged), and the expansion of Australian publishing which enabled this, meant that there would be great student interest when tertiary institutions began to challenge traditional forms of literary education in the early 1970s, often following the lead of schools and replacing what Ian Reid has called the 'Literature Gallery', and its role as a pedagogical custodian of canonical traditions, with the 'Literary Workshop', focusing on play as a means of encouraging students to engage creatively with the texts and critical methods they study (1984: 10–33). There is a further connection here with the 'new' writing in Australia. In their 1974 anthology, *Classic Australian Short Stories*, Judah Waten and Stephen Murray-Smith drew attention to assertions that the short story was a dying art in Australia. They claimed that this could not be upheld since so many new collections were being published, and their own anthology included a selection of modern writers such as Carey, Moorhouse and Wilding. Furthermore:

The revival of the short story is also reflected in the interest being shown in it in educational institutions. Indeed, it seems that the short story is being seen increasingly as the ideal medium for experimentation in creative writing in many English courses. There are certainly indications that English 'language' or 'expression' courses are beginning to acknowledge the importance of creative writing as opposed to formal grammatical accuracy in effective communication.

(x)

This 'creative' approach to literacy was the cornerstone of the New English in schools and the above observation reminds us that Creative Writing tended to develop in tertiary institutions out of the same desire to expand the boundaries of literary education or professional writing instruction. The dynamic emergence of the 'new' Australian writing and the changes in literary marketing and publishing which followed it, alongside the new methods of self-expression in schools, helped generate student demand for tertiary writing courses. And the increasing presence of writers in universities, especially as Australian literature came to be accepted as an area of study (the Association for the Study of Australian Literature was founded in 1977), provided the personnel and literary authority for these courses. Nonetheless, rather than developing as part of a network of apprenticeship and patronage, Creative Writing was a product of institutional and disciplinary changes between 1960 and 1990.

Vocational education

In 1961 the Commonwealth appointed a special committee, chaired by Sir Leslie Martin, to investigate and provide recommendations for the development of tertiary education in Australia. Reporting in three volumes over 1964–5, the Committee argued strongly in favour of encouraging a greater diversity in higher education and called for the expansion of technical education through the creation of colleges of advanced education. There would thus be three distinct types of tertiary institutions in Australia: universities, teachers colleges, and colleges of advanced education (see Martin 1964).

Formed out of technical colleges, the CAEs were geared towards a practical, vocational education for those students with different capacities and needs from the academically inclined students which a university would naturally attract. Hence an education could still be provided for those not able enough or interested enough in university study, with the benefit of a direct boost to the industrial, technological and economic growth of the nation. This marked the beginning of what became known as the binary system of higher education in Australia, comprising universities dedicated to research and the acquisition and dissemination of knowledge, and a vocational sector concentrating on teaching and professional training (teachers' colleges were incorporated into the CAE sector in 1975).

How did Creative Writing develop out of these technical institutions? Even if it were viewed as a practical subject, graduates of a writing course would have dim vocational prospects, nor would they provide any advances in technology. There are two answers. In order to raise the status of CAEs in the eyes of the public, the Martin report recommended the development of courses in the humanities and social sciences. Secondly, in order to provide a broader and more developed education for technical students (rather than mere training in a profession) it encouraged the introduction of 'relevant and integrated liberal studies' (Martin 1964: 171), which would develop the 'critical, imaginative and creative abilities' of students (182). The following passage suggests that any education in the liberal arts would have to be adapted to the professional needs of the students, rather than being concerned with the dissemination of knowledge, the passing on of a cultural heritage, or the development of the 'whole' person:

> It is imperative that students of technology should learn how to express their thoughts clearly and with an economy of words; for this purpose essay writing and precis are important. The study of literary masterpieces would, no doubt, constitute an important component of such courses, but emphasis should be on the use of language as a means of communication.
>
> (165)

The Canberra College of Advanced Education, the Western Australian Institute of Technology, and the NSW Institute of Technology all pioneered degrees or majors in writing before becoming accredited as universities in the late 1980s and early 1990s. All three have claimed, at some stage, to have been the first tertiary institution to establish writing programmes in Australia. Brief case studies of these institutions demonstrate the diversity of influences out of which Creative Writing developed.

The Canberra College of Advanced Education (now the University of Canberra) was established in 1967. In 1970 a diploma course in Professional Writing was introduced under what a former student called 'the sympathetic blue eye and relentless red pen' of its 'founding father', David Swain (Borthwick 1977: 18). Swain notes that although the first title chosen for the course was 'Creative Writing', it was subsequently rejected in order to distance it from negative associations with American college programmes.[1] 'Professional Writing' was agreed upon as the term most suited to an educational institution with a charter to provide vocational training. An emphasis was placed on getting students published as quickly as possible – partly because of the confidence which they would gain from this, but also because of the pressing need to convince the administrative powers that Professional Writing was a valid course within the college.

Journalism, copywriting, scientific and technical writing were included in the curriculum, as well as fiction, poetry, drama and scriptwriting for radio, film and television. Nonetheless, instead of offering strict rhetorical training in various modes of composition the degree was geared towards a general education in writing. For Swain, 'the true subject of the course is the student' (1970: 49). Work consisted of journal keeping, formal exercises, research-based articles, workshops, and a programme in poetry, 'not as a critical study but to explore the help it might give to writers of prose' (50). Here we see an open-ended approach to education: interactive pedagogy with a mixture of vocationalism, free expression, and craft-based writing all geared towards producing writers 'whether artists or craftsmen' (49). This recalls that figure from an earlier era, the man of letters, the 'near-creative writer' (1973: 324) as John Gross put it in *The Rise and Fall of the Man of Letters*: the literary journeyman with a respect for quality and a pen for hire.

In 1974 Professional Writing became a three-year degree course and John Hay was able to claim that it was 'the only degree course in this subject in the world' (1974: 34). By 1977 John Borthwick reported that 'sixty per cent of the Professional Writing course is not about writing at all: it's about such things as Politics, Geography, Economics, Biology, Computing, or Secretarial Practice. You may think (as I did) that you're going to do a Shakespeare. In reality, you're going to do a BA' (17).

According to the Curtin University website, the Creative Writing major in the School of Communication and Cultural Studies 'was the first three-year major course of study of its type in Australia'.[2] Curtin was originally the Western Australian Institute of Technology (WAIT), a vocational college established to offer professional training and educational alternatives to traditional degree courses in universities. At WAIT English began under the auspices of General Studies, mainly as a service department offering communication skills to other disciplines, but with one elective class in Creative Writing.

In 1973 Brian Dibble, who had taught Creative Writing and Literature in America, became Foundation Head of the Department of English and Language Studies within the School of Social Sciences. The following year the department moved to the School of the Arts and Design, and a Creative Writing major was established alongside Literature, Australian Studies, Journalism, Film and Television, and Theatre Arts. For Dibble, Creative Writing is 'a praxis which, therefore, should be conducted in the context of the assumptions, theory and principles of some discipline' (1997: 4). That discipline was English. As a result, Dibble recalls, 'the Creative Writing major was defined as complementary to our Literature major, the opposite side of the coin, so to speak. If you wanted to do second-year Creative Writing, you also had to do the counterpart second-year Literature unit. More provocatively, Literary Criticism was also required of Creative Writing students' (4).

The New South Wales Institute of Technology (now the University of Technology, Sydney) was established in 1965 with a charter to 'provide higher education for vocational purposes, that is to say, to offer courses for those wishing to enter or to advance in professional work' (*NSWIT Calendar 1975*: 11). In 1972 the School of Humanities and Social Sciences was primarily a servicing course which provided basic writing skills to students from other departments. It offered, however, a Diploma in Technology (Public Relations) with a subject called Writing I. This subject was concerned with the 'fundamentals of professional and creative writing' within a rhetorical, transactional and highly practical theory of writing (*NSWIT Calendar 1972*: 230).

When the Whitlam government came to power in 1972, full financial and policy responsibility for universities was assumed by the federal government. This precipitated a large expansion in higher education and enabled NSWIT to establish a Bachelor of Arts in Communication by 1975 (it also enabled Canberra CAE's Professional Writing course and WAIT's English course to attain degree status). Two compulsory subjects in this new degree – which was designed for those wishing to work in journalism, advertising and public relations – were Professional Writing I and II. Graham Williams, who was hired initially to teach technical writing, remembers these as truly awful and totally functional courses, with exercises such as the compilation of weather reports from bureau data.[3] The course outline for 1975, however, lists 'imaginative prose, fiction and verse' as genres attended to alongside technical writing, and indeed the university website dates its writing major back to this year.

In 1976 Bill Bonney arrived to take up the role of Dean and Associate Head of School, having left a Philosophy department at Sydney University which had been split with virulent intellectual and curriculum debates. In a whirlwind overhaul of the new degree he gathered around himself a body of recruits energised by radical Marxist and feminist views of society, as well as interdisciplinary approaches to knowledge and education.

The continual adaptions and restructurings of the Communication degree which followed were based on anything but vocationally oriented education. Most of the staff members, Helen Wilson recalls, distanced themselves from the functional model of communication which was developing in American universities by taking a much more radical approach which had its theoretical roots in the work of the Frankfurt School, as filtered through British Cultural Studies. In her insider's account of these years, which were charged with revolutionary fervour and little practical knowledge of media institutions, Wilson writes:

> The major intellectual development for some of us was the capture of the Mass Communication courses, formerly taught, it was decided, without sufficient theoretical rigour or attention to social context . . . At the time the theoretical perspectives were what mattered, and it had to be Althusser's development of Marx on ideology, because this placed the media, as 'ideological state apparatuses', in a sophisticated social theory.
>
> (1989: 279–80)

How did Creative Writing, which supposedly is antipathetical to theory, fit into this new degree? The workshop approach, for a start, was well adapted to both the teaching style and the ungraded pass/fail mode of assessment. 'We tried to adopt', Wilson notes, 'a non-authoritarian pedagogy: small classes, team-teaching and the valuing of non-academic knowledge' (280).

By 1978 Professional Writing had become a major in the Communication degree. In the following years, as journalism and public relations developed into separate majors, the writing strand became increasingly concerned with 'creative' or literary genres and the prefix 'Professional' was dropped. Apart from Graham Williams, who was keen to escape his engineering and technical-writing background, the main influences on the development of the writing major were Arnie Goldman, who brought with him experience of the American workshop model, and Drusilla Modjeska, who was best known for *Exiles at Home: Australian Women Writers 1925–1945* (1981) but is now also a respected 'literary' author. Modjeska was concerned with feminist theories of writing and what constituted women's writing. She was also keen to use Australian literature as a model and to encourage writing about Australia.

The emphasis, as always, was on craft as a means of breaking down the myth of the writer as inspired and isolated genius. Informal visits by publishers and editors were arranged, and guidance from teachers was always backed up by practical knowledge of the industry and market. There was less concern with producing published writers, however, than with the political ideas emerging from other parts of the department. The textual studies major, commonly taken by writing students, was not concerned with traditional English Studies, but with new Theory. Although there was an incredible diversity of ideas and motivations among the teaching staff, the central concern, Graham Williams relates, was a vision of the writer as 'a worker with a particular kind of position in society' (personal interview, 1998). It was this vision which situated the writing major within the broader theoretical and political considerations of the Communication degree. The dominant ideology of authorship was Marxist, in the form popularised by Terry Eagleton's *Marxism and Literary Criticism*:

> For Brecht and Benjamin, the author is primarily a *producer*, anal-
> ogous to any other maker of a social product. They oppose, that
> is to say, the Romantic notion of the author as *creator* – as the
> God-like figure who mysteriously conjures his handiwork out of
> nothing. Such an inspirational, individualist concept of artistic
> production makes it impossible to conceive of the artist as a
> worker rooted in a particular history with particular materials at
> his disposal.
>
> (1976: 68)

Eagleton goes on to describe the similar views of Pierre Macherey, who was himself influenced by Althusser. So even though students might draw on inspiration or write for therapeutic reasons, they were compelled to do this within an environment which saw the writer as possessing a social responsibility. One text which came to embody this position was Nadine Gordimer's 1985 essay, 'The Essential Gesture: Writers and Responsibility', which argues that 'society's right to make demands on the writer is equal to the writer's commitment to his artistic vision' (141). For Gordimer, the very act of writing is, in the words of Roland Barthes, the 'essential gesture' which articulates a writer's position within society.

The Communication degree at UTS was greatly influenced by the 'death of the author' debates in the 1970s, which served to dispel Romantic concepts of authorship and hence authorial criticism. The writing major which evolved out of this took the craft-based workshop model and emphasised the figure of the writer as an intellectual rather than an artist, closer to Barthes' Reader than his Scriptor. Instead of being a cut-and-paste attempt to understand literature from the point of view of the author, this view regarded the work produced as the product of a writer rather than the classroom exercise of a student. In this model of textual production, writers are not so much professionals with an eye on the literary market as intellectuals engaged with their position in society. This view of the author survives to the present day. 'At UTS,' the website for the degree currently states, 'great emphasis is placed on the position of the writer within society. This position is one of critical engagement, and it is for this reason that writing is studied in conjunction with a broad array of reading and analysis in contemporary cultures.'[4]

When WAIT became the Curtin University of Technology in 1987, this was the catalyst – according to its historian, Michael White (1996) – for massive higher-education reforms carried out by John Dawkins in the following year. The crux of the 'Green Paper', a policy discussion paper on higher education issued in 1987, was that the binary system in Australian higher education perpetuated an 'artificial' divide. Distinctions between the two sectors had become blurred.

Under the Dawkins reforms a Unified National System was introduced in 1988 which, through a series of amalgamations, mergers and consolidations, attempted to dismantle what was seen as an unproductive educational structure. New universities were established out of vocational colleges; institutes of technology were awarded university status; smaller institutes, CAEs and specialist colleges amalgamated with larger establishments; and links were established between the TAFE system and universities. A new system of funding was based on the performance of individual institutions, not on classification or historical precedent (in practice, of course, the older universities continued to receive a greater share of the funding due to their greater resources). The various reasons for these changes included: greater access to and equity within higher education for a larger proportion of the population; the need to develop Australia's international competitiveness through broad skills-training and education for the population; a drive towards greater economic and administrative efficiency; and the forging of more productive links between education and industry, research and practice.

The Dawkins reforms brought many writing programmes into universities (such as Deakin University's Professional Writing course, which began at Prahran CAE in 1976 under John Powers), and many have since developed in older universities (such as the masters degree in Creative Writing at Queensland University). Some factors contributing to this, according to a recent review of the state of English Studies by Robert White, were the need to attract more students and the desire of individual universities to increase their research output by recognising the fictive work of staff and post-graduate students (1998: 103). Nigel Krauth and Tess Brady have put this more bluntly. Once writing courses in CAEs 'started producing almost instant giant names in literature and entertainment', they claim, 'the universities rushed with indecent haste, it seemed, to get onto the bandwagon they had formerly despised' (1997: 47). But in fact Creative Writing had already been developing in universities with as much diversity as in the vocational sector. The Dawkins reforms hastened the expansion of Creative Writing in universities rather than introducing it. In 1972 P.H. Partridge had commented that 'because of the nature of the educational issues that are involved, it is impossible to conceive of a clear and rational division between *all* of the work of the universities and *all* of the work of the colleges. There will be certain to be many courses in both sorts of institution barely distinguishable from one another' (181). The Creative Writing courses which developed in universities before the Dawkins reforms are barely distinguishable from those already described in vocational institutions. 'There were precursors and prophets,' according to White, 'but as a kind of mass movement this is a phenomenon of the 1990s' (1998: 103). It is worth examining here the groundwork which these 'precursors and prophets' laid.

Universities

In the mid-1960s the Martin report endorsed a recommendation to establish the universities of Macquarie and LaTrobe. It did so in the hope that they would not replicate the educational paradigms of the traditional universities, but instead forge new methods of creating and transmitting disciplinary knowledge by taking the opportunity 'to experiment with the nature and structure of courses offered, and in the techniques of teaching' (Martin 1964: 177).

The echo and scuffle of student footfalls were first heard in the hallways of Macquarie University in 1966. According to a recent postgraduate handbook, Macquarie 'set out to provide a genuine alternative to existing universities in its approach to the academic curriculum and to teaching and learning methodologies' (Macquarie University 1997: 7). This was the first Australian university to run classes in Creative Writing. 'Literary Craftsmanship' was taught in the School of English Studies from 1970 by the Australian poet Alexander Craig, who had also been a student and teacher in the MFA programme at the University of Iowa. According to the university calendar for that year, the course was concerned 'with craftsmanship of original writing in poetry or prose fiction' and was to be 'conducted in critical seminars, based on the students' own work and intended also to clarify more general principles and problems' (361). The following year playwriting was added, along with a follow-up class, 'Literary Craftsmanship B'. In 1979 the range of genres was expanded to include 'writing for television, radio, film and "quality press"'. By 1989 Creative Writing had shifted from English Studies and become a major unit leading towards a BA in Mass Communication or Communication and Journalism.

Deakin University (founded in 1974 as Victoria's first regional university) established classes in Creative Writing in its Literary Studies stream in 1978. These were taught by the poet Graeme Kinross-Smith. The course handbook for this year describes the class as a

> practical study of the techniques of poetry writing and of contemporary prose. Particular attention will be paid to the 'New Journalism' and the coming together of creative prose and poetry in response to mass communications and film. The course emphasises student writing, together with its assessment by workshop, discussion and folio.
>
> (Deakin University 1978: 145)

From 1979 there was also a class taught by Trevor Code called 'Life in Words'. This was described as a

> course which combines literary study with creative writing. Students will study and practice four approaches to writing under the following headings: i The Writer's Self, ii The Pursuit of Reality, iii The Created Voice, iv Protest and Polemic. Literary works have been selected for their interest to the writer who is developing the craft of writing.
>
> (Deakin University, 1979: 143)

The pedagogical philosophy of Literary Studies in the School of Humanities was articulated by Ian Reid, the department's foundation professor, in his article, 'The Crisis in English Studies', published by *English in Australia* in 1982. Reid suggested several curricular changes which this crisis might prompt, along the lines of accepting the methodologies grouped under the names 'critical theory' and 'cultural studies'. Furthermore, while pointing to 'honourable exceptions', he argued that the emphasis on the formal essay in university English departments needed to be challenged, and that the development of 'more varied communication skills has been hampered mainly by the barriers of silly prejudice which in this part of the world still separate "creative writing" from literary criticism' (16–17). While allowing 'some scope' for the higher-degree professional model, he was more interested in prescribing writing exercises as a means for understanding narrative method. His argument was that 'the critical and the creative belong together, resting on the fundamental educational principle that the most enlightening way to learn about something is by trying to do it yourself' (18). This differs from Foerster's concept of reading from the inside because, rather than a means of appreciating the ethical or aesthetic qualities of literature, practice in writing was a means of *interrogating* literature, hence aligning it with the moves of contemporary theory.

The University of Wollongong was the first university to offer an entire undergraduate major in Creative Writing, and the first where it was possible to attain a postgraduate degree by submitting a work of fiction, poetry or drama. Starting in 1962 as a College of the University of New South Wales, it became an autonomous university in 1975. Although its Department of English and Drama did not offer Creative Writing, the development of scripts was carried out in performance classes. When the university amalgamated in 1982 with the Wollongong Institute of Education (which had previously been a teachers' college founded in 1962), it inherited a large Department of Education. Many academic staff members from the WIE formed the nucleus of the new School of Creative Arts, which was established in 1984. One of these was the poet Ron Pretty, who was responsible for instituting the Creative Writing major within the school, and whose secondary-school textbook, *Creating Poetry* (1987), can be seen as a legacy of this history.

The diversity of Creative Writing, which previously had developed within Literary Studies, Communications and Professional Writing, is demonstrated by its placement in this new school alongside the Visual and Performing arts, as well as Ceramics and Woodwork.

According to the course handbook for 1985 (the first year of its offering), the Bachelor of Creative Arts 'seeks to train a creative artist with a high degree of skills flexibility' (Wollongong University 1985: 392). A multi-disciplinary view of the arts was adopted under the ungainly title of 'fusion-training'. Here students would be able to 'enrich the palette of their single major talent' by acquiring a 'working practical and theoretical experience' of other art forms (392).

The course hoped to see its graduates emerge as 'fully trained "modern" Arts person[s]' able to work either as professional executants or in the teaching profession or the Media Arts. The writing major itself was little different from similar courses in other universities, however. It adopted the workshop approach of group critical appraisal of individual student work, supported by a study of techniques in fiction, poetry and drama, plus considerations of the creative process. And, unlike other strands in the degree, the writing major was supplemented by 'link subjects' offered by the Department of English, Literature and Drama. Students majoring in poetry, for example, could back up their practical workshops by attending classes such as 'Eighteenth Century Poetry' with literature students.

The more radical of Wollongong University's offerings were its postgraduate degrees, namely the Master of Creative Arts and the Doctor of Creative Arts. In 1986 these were offered in the areas of Musical Composition, Musical Performance, Painting, Drawing/Printmaking, Ceramics, Sculpture, Textiles and Creative Writing (including poetry, fiction and drama). The head of the School of Creative Arts at this time was Professor Edward Cowie. In a brief overview of the history of the DCA, Sharon Bell notes that Cowie, 'reportedly a charismatic presence on the University of Wollongong campus', was chiefly responsible for gaining official acceptance of the proposed doctorate (1998: 109). The first radical departure from postgraduate tradition for which he gained institutional approval was in relation to the requirements for admission. The postgraduate handbook for 1986 states that candidates need not have any academic qualification, although they must be 'artists of very high standards' and have received 'an Arts training of very high standards' (Wollongong University 1986: 169). Furthermore, in his proposal to the university's Academic Senate, Cowie pointed out that since many artists articulate theories of their creative process,

> [t]he award of a degree to an artist who theorises about his or her work, and couples thesis with practical submission, is therefore accepted as a viable assessment practice in the tertiary

education world. To go beyond that is truly breaking new ground, and yet there is surely a need to recognise that the actual creative work of an Artist constitutes an equivalent to the language of scholarship.

(qtd in Bell, 1998: 110)

While Cowie's proposal for the award of a doctorate based solely on the submission of a 'creative' work was formally approved, Bell points out that this was never implemented. Both Cowie's colleagues and 'corporate memory' are vague on the details as to why (111). Within a few years the official course handbook stated that the degree required a substantial theoretical analysis of the submitted work, and written documentation of the creative process.

What these examples show is that Creative Writing evolved within newly established universities which were willing to try non-traditional approaches to literary education. The University of Melbourne was the first sandstone university to offer any form of Creative Writing. While a post-Dawkins merger with the Victorian College of the Arts brought Creative Writing within a multi-media arts school into the university, the English Department had been experimenting with Creative Writing long before then. The department has a tradition of poet-critics including Vincent Buckley, Chris Wallace-Crabbe, Evan Jones, Andrew Taylor and Peter Steele. In the 1950s and 1960s Buckley and Wallace-Crabbe were often referred to as the main representatives of the 'Melbourne academic poets'. Buckley refused to teach Creative Writing, however, and it is Wallace-Crabbe who showed the most enthusiasm for this new area.

Wallace-Crabbe established the university's first Creative Writing class in 1981. This second-year subject followed the traditional work-shop model, emphasising the development and revision of work, but also included, according to the course outline, 'seminars on the study of prose and verse forms, prosody, language and narrative' (Melbourne University 1981: 184). Furthermore, students were required to submit alongside their stories or poems a 'critical project on some aspect of the writer's craft' (184). As well as Wallace-Crabbe, Kerryn Goldsworthy displayed an interest in Creative Writing when she joined the department. By 1993 another poet-critic, Philip Mead, was able to comment on the 'unique version of Creative Writing that has evolved in the English Department, namely a combination of and negotiation between critical, theoretical and creative writing' (3).

It may be that in order to gain acceptance in a traditional English department, any class which experimented with Creative Writing also had to be bolstered by critical and theoretical elements to assuage complaints that it lacked academic rigour. Nonetheless, those writers who taught Creative Writing – Wallace-Crabbe, Goldsworthy and Mead – also taught and wrote scholarly and critical works. In fact, one cannot teach Creative Writing without a critical awareness of one's own writing and its relationship to literature in general. The university has since developed an undergraduate major and a masters degree, although Creative Writing now seems to be situated as a separate stream alongside English and Cultural Studies rather than being integrated with them. This is likely to have more to do with catering for the popularity of Creative Writing than with severing theoretical links with other sections of the department.

Professionalisation

It is obvious that Creative Writing developed in Australia out of educational agendas opposed to traditional English Studies. And this is how Krauth and Brady have characterised the rise of Creative Writing (1997: 47). But much of this occurred *within* the parameters of the discipline of English. Creative Writing may have offended British sensibilities, but it is not 'outside' English Studies. It is part of an ongoing series of reforms to literary education, carried out in response to the intellectual and pedagogical challenges created by the crisis in the humanities. While in America the rise of Creative Writing was intimately connected to the New Criticism and its campaign against literary scholarship in the form of history and philology, in Australia in the 1970s and 1980s the critical climate was beginning to challenge what John Docker termed the 'Metaphysical ascendancy' of New Criticism and Leavisism. 'The crisis faced by the orthodoxy in Australian university departments of English', Docker argues, 'is in many ways part of an international crisis in the teaching of literature' (1984: 181). This international crisis, Docker goes on to explain, was the challenge to New Criticism as 'a teaching practice in Anglo-Australo-American universities' by what we know as Theory. Docker, in fact, asserted that the influence of deconstruction could create a 'new formalism' and instead argued for the institutional validity of Cultural Studies.

There were local institutional reasons for the development of Creative Writing in Australian universities, but these occurred within an international shift away from traditional Literary Studies and the very real pedagogical and curricular changes which accompanied this. In 1990 John Frow wrote that the 'discipline of English in Australia, which is now a little more than a century old, was formed in a context of political and cultural colonialism, and of the teaching of a high culture which was specifically that of the English ruling class' (7). He then asserted that 'the discipline has been falling apart for some time now' and linked this to the rise of Australian Literary Studies, feminist criticism, Cultural Studies and Theory (8–9). The impetus for this fracturing came from within English, however. As Ian Donaldson noted in the same year, '[n]ew systems of theoretical and method-ological enquiry, often originating in what were once thought of as the "softer" academic subjects, such as English, have permeated large tracts of the humanities and also the social sciences, including some of its craggier reaches' (1990: 26–7). An account of these changes can be found in *Knowing Ourselves and Others: The Humanities into the 21st Century* (1998), the first comprehensive review of the humanities in Australian universities in forty years. Creative Writing was not always in allegiance with many of these changes to English Studies, but it is a result of them. The difficult relationship of this corollary is charac-terised by Robert White in his review, in *Knowing Ourselves and Others*, of 'The State of English Studies in the 1990s':

> It was, by and large, literary theorists who helped to 'open the box' of English Studies, prising the way for creative writing as a respectable research pursuit. And yet the creative writers, generally speaking (and with some notable exceptions) are the ones within our English departments who are most suspicious of theory. After all, what author would want to embrace a move-ment that made its reputation by killing off the author?
>
> (1998: 103)

The Dawkins reforms recognised that many tertiary institutions which offered programmes in Creative Writing were universities in everything but name and accredited them accordingly. It amalga-mated many other courses being taught at CAEs into new universities, or absorbed them into pre-existing universities. This enabled the tentative movement towards new types of literary education, gener-ated by 'precursors and prophets' at established universities, to fully effloresce. The greatest impact of these reforms has been the rapid emergence of Creative Writing courses at the postgraduate level. While universities such as Curtin, Wollongong and Western Sydney allowed the option for a creative dissertation in their masters degrees, the University of Technology, Sydney, from 1990, was the first to offer a higher degree in Creative Writing by name, and backed up by undergraduate classes (Jurman 1990: 72).

In the search for more government funding, older sandstone universities, known as the Group of Eight, are cementing their reputations as research centres, with the effect of reduplicating the binary divide which the Unified National System attempted to collapse. Many of these universities have participated in the establishment of postgraduate research and coursework degrees in Creative Writing from the early 1990s onwards. In one sense this process can be seen as something of a bandwagon approach – a response to the pecuniary benefits of student demand, the possibility of garnering prestige through student publication, and a nod towards the pressures of vocationalism. It has occurred within a process of assimilation, however, geared towards the integration of the writing workshop and editorial mentorship with traditional postgraduate research and supervision. Establishing the theoretical and institutional parameters of 'research' in a particular area is a major means by which disciplines are established, and it is around disciplines that professional bodies are organised in the academy.

In 1996 Graham Williams and Jan Hutchinson, from Macquarie University (formerly of UTS), organised a conference under the auspices of the two institutions, entitled 'Teaching Writing'. Until this stage there had been no formal communication between Creative Writing programmes and no knowledge of the extent of their existence in the university system. The conference was held at UTS and promoted under the banner of the 'Association of University Writing Programs'. No such organisation existed at the time, but Williams and Hutchinson hoped that its formation would be an outcome of the conference. At the plenary session the possibilities of such an organisation were discussed. Representatives of technical and further education (TAFE), adult education and community writing courses (who had been invited to attend and contribute to the conference) felt that the word 'university' would exclude their areas, or at least mask their presence in the organisation. It was pointed out that many teachers of Creative Writing first teach in these areas before entering the university, and that the more writing courses represented in the Association the more potent would be its political voice. After lively debate it was agreed that the new organisation would include all writing programmes and courses, regardless of their institutional location. It was named the Australian Association of Writing Programs. If, according to D.G. Myers, the establishment of the Associated Writing Programs in 1967 marked the point at which Creative Writing became professionalised in America, then 1996 can mark the point at which it became professionalised in Australia.

5 Negotiating Theory

This case study of Australian universities demonstrates that Creative Writing programmes do not have to be conceived as an institutional anomaly existing in splendid isolation within the postmodern university. Creative Writing has an interdisciplinary presence in Australia, and would find itself covered by three of the ten electoral sectors of the Australian Academy of the Humanities: English; Cultural and Communication Studies; and Fine Arts. Until the 1990s, critical reflection on Creative Writing tended to take the form of handbooks which formalise craft-based workshop techniques into a how-to guide for students. The last decade has seen a massive increase of scholarly interest in Creative Writing as an area of academic study. The most important initiative of the Australian Association of Writing Programs has been the establishment of an electronic refereed journal, *TEXT*, which has been publishing academic articles about Creative Writing since 1997. The debates which have been conducted in this journal have facilitated a much greater self-awareness about the institutional location of writing programmes and the opportunities and problems arising from this.

This scholarly interest is part of a growing international dialogue on writing programmes. For instance, it has only recently been recognised that the emergence of Creative Writing in British universities has been strikingly similar, both chronologically and institutionally, to that in Australian higher education. In a 2003 article published in *TEXT*, Graeme Harper, from the UK Centre for Creative Writing Research Through Practice, pointed out that there has been a 'phenomenal' growth of Creative Writing in the UK from the early 1990s, citing the presence of over 140 undergraduate courses, over 70 masters courses, and around 20 PhD programmes. Harper writes that the growth of Creative Writing in the UK has been generated by two things: the founding of the 'new universities' – those polytechnic institutions 'renamed' as universities in 1992–3 and thereabouts – and by the general decrease in student applications for what might be called 'traditional' English Literature degrees. Not to say English Literature, as a subject in British tertiary education, has entirely lost its ground. However, the impact of Cultural Studies, Media Studies, Gender Studies and various other developments, amalgams, and off-shoots, has taken in its toll on single honours Literature study, particularly in the less traditional UK institutions.

(1)

An inevitable result of this growth has been a proliferation of research activity in the last few years as teachers of Creative Writing develop a sense of professional awareness and disciplinary identity. Much of this activity has been of a fact-finding nature: encouraging a national dialogue between British universities which offer writing programmes; and acquiring comprehensive and systematic information from students about what they gain from these programmes. The central concern is an ongoing discussion about what role Creative Writing can play in contemporary English Studies. The English Subject Centre, established in 2000, has run a series of annual events at various universities, including Sheffield Hallam University, Bath Spa University College and the University of Glamorgan, as well as producing a number of research reports on the emerging discipline of Creative Writing, including *Creative Writing: A Good Practice Guide* by Siobhan Holland in 2003. The National Association of Writers in Education, which, according to its website, 'is the one organization supporting the development of creative writing of all genres and in all educational settings throughout the UK', has also contributed to the debate about Creative Writing in universities, recently publishing cases studies of student experiences in Creative Writing courses.[1] Furthermore, the *International Journal for the Theory and Practice of Creative Writing* has recently been founded.

The United States, as we have seen, has a different history to deal with, but in the handful of years since the turn of the century, journals such as *Electronic Book Review*, *College Review* and the *Iowa Review* have all devoted their pages to special issues or ongoing debates about Creative Writing. As well as this, there are now regular conferences at which an international cross-pollination of ideas is taking place. Annual gatherings for the Australian Association of Writing

Programs, 'Craft, Critique, Culture: An Interdisciplinary Conference on Writing in the Academy', which has been held each year at the University of Iowa since 2000, and annual 'Great Writing' conferences in Britain, all provide a forum for discussion of Creative Writing as an expanding discipline.

Rather than maintaining a division between writers and critics, this new industry sees both as teachers, and has been concerned with understanding the place of Creative Writing in the contemporary humanities as an academic discipline, and hence with negotiating contemporary critical practices to devise not just new pedagogical approaches to the teaching of writing, but new ways of contributing to Literary Studies via Creative Writing. Most of this research output is being generated by teachers and postgraduate students who wish to engage with the interdisciplinary institutional climate in which they are located, both intellectually and professionally, rather than sectioning themselves off as writers. It is the product of writers who publish creative work and teach in writing programmes, but who also teach and publish in areas of scholarly enquiry such as Literary and Cultural Studies, Communications, Gender Studies, Postcolonial Theory and New Media Studies.

If we view writing programmes only as a practical apprenticeship for literary aspirants, then any introduction of 'Theory' to the writing workshop, or any attempt to engage with contemporary critical debate, tends to be seen as a desire to cure the intellectual naivety and theoretical ignorance of writing students by propping up the workshop with critical theory. However, it seems unproductive to dramatise the presence of Creative Writing in universities as a struggle between writers and critics over the integrity of literature or the importance of aesthetic value. The history of Creative Writing demands that it be seen as a flexible and continually developing set of pedagogical strategies for challenging and reinvigorating Literary Studies.

In a brief contribution to the 'Special Millenium Issue' of *PMLA* in 2000, Nicole Cooley argues that the 'relation between literary studies and creative writing is in crisis', and that to invigorate English Studies in the new millennium a dialogue between the two needs to be opened (1998). The dialogue she proposes, however, seems to be based on one party listening and learning, rather than on an equal exchange of ideas. For Cooley, two 'questions arising from literary studies demand our attention in the creative writing classroom' (1998). One concerns the role of identity politics. If Creative Writing is concerned with 'giving students voice' this must be accompanied by an examination of 'the critical and theoretical assumptions surrounding identity' (1998). In regard to the second question, 'we must foreground the relation of literary texts to criticism and theory, asking student writers how texts and theories work together' (1998).

So the challenge presented to the discipline of Creative Writing at the beginning of the new millennium is to negotiate a theoretical and political stance in relation to current intellectual work in the humanities. Creative Writing needs to answer the critique of authorship and of the category of literature offered by Theory, rather than simply rejecting this critique as unhelpful or deleterious to literary culture. But what would answering these charges of theoretical naivety entail? Is it enough simply to put the 'Theory canon' on reading lists for students of Creative Writing and hope it will have some effect on their work? Is it necessary for teachers of Creative Writing to develop some new eclectic theory of literature which accommodates the writer's point of view? What would a new pedagogy based on this grand synthesis look like? And, most importantly, would, or should, this theoretically informed pedagogy alter the sort of work being produced in Creative Writing? How do writing programmes negotiate the insights of contemporary theory, and the critiques of literature which these offer, while still retaining the central pedagogical aim of Creative Writing, which is to teach students how to develop their writing skills in order to produce literary works? The many ways in which various writing programmes and individual teachers of Creative Writing across the world are currently attempting to negotiate a relationship with contemporary Theory can be organised, for convenience, into three categories: the *integration* model; the *avant-garde* model; and the *political* model.

Integration model

The integrated pedagogy model is based on the assumption that there is a fundamental conflict between writers and critics over the nature of literature, and sees the writing workshop as a means of establishing a dialogue between the two, particularly via a practical engagement with poststructuralist theory. An example of this integrated model, which seems especially prominent in the UK, can be found in the 2003 publication from the St Edmund Hall Poetry Workshop at Oxford University: *Synergies: Creative Writing in Academic Practice*. This book is an anthology of sonnets written by students, accompanied by critical analyses performed by the students on each other's work. It was deemed newsworthy enough to receive a write-up in the *Guardian* (Alden 2003) because, rather than being the product of a former polytechnic, institutions which were the driving force for the emergence of Creative Writing in British higher education, it was a product of an ancient and conservative English university. The metaphor of synergy offered by the editors, Lucy Newlyn and Jenny Lewis, indicates a belief that Creative Writing can provide an educational environment which facilitates a mutually enriching combination of the creative and critical faculties, of literary theory and practice.

Newlyn and Lewis present a 'new teaching model' for the workshop, which involves a 'six stage process of creative and critical writing' (2003: xvii). These stages include: collaborative writing, individual writing, collaborative criticism, individual criticism, editing and feedback. The practice of writing sonnets is designed to give students an insight into the creative process and to foster a greater understanding and appreciation of how literature works. This is a familiar enough argument in favour of the writing workshop. Newlyn also claims, however, that this process allows students to explore 'questions fundamental to literary theory. Through the practice of collaborative and individual writing, we had investigated such topics as authorial intention, reader-response, ownership of texts, canon-formation, intertextuality, and the anxiety of influence/reception' (67). She concludes: 'Having observed the ways in which practice can enlighten theoretical issues, I have become convinced that creative writing could usefully be integrated into the teaching of elementary literary theory, as well as critical analysis' (67).

The ultimate outcome of this pedagogical synergy for Newlyn is that it 'produced better essays from the undergraduates, and some good poetry. The most important product of all was a happier, more purposeful group of students, who felt that their creative identities were valued' (xvi). While the benefit of such an outcome cannot be dismissed, this project strikes me as somewhat unambitious, neither producing innovative writing aware of its context within contemporary literature, nor providing an indepth understanding of Theory, content with catering to the ethos of the Creative Class rather than fostering a sense of responsibility to literature as a field of knowledge. Furthermore, poststructuralist theory may be counter-intuitive, but its domain of enquiry is linguistic and textual meaning, not the creative process. So attempts to illuminate or interrogate it through the practice of writing seem to be beside the point.

I am also sceptical of publishing the 'results' of such writing classes as an anthology of student work. Integrated programmes share with the school model of expressive writing an argument that what is produced in the workshop is not the point so much as what is learned in the act of producing literature. The catch here, of course, is that the work is presented as the practical outcome of the literary knowledge and appreciation gained by students. Can the poems published in a student anthology be seen as evidence of the success of an integrated course, and therefore be judged as examples of a well-honed appreciation of literature? What if the piece of writing is of poor quality? Does this mean the student has not demonstrated good reading skills? The assumption here is that the better the writing, the more acute the critical insight or appreciation, which is obviously an unsustainable and unprovable link. Yet anthologies of student writing, from Hughes Mearns's *Creative Youth* to *Synergies*, continually insist that their goal has not been to produce writers before upholding the work as examples of good writing, as if this is proof of the success of the pedagogical practice. Improved literary appreciation is a valid by-product of a workshop-based writing course, but is not a sustainable justification for the existence of Creative Writing as a discipline.

The way in which *Synergies* claims to heal a wound or cross a divide between writers and theorists for the good of students builds on an earlier call to negotiate the division between Creative Writing and Theory by Robert Miles. 'I believe', Miles wrote in 1992, 'that at bottom there is an irreducible tension between the manoeuvres of contemporary theory and the practice of teaching writing' (36). He argues, however, that this can be a productive tension in the workshop, because it 'affords the student the opportunity of comparing theories of how texts come into being with the actual experience of bringing texts into being' (37). But, as I have said, poststructuralism (which stands in here for 'contemporary theory') does not provide a theory of the creative process. It provides a theory of the production of textual meaning, based in a linguistic unconscious. In which case, to pit empirical practice against theoretical speculation in the writing workshop only provides a domestication of the insights of Theory. It leads Miles to claim that Barthes's theory of the author entering his own death at the moment of writing enables students to understand how writers assume a narrative persona or enter the voice of their characters. In turn, discussion of craft, as a series of technical decisions, recentres the authorial subject, supposedly questioning Theory.

While Miles's account purports to be an examination of 'contemporary theory', his only reference is to Barthes's 'Death of the Author', which, even in 1992, would have been virtually antiquated. Too many writers see the death of the author as the apotheosis and end point of Theory, as if it had never moved on from Barthes's 1960s polemic, and seem to believe that their living existence somehow disproves his thesis. For instance, novelist and teacher of Creative Writing Jan McKemmish equates intertextuality with authorial influence by claiming that 'literature has a history, there are lines of descent, and influence – intertextuality is not a new idea' (1996: 71). Even Harold Bloom, who merged the Oedipal drama of psycho-analysis with poststructuralist theories of intertextuality in his idea of the 'anxiety of influence', has claimed, in an attack on New Historicism, that '[t]he death of the author is a trope, and a rather pernicious one', but 'the life of an author is a quantifiable entity' (1996: 37).

The tension between theory and practice, Miles suggests, is also 'the conflict between regarding writing from the point of view of the professional writer' and 'regarding texts from the vantage point of literary criticism', or between a verbal arts degree and a Literary Studies degree (1992: 37). Miles argues for Creative Writing as a verbal art injected into Literary Studies, which means less emphasis on the student as an aspiring writer and more on the student as a critic. This does little to help the majority of writing programmes taught in the former mode, which is typical of attempts to construct 'integrated' programmes of Creative Writing and Critical Theory.

The integration model offers a practical interrogation of Theory via the writing workshop which ultimately will reassert the value of literature in the postmodern academy; it employs Theory as a means of literary appreciation as much as a means of critique. The writing workshop as we know it emerged at the University of Iowa when Norman Foerster's 'reading from the inside' became 'reading as a writer'. Whenever it is claimed that the real benefit of writing programmes is their ability to develop a student's reading skills it strikes me as a defensive attitude which returns to Foerster's model, reducing the value of Creative Writing to an adjunct or pedagogical tool for Literary Studies. Whatever educational benefits this may provide students, it is certainly not sufficient for research higher degrees in Creative Writing where students must produce a signifi-cant body of writing. While it is fine to argue that Creative Writing can perform a mediating role in literary education, healing a supposed rift between creativity and criticism, we should also ask: if universi-ties are interested in contributing to literary culture in general via the production of new writing, what role can Theory play in this endeavour?

The avant-garde model

Jonathan Culler pointed out in 1988 that critical theory has been greeted with scepticism because it 'cannot be seen as explicating or promoting some new literary practice', in the way that the New Criticism gained prominence in the academy by interpreting modernist poetry (39). He suggests, however, that 'the power of innovation and defamiliarization, which previously lay with a literary avant-garde, behind which academic criticism lagged, has now passed to criticism' (38). One way in which Creative Writing programmes have tapped into this avant-garde sensibility in recent years has been to encourage an aesthetic engagement with contemporary Theory in order to produce 'experimental' writing which challenges assumptions about lyric poetry, literary realism and linear narrative.

There are precedents for this sort of avant-garde literary dialogue with Theory which can be drawn upon. The self-reflexivity of metafiction has led to its being positioned by academic criticism as an exemplary genre of postmodern fiction, and hypertext has been described as a manifestation of poststructuralist theory, most prominently by George Landow (see Landow 1992). Those writers associated with the Language Poetry movement have often invoked the critical insights of Barthes and Derrida as one of the influences on their poetics. In *The Marginalization of Poetry*, Bob Perelman refers to Derrida's *Glas* and asks: 'Doesn't it use / the avant garde (ancient poetic adjective!) device / of collage more extensively than most / poems?' (1996: 9).

These forms of avant-garde writing have all been encouraged in Creative Writing programmes. Metafiction has always been a useful genre for those who are interested in the craft of writing because its self-reflexivity draws attention to the art(ifice) of fiction. In retrospect, it is easy to read John Barth's seminal metafictional short story of 1969, 'Lost in the Funhouse', as a handbook of fiction writing as much as a self-reflexive parody of realist fiction. Barth himself is a teacher of Creative Writing, and it is instructive that in David Foster Wallace's ironic homage to this story, 'Westward the Course of Empire Takes its Way' (1997), Barth's adolescent protagonist, Ambrose, has become a professor of Creative Writing.

Two American universities have developed an international reputation for fostering avant-garde writing. Since 1990, Robert Coover, another writer of metafiction, has taught workshops in hypertext fiction at Brown University. The Creative Writing Program at Brown is a recognised leader in the field of electronic writing, as evidenced by another Coover initiative launched in 2002: the Cave Writing

Workshop, which is a collaborative and interactive environment for an interdisciplinary team of artists across the field of the Creative Arts, along with computer programmers and sound engineers. According to its website: 'The Cave Writing Workshop is an advanced experimental electronic writing workshop, exploring the potential of text, sound, and narrative movement in immersive three-dimensional virtual reality'.[2] The Poetics Program was established at the State University of New York in 1991, with Robert Creeley and Charles Bernstein as founding directors. Both of these poets were associated with avant-garde movements: the Black Mountain School and the Language Poets, respectively. This programme shares the same ethos as the integrated model, insofar as it takes an interdisciplinary approach to the writing and studying of poetry in an academic environment. However, as the course syllabi made available on the programme's website indicate, the ultimate goal is not to illuminate Theory through practice, but to remake it, and to encourage innovative writing through experiments with such avant-garde practices as collage and found poetry.[3]

'If I speak of a "politics of poetry",' Bernstein has written, 'it is to address the politics of poetic form not the efficacy of poetic content' (1999: 4). This statement reminds us that the common ground of avant-garde movements has typically been a faith in the link between formal experimentation and political critique. Critical theory offers the intellectual apparatus of critique for a contemporary avant-garde, while writing programmes, as a result of their proximity to academic criticism, offer a potential site for literary renewal. Such a practice seems paradoxical: to encourage an avant-garde sensibility within an institutional setting. However, given the economic realities of commercial publishing, it could be argued that the university is well placed to foster an alternative literary culture. The existence of these programmes is a welcome sign of diversity, although the drawback of offering them as a general model for Creative Writing is that such an enterprise can lead to the neo-confessional workshop poem and minimalist fiction being replaced as ideal modes of writing with 'experimental' writing, and to a poetics which cannot accommodate students who wish to write in 'conservative' genres.

The most overt example of the influence of Theory on Creative Writing is the presence within Australian universities of that hybrid form of writing known as fictocriticism. The prevailing trope of fictocritical discourse is that of a 'space between' the categories of fiction and criticism created by the epistemological collapse of critical distance in postmodern theory: a textual no-man's land in which a generic intermingling and hybridity of form takes place. Writing identified as fictocritical tends to shift between fragmentary modes of experimentation, from essayistic to poetic to theoretical, employing autobiographical elements and story-telling techniques, and is often supported by the scholarly apparatus of quotation, referencing and footnoting. Some prominent examples of fictocritical writing include *No Road: Bitumen all the Way* (1997), a genre-defying work of prose by Cultural Studies intellectual Stephen Muecke, and the anthology *The Space Between: Australian Women Writing Fictocriticism* (1998), edited by Heather Kerr and Amanda Nettelbeck, which contains writing by women who largely work in the academy.

Fictocriticism could perhaps best be described as a term around which a number of theoretical and institutional negotiations between the creative and the critical take place, which is why an analysis of its relationship to Creative Writing is instructive. I would argue that, as a mode of writing, fictocriticism develops out of a tradition of liberating criticism from its parasitical dependence on literature. This tradition of liberation has two strands: either a *distancing* from literature as an object of study, hence making criticism into a science (from philology to structuralism); or a move *towards* literature by claiming the use of a creative faculty in criticism (aestheticism and impressionism), or collapsing the generic boundaries between literature and criticism (poststructuralism).

In 1981 Rosalind Krauss argued that the 'literary products of postmodernism' are not the fictional heirs to Modernist experimentation, but 'paraliterary' works by Barthes and Derrida which deliberately blur distinctions between literature and criticism. 'And what is clear,' Krauss wrote, 'is that Barthes and Derrida are the *writers*, not the critics, that students now read' (1985: 295). Fictocriticism has often been characterised as the Australian counterpart of the paraliterary because of the influence of Barthes and Derrida on theorising the collapse of generic boundaries. However, the strong presence of a personal voice in most fictocritical writing suggests that it would be more accurately described as the counterpart of what, in the United States, is called confessional or autobiographical or personal criticism (as well as autocritique and autocritography), a mode of writing popular enough to be anthologised in the book *Confessions of the Critics* (1996), edited by H. Aram Veeser.

The term 'confessional criticism' appears to derive from Elaine Showalter's introduction to *The New Feminist Criticism* (1985), which is indicative of its own indebtedness to feminist challenges to androcentric academic objectivity, where the critical 'I' is deployed as an embodiment of the axiom 'the personal is political'. But confessional criticism is also indebted to the poststructuralist critique of critical and philosophical modes of writing as metalanguages, and its subsequent rejection of the epistemological relationship between these modes and an unquestionable truth. If the disinterested and impersonal prose of academic writing can no longer provide access to knowledge, then the intellectual as a political subject becomes the only enabling motivation of critical activity. The move beyond poststructuralist theory characterised by confessional criticism is realised in localised narratives which are embodied in the contingent truths of the anecdote, and a naming of personal and political investments in the object of study. Each act of criticism is an occasion to enact a form of identity politics, where the critic does not so much express an essential self as perform the role of critic.

In a similar fashion, fictocriticism can be seen as a mode in which the ethical formation of the critical subject is foregrounded as the originating motive of criticism, but evades Romantic notions of selfhood by seeing this critical subject as the *product* of a textual performance. It has proved most popular amongst women in the academy, which has led some to question the reliance on male poststructuralist critics to explain its origins. Anna Gibbs argues that fictocriticism made its appearance 'in the writing (mostly non-academic) of women very well aware' of works by feminist figures such as Cixous and Irigary (1997: 1). Gibbs posits three institutional trajectories for the spread of fictocriticism in universities. It 'began to make its way into the universities', she claims, 'initially through women's studies courses, and then through the advent of courses in "creative writing"', as well as through the influence of 'the so-called "autobiographical turn" of cultural studies' (1).

The sort of writing which circulates under the name of fictocriticism tends to appear in academic journals and conferences, as well as anthologies associated with universities. Complaints exist that fictocriticism caters to an academic readership, but an academic market is as legitimate as any other in the age of niche marketing. And much fictocriticism is being produced by students for assignments in writing workshops and theses for research degrees in Creative Writing. In 1996 Anne Brewster presented a paper entitled 'Fictocriticism: Undisciplined Writing' at the inaugural conference for the Australian Association of Writing Programs. Brewster argues that an 'event contiguous with the emergence of ficto-criticism is the burgeoning of creative writing programmes in Australian universities. Indeed a number of the academics interested in and writing ficto-criticism are involved in creative writing programmes' (29). These programmes, she suggests, 'on account of their own anomalous and anxious positioning', open up a space for the introduction of 'hybrid and cross-generic projects', one of which is the 'conflation of fictional and critical discourses' (30). Creative Writing classes become a literal place where students can explore the fictocritical 'space between'. 'The enthusiasm with which students versed in theory take to ficto-criticism in creative writing classes', according to Brewster, 'suggests that in a creative writing programme they have a license to do what can't be done in the more formal literary or cultural studies essay, that is, personalising the theory and making it over in their voice' (31).

Brewster does not state that fictocritical writing necessarily should be taught in Creative Writing classes, claiming instead that she is merely tracing a genealogy of the form, articulating the institutional sites at which it is appearing. No account is provided, however, of how fictocriticism might provide options for the student of Creative Writing who is not 'versed in theory', of what sort of licence it might provide for the writer of traditional literary genres, or of why its practice is not allowed in classes devoted to the study of theory.

A cynical way of considering this is to see Creative Writing as a way of accommodating fictocriticism by bringing it into the academy through the back door, but leaving it on the doormat. As a 'genre' fictocriticism imparts a certain amount of academic credibility to Creative Writing because of its overt and reflexive engagement with critical issues. In turn writing programmes can act as a form of generic containment, protecting the boundaries of the traditional academic dissertation from fictocritical contamination. Fictocriticism emerges in the institutional circumstances where those teachers and students who have the desire to write and hence become involved in Creative Writing are also influenced by poststructuralist/feminist theory. This is due to the fact that Creative Writing and 'Theory' developed in Australian universities at the same time. If fictocriticism is a metaphorical (postmodern) space between theoretical and literary genres, the discipline of Creative Writing is an institutional juncture for this space, a literal site for negotiation between the demands of the academy (theory) and the demands of the literary market (literature), plus the attendant theoretical binaries of objectivity/subjectivity and exteriority/interiority. Fictocriticism can thus be seen as a product of *institutional* forces: the teaching of Creative Writing alongside the teaching of Theory in Australian universities.

In 'The Investigation', Helen Flavell constructs an 'academic fiction' around two protagonists: a male, moustached, professor at a traditional sandstone university who is made nervous by his students' enthusiasm for the 'new critical genre' of fictocriticism, their desire as students of Theory for a more personal and lyrical response to the texts they study; and a young female student known as Anna. 'Anna is 24 and a postgraduate student. Her university doesn't have sandstone arches and ivy creeping; she's been brought up on a trans-disciplinary diet of various subjects levelled under the umbrella of "communications". She's studied creative writing, journalism, won a prize for an essay in cultural studies, and thrives on reading contemporary theory' (1999b: 105). What is being constructed here is a generational (and gendered) narrative describing the institutional and interdisciplinary conditions for the emergence and popularity of fictocriticism. This narrative may be too stereotypical to function as an accurate description, but it is instructive concerning the way in which proponents of fictocriticism wish to position it as a marginal yet dynamic practice within institutional power structures.

If one decides to write fictocriticism one consciously determines to blur generic boundaries in their writing, via a hybridisation or mongrelisation of disparate textual elements, and thus enact or perform a critical operation. If generic boundaries are blurred, however, this only takes place *within* the hybrid form; it is performed each time by a fictocritical act. This is why it is a performance of the critical self rather than a stable genre. As Anna Gibbs writes, it is 'a hit and run guerilla action, tactical rather than strategic' (1997: 1). These last two terms recall the work of Michel de Certeau, who described strategy in spatial terms and tactics in *temporal* terms. So it is a tactical, temporary raid on strategic divisions and hierarchies. It prises open a 'space between' genres and knowledges.

Unfortunately, this temporary mongrelisation, tied to an ethical performance of the critical self, is often accompanied by a narrative of supersession, as if the *epistemological* breakdown of the barriers between literature and criticism effected by post-structuralism had also made a *generic* collapse inevitable. Brian Attebury claims that metafictional and fictocritical 'violations of boundaries tend to make people very nervous' (1998: 1), as if these 'people' might feel an impending redundancy for their conservative genres. 'When ficto-criticism arrives,' Noel King wrote in a 1991 article with Stephen Muecke which gave fictocriticism its name, 'what departs? Presumably the stable and separated bodies of "fiction" and "criticism", replaced by compounds, mergings, mutations and mistakes' (Muecke and King 1991: 13). For King, it was the separate bodies of fiction and criticism. But what is meant by this departure? These bodies have obviously not departed, they are not redundant, they only depart within the fictocritical text itself, within its own performative moment of hybridity. The suggestion that fictocriticism may serve as some exemplary dialectical resolution between the poles of writing and criticism – or, more precisely, between literature and critical theory – cannot be sustained. Rather than negating or rendering obsolete the distinctions it challenges, fictocriticism requires their continued opposition for its aesthetic dynamism and offers yet another mode of writing within a plurality of options available to the writer.

The postmodern project of 'hybridisation' is to break down barriers between genres, to recognise that genres are institutionally conferred categories, or at least rhetorical conventions, rather than essentialist modes. If followed to its logical extreme, however, collapsing boundaries within literature, and between literature and criticism, into a generalised 'writing' means *erasing* rather than celebrating or multiplying difference. Obviously this erasure is neither possible nor desirable. Hence postmodernity is best described as a plurality of genres, and each new hybrid splice (fabulism, magic realism, metafiction, fictocriticism, creative non-fiction, confessional criticism) is an addition to this plurality rather than a negation of pre-existing options; an addition which, moreover, requires the existence of the genres it spliced in order to retain its hybridised identity. This plurality means an erasing of *heirarchies* rather than generic differences, and a loosening of boundaries, retaining the conceptual differences of genres but exploiting their practical possibilities of permeability (rather than contamination).

Political model

One critique of poststructuralist theory as it has been applied to literary study is its lack of a social dimension, its introspective self-reflexivity and political quietude. Deconstruction has been called the 'new New Criticism' by Edward Said because its literary appropriation by the Yale School in America enabled critics to continue their hermetic interest in texts without considering the Foucauldian strain of poststructuralism (1983: 159). As Said points out, 'Derrida's criticism moves us *into* the text, Foucault's *in* and *out*' (183). How can Creative Writing also get outside the text and explore how literature operates in society – not, in Foucault's words, as a substitute or 'general envelope for all other discourses' (1990: 308), but as an active social agent alongside other discourses? That is, how can it facilitate an understanding of authorship and literary production in its social context? This question informs the third model of negotiation, which is based on a desire to demystify cliches of literary creativity and reform the writing workshop as a site of political contestation. The focus is not on formal experimentation but on the pragmatics of production and reception within the framework of Cultural Studies. In this model of teaching, the workshop is not a neutral zone for the development of literary craft, but a site at which critiques of the politics of representation and analysis of the circulation of literature across different institutions become part of the ethical and professional training of students who will emerge, not as writers who know the avenues of commercial publication, but as professionals who have a critical awareness of the power relations at work in the field of writing.

In 2001 *Electronic Book Review* published a long article by Joe Amato and Kassia Fleisher entitled 'Reforming Creative Writing Pedagogy: History as Knowledge, Knowledge as Activism'. The number of formal responses to the journal which this article generated is indicative of a general mood of frustration which it had tapped into. Amato and Fleisher ask if the Creative Writing classroom is 'a place simply for fortifying the mysteries of creativity, or can something more concrete, more palpable, more critical, more *urgent* therein be attended to?' (1). What follows is a shambolic and meandering analysis of the limitations of Creative Writing and the need for a more radical approach to teaching. It is difficult to ascertain exactly what the authors hope to achieve, but it is clear that they feel Creative Writing programmes need to overcome their intellectual isolation and be more open to current changes in technology, theory and teaching. They claim that 'craft-based criticism has become a rather rudimentary application of tried and true analysis, designed primarily to promote the verbal artifacts, linguistic processes, and received wisdom of a bygone era; an analysis thoroughly resistant to considerations of race, ethnicity, gender, class, sexual orientation, disability, and how such factors impact notions of authorship and community, past and present' (11).

A more coherent article along the same lines is provided by Chris Green, whose essay, 'Materializing the Sublime Reader', was published in *College English* in 2001. Green's ambition is 'to add another vocabulary to the pedagogy of the creative writing workshop: the language of use and action, of practice and implementation-praxis' (155). According to Green, workshops in America are conducted under the gaze of a 'sublime' reader, the homogenous presence of mainstream commercial literature which students are being trained to write. 'Before asking how students can better write "good" poems,' Green writes, 'I propose we look beyond the gaze of the sublime reader and ask how students can write useful poems' (159). By useful he means poems which serve specific communities that student writers are associated with. He proposes as a guide the 'material' reader who exists in the world beyond the workshop. 'The audience in the workshop should be able to anticipate what interpretive speech community is going to receive the poem, in what form: in this capacity, readers in the workshop can grant useful evaluation' (162). In other words, the workshop can train students to understand the political responses of specific readerships, and thus will rely upon an aesthetic in which politics plays a role alongside literary craft. 'The workshop needs to address lived situations rather than assuming and perpetuating the presence of a falsely sublime (generally a white, educated, middle-class) reader' (162). Furthermore, this approach will prepare students for the realities of writing outside the university, enabling them to negotiate 'structures and institutions of publication, education, readings, employment, community, politics, and family' (155). This is not simply practical advice, for rather than producing professionalised writers, Green hopes that Creative Writing can '*serve* writers from widespread and even oppositional communities in such a way that their participation in those communities is facilitated' (162). In order to achieve such community service, Green argues, Creative Writing requires a greater engagement with Cultural Studies, which 'considers the text as being in the world, examines how it arrived, asks who uses it and why' (165).

A similar approach was presented in Australia by Jennifer Webb, in a 2000 article, 'Individual Enunciations and Social Frames'. Webb's central argument is that 'one of the skills writing students need is an understanding of the politics of identity and representation; and that the active incorporation of cultural studies methodologies within the creative writing programme is a good starting point for its provision' (1). According to Webb, a fixation on the aesthetics of literary craft in the workshop neglects crucial practical and political considerations of writers who enter public discourse through publication. As such, 'a focus on either the mechanics or the aesthetics of writing in the absence of a contextualised framework risks overlooking the equally vital attention that could be paid to the social conditions in which creative works are made' (2). The conflict which Webb seeks to negotiate is that between individual enunciation and the social frame: that is, how do students negotiate a personal vision (which is a political as much as a creative act) within the field of writing, inscribed as it is within institutional and discursive power relations?

The articles I have discussed here are all polemical interventions in the ideology of writing workshops, and as such do not really address in detail what a reconfigured workshop poetics would look like, how it might influence individual decisions relating to the structure of a work, to redrafting and editing. This is a consideration I hope to address in the conclusion. In terms of negotiating Theory, it is evident that identity politics has provided the most influential means by which the writing workshop has become politicised. According to David Galef, where 'creative writing once offered a refuge from the wars of political correctitude' (2000: 172), identity politics has now found its way into the workshop. 'Gayatri Chakravorty Spivak's "Can the Subaltern Speak?" has been translated to the creative writing instructor's dilemma, "Is It Okay to Write Like an Afro-American If You Aren't One?"' (172).

Identity politics, which developed out of the fragmentation of the New Left, is concerned with giving a public voice to members of society who have been marginalised as a result of mainstream prejudice against their 'difference' (on the grounds of gender, race, class, religion, sexual orientation, etc.). The strategy here is for these citizens to counter their marginal status by appropriating the grounds for their original prejudicial differentiation from the mainstream as the basis for a group identity. By this process marginal identities become empowered as constituencies demanding political recognition and the right for civic self-definition based on difference. The translation of this civil rights activism to the realm of Literary Studies has involved critiquing the study of canonical works (as politically neutral representatives of a timeless and universal humanity) and advocating the curricular inclusion of non-canonical works (based on the criterion of representation of marginalised identities).

How would identity politics translate to the Creative Writing classroom, and especially to the concerns of white, middle-class would-be poets who do not possess the cultural cachet of marginalisation? The first step would be to assert in the workshop that individual identity must be seen in relation to group identity. Is the writer also representative of a constituency, formed by race, class, gender, sexual orientation, age or religious affiliation? In which case, is the writer legitimised to form an identity, or discover a voice, through the literary representation of other constituencies? This question certainly encourages a vision of social agency, but can have the effect of simply reinforcing the doctrine that apprentice writers ought to write only from their own experience, and does not really move us beyond the idea of voice as a means of discovering an essential self – the practice of individuation is merely carried out in a social context. Nor does it move us beyond the idea that the practice of writing is an act of ethical self-formation, and that the role of Creative Writing is to foster this practice. Whether or not identity is construed as anti-essentialist in the workshop, identity politics would still focus on the role of students as social agents relating to a particular constituency and how this identity is realised in their writing. Charles Bernstein has provided a stinging critique of identity politics in the workshop, asserting that it often amounts to nothing more than poets replacing 'I see grandpa on the hill / next to the memories I can never recapture' with 'I see my yiddishe mamma on hester street / next to all the pushcarts I can no longer peddle' (1992: 6).

Furthermore, not only has John Guillory provided a convincing and widely known refutation of the relationship of identity politics to the canon debate in *Cultural Capital* (which I outlined in Chapter 4), but identity politics itself has undergone critique and revision since its prominence in the last two decades, evidenced by the recent special issue of *New Literary History* (autumn 2000) entitled 'Is There Life After Identity Politics?' The writing workshop might be better conceived as an arena in which to interrogate the assumption that literature represents social experience, and thus to explore the extent to which it constitutes a zone of public and critical contestation over issues of identity.

The various models for negotiating a relationship with Theory which I have outlined are based on a critique of the traditional writing workshop. However, there remains a strong sense of continuity in the self-defining claims for Creative Writing from its origins to the present day. Proponents of Creative Writing have always argued that what defines it as a discipline is its emphasis on praxis, where students learn *how* literature is made, not just about it, developing an understanding of literature as a process rather than a product (although, as I demonstrated in Chapter 3, such an approach is not alien to literary criticism), and students write their own literary works rather than simply read literature, thus becoming producers rather than receivers of knowledge (although I fail to see why writing essays is not also practical). Traditional boundaries between reading and writing, the creative and the critical, have been challenged by an engagement with poststructuralist theory, but the argument remains that Creative Writing offers students more personal freedom and practical skills than an essay-based

Literary Studies class. Hence what remains constant in the demarcation of Creative Writing as a discipline from the early twentieth century to today is an emphasis on empowering students. In a reference to the advertising slogan for Nike footwear, Nigel Krauth writes: ' "Just do it" is the ad for Creative Writing departments; "Just wear it" might be seen as the ad for old-style English departments' (2000: 1).

While writing programmes have typically been positioned in conservative opposition to developments in critical theory, or at least in anti-intellectual ignorance of them, Creative Writing has also been forwarded as a means of critiquing traditional English Studies alongside Theory. This once again relies on the idea of empowering students to challenge received ideas of canonicity. In a 1986 editorial article for *Critical Quarterly*, called 'Broken English', Colin MacCabe outlined various changes to literary education as a result of the crisis in English Studies, before suggesting that 'both composition and creative writing must become central within the curriculum' (13). His argument is that Creative Writing would operate, not as an antidote to this crisis, but as an active participant (if it moved beyond the ethos of free expression):

> If the cultural tradition is there to be interrogated rather than simply transmuted, it is essential that students should be able to participate positively in that interrogation. Pedagogy cannot be reduced to a question of handing on a critical attitude – that critical attitude must find form in cultural production. If we are to teach students to read then we must also teach them to write.
>
> (13)

In 2001 Marcelle Freiman argued that 'the teaching of creative writing' is positioned 'as "other" to the "main" teaching of Literature, within the boundaries of the discipline' in Australian universities (1). In other words, because Creative Writing is institutionally marginalised it can, metaphorically, partake of the interrogative dynamic of postcolonial criticism as a challenge to the hegemony of English Studies. Postcolonial theory proceeds from the assertion that English Studies was conceived as a means of exercising imperial hegemony over its subjects, and Freiman argues that Creative Writing offers a means of productively transforming the discipline because it encourages students to explore the 'chaos and unpredictability of literary creation' as well as introducing 'lived experience into the classroom' (1).

In this light, Creative Writing does not have to be radically undermined by negotiations with Theory; it can be productively adapted to a range of educational strategies. Despite the range of arguments I have presented about how the writing workshop ought to operate, they all stem from the idea that it can empower individual students. Depending on one's ideological approach, the practice of writing can enable students to appreciate the aesthetic and humanist qualities of literature, or to interrogate the assumptions of Literary Studies; it can facilitate the therapeutic discovery of a neo-Romantic expressive voice, or encourage students to perceive themselves as active participants in identity politics; and it can ultimately help them to become better citizens, whether this is in the liberal arts tradition of well-rounded persons, or in the critical pedagogy tradition of socially conscious activism. This educational strategy lies at the heart of the origins of English Studies as a discipline within the humanities: studying literature will make students better people if only we know the right way to teach it.

Another constant within Creative Writing is an emphasis on the crucial importance of reading. 'I don't teach writing workshops but reading workshops,' Charles Bernstein asserts (1999:11), echoing the statement of Allen Tate from fifty years earlier (1940: 506). What *is* changing is the sort of reading being taught, from one informed by the New Criticism to one informed by an engagement with contemporary critical theory. As I pointed out in Chapter 3, this emphasis on reading is not simply to make students better readers, but to demonstrate the importance of reading to the craft of writing. I have argued that the traditional writing workshop is founded on the Modernist premise that criticism is an essential part of the creative process, most clearly articulated by T.S. Eliot in 'The Function of Criticism'. And while debates exist about what forms of criticism should be taught in the writing workshop, there is no debate about the importance of the critical *faculty*. In the article cited earlier, Marcelle Freiman argues that a postcolonial approach to Creative Writing can interrogate and disrupt conservative notions of genre, canonicity, culture and identity within English Studies, but she also points out that Eliot's

> statement about the critical labour involved in creativity remains both pragmatic and pertinent to the process and its craft. Creative writing involves re-reading and rewriting which develops critical ability in an acutely practical, and experiential, context. Developing this critical-reading faculty is a vital part of the teaching of writing. Criticism can be further incorporated into the subject as self-reflexive analysis and commentary.
>
> (2001: 4)

Creative Writing programmes are centred on the empowerment of individual students because, unlike in traditional disciplines, there is no coherent body of knowledge to be passed on. Debates about the teaching of Creative Writing in undergraduate education are important, but it is developments at the postgraduate level which are crucial to the subject because academic disciplines are based on the idea of research. In research higher degrees in Creative Writing the emphasis is no longer on what students can be taught, but on what they can produce which will be both of 'publishable' quality and analogous to scholarly research. This is particularly important as writing programmes at the doctoral level become more popular. Not only is the PhD the highest academic qualification a student can receive, a qualification for which an original contribution to knowledge is expected, but it is increasingly necessary if a graduate wishes to secure permanent full-time employment in a university.

One way to conceive of Creative Writing as a discipline is to understand that it produces knowledge by an interaction between formalist criticism and practical craft. This is because a practical device of literary composition, such as point of view or narrative voice (a technical choice made by the writer as to who sees and who speaks in the work), is also a critical tool of analysis (a formalist category for the classification and study of literary works). By exploring and expanding the aesthetic possibilities of composition, a literary text interrogates methods of reading. If poetics, in Todorov's formulation, negotiates the boundary between literary structure and individual work, or between science and interpretation, then the same negotiation occurs in literature itself. A specific work of literature not only *reveals* the structure or general laws of literature, but interrogates and expands them. It is a contribution not just to the practical creative art of writing, but to the study of literature as well.

This requires a recognition that knowledge in Literary Studies does not consist of a list of methodological approaches which can be applied to the study of literature, and nor does it reside in a body of canonical works awaiting critical excavation, but that it is formed at the dialogic junction between the two. Knowledge is constituted by the interaction of literature and criticism. This does not entail a poststructuralist collapse of linguistic and epistemological boundaries into a unified critical enterprise. Nor does it entail a dialectical tension between the two modes. It is, rather, a dialogic process, a ceaseless interaction between permeable modes of writing.

What I am arguing for, then, is a concept of intellectual exchange, of literary and critical writing as complementary practices, of the discipline of English involving a dialogic interaction between two modalities of intellectual work within a specific field of knowledge. If English Studies is founded on the study of literary texts then obviously those texts contribute to what constitutes knowledge in the discipline. English is a dialogic engagement between literature and criticism, not in a hierarchical sense of host and parasite text, first-order artistic practice and second-order intellectual apprehension, but in the sense of an ongoing series of interactions between complementary modes of *writing*. In this case Creative Writing is not necessarily the teaching of writing literature alongside the teaching of writing criticism, but a mode of literary research within the academy.

Ultimately, however, I feel the most important question for writing programmes to consider is what sort of graduates they should be producing at the postgraduate level; the graduates who, presumably, will be trying to contribute to a national literary culture via publication, and who will be qualified to teach, and hence will bear responsibility for perpetuating and regenerating the discipline. The integrity of the discipline relies on what sort of writers it produces. To argue that most students won't go on to be published authors is an evasion, for most standard PhD students will not publish their theses, nor will many of them find academic jobs. If, since the inception of writing programmes, the focus of Creative Writing has been on the development of critical reading skills and on the empowerment of individual students, it is the figure of the writer as an intellectual which is the final product. Here, in the figure of the writer, is where Creative Writing does or can overlap with the aims of the contemporary humanities.

The idea of the university has fundamentally changed as we enter the new millennium. Funding structures for and public expectations of the Enterprise University demand a greater emphasis on socially beneficial and economically productive research from academics, and more focus on identifiable skills for graduates which will enable them to contribute to a national workforce. The intellectual paradigm of the New Humanities is a response as much to these changed institutional conditions as to the disciplinary challenges of Theory. And it is in this context that the idea of a literary intellectual needs to be elaborated.

6 What is a literary intellectual?

In the introduction to his 1995 book, *From Outlaw to Classic*, Alan Golding argued that 'the place of creative writing in the academy, and its relation to "theory," deserves a substantial treatment that I have not attempted here' (xvii). As I pointed out in the previous chapter, these questions have been addressed in a variety of ways by academics who teach in writing programmes. In the same year, however, the term 'posttheory' was coined by Jeffrey Williams, suggesting that Creative Writing might now need to situate itself in relation to a new academic paradigm. In an article entitled 'The Posttheory Generation' Williams discusses the specific identity of 'the generation of intellectual workers who have entered the literary field and attained professional positions in the late 1980s and through the 1990s' ([1995] 2000: 25). Williams defines this generation not in terms of age, but in terms of institutional conditions determined by two interrelated factors: 'first, what seems to be the dispersion or breakdown of the paradigm of Theory; and second, a drastically reconfigured job market, pinched in the vice of a restructured and downsizing university' (25).

The 'posttheory generation', Williams asserts, has been educated in an academic climate governed by Theory, but nonetheless possesses a sense of belatedness, of appearing after the revolutionary polemics of poststructuralism, Marxism and feminism became institutionally sanctioned as part of graduate-school training and as a mark of professional attainment. 'In short, the posttheory generation was taught to *take theory* – not traditional scholarly methods, not normal practical criticism – *for granted*, and theory in turn provided a threshold stamp of professional value' (29). The academic work of this new generation has not produced new theoretical paradigms. Instead, Theory has become fragmented and applied to areas such as Cultural Studies and Race Studies; it has 'dispersed to provisional, localized, pragmatic interventions, rather than building to or drawing from a systematic critique' (33). This eclectic microspecialisation of Theory, Williams argues, is the product of institutional changes to the university:

> To bring the theory story up to date, the recent turn from high theory to cultural criticism, and from characterizing ourselves as theorists to public intellectuals, indicates not so much the 'exhaustion' of theory or a revival of social conscience; rather, it responds to a shift in the role of the university, to the defunding of welfare state entitlements such as education, and to imperatives for 'accountability' of public institutions.
>
> (31)

If, in the 1960s and 1970s, universities were burgeoning with research funding, the 'internal rationale' (31) that Theory provided has now given way to 'a more public rationale' (32) in the corporatised university. Cultural criticism and public criticism, which attempt to engage more directly with concerns beyond the academy, can be seen as a response to demands for accountability, but also to the 'PC debates of the early 1990s' which 'registered a crisis of legitimacy for the university and its social role' (35). Williams argues, however, that if this shift is to be a genuine academic achievement for the posttheory generation, criticism must work for the public good, rather than simply as a public-relations exercise (36).

Wiliams's article was reprinted as the lead essay in the recent book *Day Late, Dollar Short, The Next Generation and the New Academy*. In the introduction to this anthology, entitled ''60s Theory/'90s Practice', Peter C. Herman designates the *Next Generation* as 'critics who are now at the beginning of their careers, people who are in graduate school or are assistant professors. If tenured, then tenured only recently' (2000: 1). The *New Academy* is described as a university system faced with dwindling funds and hence with the necessity to adopt corporate adminstrative structures and values as well as to establish links with business. *Day Late* refers to the sense of belatedness in regard to the baby-boomer excitement of the 1960s, since Theory is now 'something that comes along with graduate education, a body of knowledge and a language to be mastered. It is, in this sense, institutionalized, packaged, and commodified' (1). *Dollar Short* refers to the disastrous paucity of available jobs for the next generation: the diminishment of tenure-track positions and the increase of adjunct and part-time work as a result of the 'down-sizing' mentality of increasingly corporatised universities.

This next generation, according to Herman, uncritically accepts the 'hermeneutics of suspicion' of their predecessors, the notion that there are texts to be interrogated rather than works to be read. There is, however, a timidity and caution in regard to new thinking, which is supposedly a result of the need for 'professional survival' in a job market governed by entrenched members of the Theory generation. The turn to a greater presence in the public sphere is a result of the tenuous financial position of the humanities and the need to ensure funding by producing results with visible public benefit.

How is Creative Writing situated in this post-Theory academy? David Galef's essay in *Day Late, Dollar Short* provides little help. In the 1980s, Galef argues, 'Big Theory' was at its height, composition was the workhorse of the academic industry, and Creative Writing a nebulous area in the university. Today, Theory is declining in cultural capital while writing instruction expands. 'As with comp/rhet, the trend is economically driven: creative writing is a cash cow, a popular offering with a low overhead and a big return' (2000: 171). So Creative Writing is to be understood as the product of student demand in the corporatised university.

In Australia the intellectual climate and institutional conditions which constitute the post-Theory academy would be described by the term 'the New Humanities', albeit without the connotations of generational conflict contained in the word 'New'. The term was first used by Ian Donaldson at a symposium for the Australian Academy of the Humanities in 1989. Donaldson pointed out that in the previous few decades new modes of theoretical and methodological enquiry had contributed to a breakdown of the traditional divide between the humanities and the social sciences, between a refined liberal humanist world of the arts and a more rigorous analysis of society. The New Humanities, as he describes the work of research centres in America, are concerned with 'reconfiguring knowledge . . . bringing together new combinations of scholarly and theoretical enquiry' and 'redrawing old taxonomies within the academy' (1990: 31).

What Donaldson is referring to here are the disciplinary, curricular and policy changes wrought within the academy by the impact of Theory. His tentative phrase was solidified into an institutionally accredited term when the Academy's symposium of 1991 was entitled Beyond the Disciplines: The New Humanities. In the introduction to these proceedings Ken Ruthven writes that those 'who are making the running in the new humanities' use critical theory as a 'heuristic device' for identifying occluded knowledges (1992: viii). The papers published, by critics such as John Frow, Meaghan Morris and Tony

Bennett, were all concerned with the new interdisciplinary enterprise of Cultural Studies. And indeed, in 1996, Cultural and Communication Studies was included as the tenth electoral section of the Academy, thus becoming the exemplary discipline of the New Humanities. As Jonathan Culler has claimed, in an almost too neat formulation, Cultural Studies is Theory put into practice (1997: 43).

In 1999 the academic journal *Southern Review* changed its twenty-five-year subtitle, *Literary and Interdisciplinary Essays*, to *Essays in the New Humanities*. As Cathy Greenfield explains in her editorial, the word 'literary' was dropped because this was no longer the journal's primary focus. Rather than privileging literature as an aesthetic category, the journal is interested in its function as a discourse alongside other cultural practices and forms of media. Interdisciplinary analysis is foregrounded by the adoption of the rubric 'New Humanities' because, as Greenfield argues, 'the reforming practices of interdisciplinarity' are the 'enabling condition' of its existence (1999: 118).

Greenfield characterises work in the New Humanities as a move *beyond* Theory. For instance, such work seeks new ways of understanding agency, rather than dismissing it as a bourgeois myth, and ways of engaging with questions of policy instead of relying on critiques of ideology. It is worth noting here the 'aims and scope' of the journal, which can be found on the verso of the front cover in each issue. According to these, *Southern Review* 'publishes essays, articles, reviews and review articles on a wide range of cultural and media matters, as well as fiction and poetry'. The journal goes on to explain that it seeks essays of an interdisciplinary nature concerned not only with texts, but also with the wider discursive relations in which they are implicated. There are no prescriptions for fiction or poetry. Is this out of deference, I wonder, to the writer's *donnée*, a retention of aesthetic criteria in the publication of literature that are being rejected as concerns for literary criticism? Why does a journal concerned with essays in the New Humanities publish fiction and poetry? And what sort of writing would be appropriate?

The UTS Review (now *Cultural Studies Review*), which was subtitled *Cultural Studies and New Writing*, claimed to offer 'an international space for academic and creative writing on culture', but 'creative writing that no longer construes "the literary" as a site of withdrawal from politics, from the worlds created by the media and other technologies, from new practices of history and from the social sciences' (Morris and Muecke 1996: 1). This is a more theoretically consistent editorial policy, although since the journal's inception in 1995 only a handful of pieces have been published under the category of 'new writing'. Many of the 'articles' published, however, could be classified as fictocriticism, creative non-fiction, or confessional criticism. What this indicates is that there is a certain type of writing which is suitable to the journal's aims. The appellation 'new' refers to a currency not only in terms of temporality but also in terms of formal innovation or experimentation, especially with generic boundaries. This suggests the possibility of an avant-garde 'writing' (as opposed to 'literature') which could be aligned with the academic work of the New Humanities.

The question for us, then, is what position does the discipline of Creative Writing, which concerns itself with the production of literary works, occupy in the New Humanities? While Creative Writing is not necessarily founded on a concept of the literary as a site of withdrawal from politics and society, this is nonetheless implicit in the workshop process because its main function is to establish a standard of literary value by which to identify what 'works' in exemplary texts and to apply these principles to the aesthetic improvement of student manuscripts. Furthermore, while Creative Writing has followed the same trajectory as the New Humanities, emerging through newer tertiary institutions in the wake of challenges to traditional forms of knowledge, its historical and theoretical ties, as we have seen, remain with the American New Criticism, which construed the literary precisely in terms of aesthetic autonomy.

Creative Writing is also generally regarded as an apprenticeship for aspiring writers. That is, it provides skills training for those who wish to enter the 'literary establishment' via mainstream publication. This is why writing programmes advertise the number of 'successful' graduates who have published their work. By the term 'literary establishment' I mean reviewers, editors, publishers and writers whose domain of professional work involves the production and reception of literature, and who conceptualise this domain as the 'public sphere' because it addresses a general readership rather than an academic audience. This literary establishment, to which students of Creative Writing are ostensibly being trained to contribute, has typically responded to the 'culture wars' by bemoaning the professional jargon of academics and the relativisation of literary value perpetrated by postmodernism, thus establishing its opposition to critical Theory. David Williamson's highly successful play, *Dead White Males* (1995), is a *locus classicus* for this response.

What is at stake in this debate between the literary establishment and the academy is less an understanding of literature than a struggle over who wields literary authority. If the discipline of Creative Writing is to assume a non-antagonistic institutional position within the New Humanities, I feel it is less important to engage in theoretical debates about what constitutes literature than to ask: what is a literary intellectual? That is, to what figure in the academy has literary authority traditionally accrued, and how can a vision of authorship be elaborated in relation to it? This figure has been the critic. In what follows I will briefly outline the various forms of literary authority the critic has assumed, and the way this authority has positioned the writer.

Practical criticism

John Dryden was the first to use the term 'criticism' in a specifically literary context, arguing in 1677 that it meant the art of judging the qualities of a literary work, rather than the practice of censuring it.[1] Throughout the seventeenth and eighteenth centuries, criticism tended to operate by judging whether a literary work had successfully applied various neo-classical 'rules' of composition. In this sense it was closely related to the craft of writing. With the birth in the 1800s of the great literary reviews, such as the *Edinburgh* and the *Quarterly*, criticism became synonomous with reviewing. In this period the figure of the man of letters developed. The man of letters was a literary journeyman – writer, critic, essayist, reviewer and journalist – a man of taste eking out a living through the professional reviews (see Gross 1973).

In 1842 Edgar Allan Poe condemned the 'cant of *generality*' (1957: 33) into which criticism was supposedly falling, as a result of the influence of the 'British Quarterly Reviews, upon which our own Quarterlies have been slavishly and pertinaciously modelled' (34). He argued that 'the review or criticism properly so termed' had degenerated into a general paper on the subject which the book under review deals with, neglecting a consideration of the book itself (34). He wished to retain the word 'criticism' for the specific commentary on a work of literature. By 1929 T.S. Eliot was complaining that 'the "critic" has been chiefly the reviewer, that is to say, the hurried amateur wage-slave', and that this has been to the detriment of criticism (1962: 617). John Crowe Ransom argued in 'Criticism, Inc.' ([1937] 1984) that reviewing could no longer be counted on to perform the serious task of criticism in any but an amateur fashion. The professionalisation of criticism by its being taken into universities was necessary if contemporary literature was to receive the criticism it deserved and required. However, Ransom's main argument, as we know, was that criticism could reform the state of English Studies.

The development of criticism in universities was not merely a case of professionalising a practice which had previously been conducted by men of letters in the public sphere. The rise of English Studies instead produced a new sort of critic, and a new sort of criticism alongside reviewing. It is here that the act of criticism comes to perform a large-scale and institutionalised educational function, and the critic takes on a pedagogical role as a guardian of our cultural heritage.

In 'The Function of Criticism at the Present Time', Matthew Arnold asserted that criticism as he understands it is not 'criticism of the English literature of the day', that is, it is not reviewing ([1865] 1937: 50). He defines criticism as 'a disinterested endeavour to learn and propagate the best that has been known and thought in the world, and thus to establish a current of fresh and true ideas' for literature to draw inspiration from (49). The key word here is 'disinterested'. For Arnold it was important for critics to pursue their 'free play of the mind' (35) on all subjects, free of any vested interest, aloof from thoughts of practicality, and untouched by the political concerns of the review pages, such as the *Edinburgh* and the *Quarterly*, which he called 'organs of men and parties having practical ends to serve' (37). Arnold does not, in this essay, say exactly *where* this sort of independent criticism ought to be conducted, but his vigorous campaigning, as a critic and school inspector, for the inclusion of literature in schools and universities demonstrates that he saw an intimate link between criticism and education. Furthermore, the relationship between disinterestedness and academic tenure made universities the ideal place for Arnold's concept of criticism.

In his greatest work, 'Culture and Anarchy' (1867–9), it is obvious that Arnold sees culture and criticism as intimately related, for he defines culture as the best that has been thought and known. In this essay, however, the goal of learning and propagating culture is not to prepare the ground for a new epoch of literary creativity, but to act as a defence against anarchy, epitomised by working-class riots, and to support the order of the nation-state against hasty political demands of the liberal middle class. Culture performs this function by encouraging an individual self-transformation amongst all classes towards a state of serene contemplation.

Modern academic criticism can trace its origins to the work of Arnold, for whom the function of criticism was to contribute to the role of culture in maintaining social stability by establishing the critical base for a continuum of literary works from age to age. This cultural mission was joined with the traditional role of evaluating literature in the professional practice and pedagogical tool known as practical criticism. The theory for this academic movement comes from T.S. Eliot's modernist notions of impersonality in art, and the technique comes from I.A. Richards's book of the same name. *Practical Criticism* was based on a series of experiments in which 'undergraduates reading English with a view to an Honours degree' ([1929] 1964: 4) were asked to read and comment upon a selection of unfamiliar poems without knowledge of their authorship or any other contextualising information. The purpose of this was to document 'the contemporary state of culture' (3). Not surprisingly, the readers and thus contemporary culture were found wanting. Richard's debt to Arnold is to be found both in his description of 'mechanical inventions' as the malaise of civilisation and in his prescription for its salve in the reading of poetry (321).

Richards based his study of poetry in its effects upon readers, and wished to apply modern psychology to a better understanding and hence improvement of communication. Practical criticism, the critical reading of poetry, is meant to improve our communication and thus help us adapt to the age of the machine by giving us a link with the past. Richards's psychological apparatus had little effect on English Studies, but practical criticism, a sensitive reading of individual poems and the communicative ability of their language, which formed the bulk of Richards's book, became an indispensable pedagogical device. Leavis and Thompson argue in *Culture and Environment* that practical criticism can be applied to 'the analysis of advertising, journalistic articles and popular fiction' in the school classroom ([1933] 1962: 6). Leavis also advocates exams in practical criticism as a means of training intelligence and sensitivity at the Honours level in his sketch for an English School (1948: 43). Describing *Understanding Poetry* as an exemplar of practical criticism, Austin Warren applies the term to both the practice of the American New Critics and the methods of literary education which they devised (1941: 36–7).

The figure of literary authority that practical criticism promoted within the academy was the critic as the moral guardian of our cultural heritage, finding in literature a spiritual balm in the face of science and mass civilisation. This figure in fact appropriated for criticism the role of the Romantic poet. Indeed it is Coleridge who first used the term 'practical criticism' in his *Biographia Literaria*. Through 'practical criticism' – as he called his critical analysis of the works of Shakespeare – Coleridge hoped to discover the essential qualities that are symptomatic of poetic power or the imagination ([1817] 1956: 175). For Coleridge, literary authority resided in the poet and, most importantly, the poetic process. And Shelley uttered the most grandiloquent pronouncements on this authority of the Romantic poet when he called poets the unacknowledged legislators of the world ([1821] 1963: 190).

For the Romantics, construing the literary as a site of withdrawal from society was in fact a political protest. Practical criticism replaced poetic composition as the base from which the scientific aridity and materialism of industrialised society were challenged by the human spirit and by human creativity. Cleanth Brooks claimed that what he and I.A. Richards shared was an agreement that 'the greatest and most enduring poetry . . . manifested to a high degree Coleridge's synthesizing imagination' (1981: 590). However, authority in the academy became vested not in the poet but in the figure of the critic-teacher – the 'priest or rabbi of literary capital' as Jim Merod has called him (1987: 1). This is because it is criticism that had the responsibility of evaluating and promoting the transformative power of imaginative literature, and its goal was to produce a readership rather than to generate new writing.

Creative Writing, as we have seen, developed alongside the New Criticism in a handful of American universities from the 1930s, but it was left with a denuded Romantic aesthetics, adopting an expressivist theory of authorship that democratised the poetic imagination as a means of self-development, and a craft-based pedagogical practice in which the advice to show rather than tell operationalises the didactic heresy at the structural and syntactic level as well as the thematic level. It thus perpetuates the dead end of the Romantic legacy known as art for art's sake. The workshop model offers no figure of the *writer* for students and teachers other than that of the artist dedicated to the discovery of a personal voice and the development of a craft. The university, in this formulation, is nothing but a garret in the ivory tower, and this attitude persists today.

For instance, the only mention of a social function for writers on the website for the AWP is the statement that in 'creative writing workshops . . . stories and poems are made as gifts for readers and listeners', which is 'a highly civilized and humane act' (Fenza n.d.: 2). In Australia to date, the main function of the AAWP has been to debate whether creative work can be construed as research for the purposes of funding and assessment. So the representative bodies of Creative Writing across two countries see the writer as a literary Santa Claus or an academic careerist, chasing professional success in the literary establishment. Is it any wonder that Creative Writing has not claimed a position of literary authority in the New Humanities if it cannot elaborate a more forceful figure of the writer?

Oppositional criticism

While the tradition from Arnold to Leavis, from the late nineteenth to the mid-twentieth century, appropriated and institutionalised the moral function of the Romantic poet, substituting criticism and the university for the poetic imagination and nature, criticism has, from the 1960s, taken on the political responsibility of that figure we would call an intellectual. This intellectual engages not in practical criticism, but in oppositional criticism. According to Leela Gandhi, the New Humanities are characterised by 'oppositional and anti-humanist criticism' (1998: 52). The term 'oppositional criticism' derives from Edward Said's 1983 book, *The World, the Text, and the Critic*. 'Were I to use one word consistently along with *criticism*,' Said states, '(not as a modification but as an emphatic) it would be *oppositional*' (29). Oppositional criticism is founded on the assumption that the concept of autonomous aesthetic value expounded by practical criticism, rather than a spiritual salve against a materialistic capitalist society, is in fact one of its chief ideological buttresses (175).

The new function of criticism, characterised by Terry Eagleton as a 'struggle against the bourgeois state' (1984: 124), breaks with the tradition of *evaluation*, preferring to uncover the invisible political work which criticism does in the realm of culture by relating literary works to the social forces of cultural production and consumption, or by undermining the metaphysical assumptions of literature. Oppositional criticism also sees this textual critique as the base for social change, rather than cultural defence. While humanistic English Studies opposed itself to modern scientifc and industrialised society, the anti-dote it provided was a politics of cultural nostalgia founded in the value of the literary text. It followed the Arnoldian model of non-intervention (see Leavis 1948: 24). Hence, for Paul Bove, 'practical criticism is a pedagogy and a theory intended for the maintenance and management of the status quo' which 'reduces what might be the complex function of modernist literature to an ahistorical training school for teacher education in cultural management' (1986: 55).

The figure of the oppositional critic no longer traces its lineage to Dryden, the 'father of English criticism', or to the Arnoldian tradition of cultural heritage, but to the tradition of the intellectual with a political responsibility, and in particular the Marxist intellectual. The typical model for the oppositional critic throughout the 1980s (the period of 'Big Theory' in Galef's words), was that of Foucault's post-Marxist 'specific intellectual'. This figure has been employed by Bove, Frank Lentricchia, Jim Merod and Tony Bennett to describe the sort of intellectual work they wish to promote, although each has a different understanding of how the specific intellectual might work as a model for literary critics. I will look briefly at *Criticism and Social Change* by Frank Lentricchia as this is perhaps the most well-known formulation, and because the term 'oppositional criticism' appears in this book in the same year as in Said's.

'I come down', Lentricchia claims, 'on the side of those who believe that our society is mainly unreasonable and that education should be one of the places where we can get involved in the process of transforming it' (1983: 2). Rather than advocating a broad political activism, however, he asks: 'Can a literary intellectual, to come to the issue that most preoccupies me, do radical work *as* a literary intellectual?' (2). Lentricchia's definition of literary intellectual is this:

> By *literary intellectual* I mean the sort of intellectual who works mainly on texts and produces texts: hence not only poets, novelists, and other 'creative' writers and literary critics in the narrow sense but all intellectuals traditionally designated as humanists; critics in the broadest sense; and not only university humanists, but also literary intellectuals in the sense of journalists, advertising experts, and all media creators and disseminators of what is called 'the news': people who read, analyze, and produce what advanced criticism calls 'representations' and 'interpretations'.
>
> (6)

Lentricchia does not attempt to argue for any sort of solidarity between this incredibly diverse range of figures. In fact, after listing them, he puts them aside because his main interest is in literary intellectuals in the education system, which, for him, means critics and teachers. 'My focus is the university humanist', he explains, 'because I think that his and her position as a social and political actor has been cynically underrated and ignored by the right, left and center' (6). He rejects the traditional Marxist view of the intellectual as 'a bearer of the universal, the political conscience of us all' (6). He also rejects the Gramscian model of an intellectual aligned in daily practice with the working class. His model is Foucault's specific intellectual, 'one whose radical work of transformation, whose fight against repression is carried on at the specific institutional site where he finds himself and on the terms of his own expertise, on the terms inherent to his own functioning as an intellectual' (6–7).

Lentricchia argues that political activism by university humanists in 'the so-called outside world' (7) is not as important or even as powerful as, nor has it any necessary relationship with, their work as teachers and writers within the specific discipline or area of study for which they are trained. For Lentricchia the idea that 'the work of culture that goes on "inside" the university is somehow apolitical – and that this is a good thing' is what needs to be struggled against (7). The intellectual must combat 'his own training and history as an intellectual, and . . . the culture that he has been disciplined to preserve' (7–8). This will be achieved not by linking traditional texts to contemporary political situations, but by analysing in the classroom precisely how they operate as traditional texts. 'This sort of interpretation, when worked through the traditional texts of the humanities, will above all else attempt to displace traditional interpretations, which cover up the political work of culture. An active self-conscious work of interpretation will show the political work that the canonized "great books" have done and continue to do' (11). The aim is to interrogate a literary classic 'so as to reproduce it as a social text in the teeth of the usual critical lyricism that would deny the social text power and social specificity in the name of "literature". The activist intellectual needs a theory of reading that will instigate a culturally suspicious, trouble-making readership' (11).

So for Lentricchia, a literary intellectual is an academic who, through teaching and research, attempts to undermine the New Critical emphasis on the aesthetic autonomy of literature and the universalising moral function of canonical texts by a critical materialist reading of literature's social context. A literary intellectual is an intellectual who practises oppositional criticism within the university and it 'is the task of the oppositional critic to re-read culture so as to amplify and strategically position the marginalised voices of the ruled, exploited, oppressed, and excluded' (15). Here Lentricchia seems to forget his claims for the specificity of intellectual work, for the oppositional critic is once again speaking on behalf of marginalised groups, representing their claims within the academy. For him the literary intellectual can be 'a social force, who at his specific institutional site would begin to make a contribution to the formation of a community different from the one we live in: "society" as the function of many things, one of them being "education"' (19). While he claims that intellectuals need to struggle against their traditional role, he does not say why they should be doing this on behalf of others. Nor does he explore the specific institutional power relations involved in this work. The university is simply the place in which oppositional critics or literary intellectuals find themselves situated, and thus they are compelled to transform their 'critical consciousness', to use Said's phrase, within the system of higher education. The role of the critic may be inverted, but the role of the teacher remains unchallenged. The social function of the university is not reconsidered: it remains a neutral site regardless of whether the knowledge it disseminates is conservative or radical. Furthermore, in this formulation there is no complementary vision of the writer, within or without the university, for literature is placed in an antagonistic relationship with criticism, and the writer is divested of agency, or at least placed in the outdated mode of the universal (and placeless) intellectual.

My interest in the intellectual is not as the central figure for a revolutionary politics or a struggle within and against 'regimes of truth', but as the focus for an understanding of the institutional conditions in which all writing takes place. A central preoccupation of Cultural Studies since the inception of the Birmingham School has been the figure of the intellectual. The most exhaustive examination (and example) of this preoccupation is John Frow's *Cultural Studies and Cultural Value*. In this book Frow draws upon the work of writers such as Alvin Gouldner, Barbara and John Ehrenreich, and Pierre Bourdieu to situate 'cultural intellectuals' within a broader professional-managerial or knowledge class. Intellectuals are defined as professionals in possession of cultural capital, or stored mental labour, which provides them with economic gain. For their reproduction they rely on a system of credentialising through education, rather than non-meritocratic authority in the form of privilege, money or state power. In the knowledge economy, intellectuals have supplanted traditional working-class labour, but while they may control the means of production through professional knowledge and skills (which maintain monopoly capital on behalf of the bourgeoisie), they do not own the means of production and hence are in competition with the ruling class. Frow argues that academics or 'cultural intellectuals' are a 'local fraction' of this knowledge class, with a 'commitment to the institutions of cultural capital, and simultaneously a set of anxieties about [their] place within these institutions' (1995: 130–1).

If one wished to locate Creative Writing within this framework, the awarding of degrees in writing can be seen as an attempt to absorb the 'placeless' writer into the institutional apparatus of the knowledge class by imposing systems of professional training and accreditation on the practice of writing. This argument, as we have seen, has often been levelled against writing programmes. Alarmist critiques such as this, however, tend to neglect consideration of literature as an institutionalised profession.

One does not become a writer simply by virtue of putting pen to paper, or fingertip to keyboard. One is *credentialled* as a writer by virtue of acquiring agents, securing publishing contracts, being reviewed, selling books, and winning prizes and grants, as well as gaining membership of professional organisations such as the Australian Society of Authors. Writers are members of a new class of intellectuals because they control their domain of knowledge (literature), but do not own the means of production (the publishing industry), and they are distinguished from unskilled wage earners by their possession of cultural capital: in this case, their talent and professional writing skills. The aesthetic, or literary value, is thus an economic commodity.

It is obvious that Creative Writing is one institutional site of the literary establishment, for it does provide employment for writers *as* writers, and skills training for aspirants. It does not, however, perform a *necessary* function in the reproduction of literature. Teachers of Creative Writing do not need university positions to write (although they may need the income to support their writing) and students do not become qualified writers by virtue of their study. In which case, Creative Writing must have another function beyond its 'official' purpose of employing and training writers: it must have a function specific to the university.

The university is a site for the reproduction of a broad intellectual or professional-managerial class via professional training and accreditation. In other words, the university is not where the knowledge class operates, but where it trains and recruits. Humanist academics, or those cultural intellectuals who are trained and accredited to stay within the university, are members of a broader class of knowledge workers, but their professional domain of knowledge remains largely within its main apparatus of reproduction. So if Creative Writing is a site for the professional training of writers, but is not a necessary system of accreditation, its main function is to contribute to the domain of knowledge of cultural intellectuals within the academy by the provision of a literary education. The performance of this necessary function in fact contributes to the goal of reproducing literature as a profession through the employment and training of writers, precisely because the domain of knowledge that incorporates Creative Writing takes literature as its object of study. This knowledge sustains the profession of literature by affording it cultural prestige – thus increasing its capital or potential to generate more capital, not to mention the direct sales generated by reading lists.

In order to reconcile its professed but not *accredited* purpose of training writers with its necessary function as a contribution to academic teaching and research, however, Creative Writing must elaborate a figure of the writer capable of straddling these two domains. The model of the writer as a professional artist for whom the university is only a place for the transmission of craft skills and a knowledge of literary models lacks the symbolic force to perform this reconciliation between unaccredited purpose and necessary function.

If, like the New Humanities (or, more accurately, like the rest of the New Humanities), Creative Writing is to go beyond Theory, it must become more than a pre-professional training ground for artists dedicated to their craft and a personal vision of the world created by their imagination and realised through their individual voice or style, and for whom Theory is an antagonistic discourse. Equally, workshops need to be more than a haven for avant-garde experimentalism where Theory provides a liberation from outmoded generic distinctions. Rather, a new vision of authorship needs to be elaborated, where literature is an intellectual practice *alongside* other non-literary discourses in the academy, and where the division between fiction and non-fiction still exists, but in a non-hierarchical relationship.

According to the AWP Guidelines for successful graduate degrees, the MFA generally requires 'coursework in form, theory, and literature, including contemporary writers' (Associated Writing Programs, 1990: 12). This coursework, however, takes place outside the workshop and hence there are no curricular guidelines for the relationship between the workshop (where the creative thesis is produced) and classes in Literary Studies. The figure of the author which emerges from this system is that of a professionally trained writer who has been provided with a supplementary education in literary appreciation.

Masters and doctoral degrees in Creative Writing in Australian universities tend to place less emphasis on the workshop, relying more on the academic mentoring system of thesis supervision, in which the supervisor adopts a role similar to a professional editor. Furthermore, rather than coursework requirements, the creative thesis must in most cases be submitted with an accompanying critical commentary, or 'exegesis', as it is often called. The critical essay must have a demonstrated relationship to the creative thesis, so that the submission takes the form of a unified piece. This mirrors postgraduate requirements in the visual and performing arts, where the creative thesis is accompanied by written documentation which acts as a record of the artistic process, explaining the theoretical underpinnings of various artistic strategies and techniques, and thus demonstrating what might be called 'research equivalent' activity. The figure of the writer here is very much in the Eliotic mode, where the critical work is a byproduct of the creative process, not fully discharged in the literary work itself.

The exegesis recalls the tradition of the English writer-critic, from Dryden through to Eliot himself, who produces what George Watson (1973) calls 'prefatorial' criticism in defence of their own work. Like this figure, the postgraduate writer is expected to produce criticism deriving from their creative practice and serving as some form of illumination of it. Unlike this figure, however, the postgraduate writer loses literary authority by the very presence of the exegesis which performs two supplementary functions: to overcome the speculative nature of evaluation by providing a corroborating statement of intent prepared by the artist, against which the success of the work is to be measured; and to act as an insurance policy in case the artistic process was deficient in academic rigour, requiring the student to demonstrate critical/theoretical skills by using their own work as an object of analysis.

The option to submit a single fictocritical thesis offers a vision of a postmodern writer-critic who enacts his or her dual identity within the single hybridised work. I suggest, however, that the distinction between the practice of artists and the theory of critics can be circum-navigated by collapsing both figures into that of the intellectual, a figure that incorporates both, without the need for hybridity, because it is based on a vision of social agency rather than a theory of generic form or of the creative process. For an artist to be an intellectual it is less important to have a theory of writing than to possess a vision of how a literary work might operate in society and to assume respon-sibility for it. In what follows I will argue that it is the pseudo-mythic model of the public intellectual who can straddle the academic world and the public sphere, and has become the exemplary figure of the New Humanities, which provides the way forward for Creative Writing.

The public intellectual

The current preoccupation with the idea of the public intellectual seems to have been prompted by Russell Jacoby's *The Last Intellectuals*. In this book Jacoby claimed that preoccupation with intellectuals as a sociological class was symptomatic of a decline in public intellec-tual life and the dearth of independent intellectuals, or 'writers and thinkers who address a general and educated audience' ([1987] 1989: 5). Rather than putting forward a class analysis, Jacoby discusses intellectuals on generational grounds. His argument is that earlier in the twentieth century intellectuals were independent thinkers who operated largely as freelance writers. The gentrification of bohemia, the expansion of suburbia and in particular the rise of the universities contributed to a decline in public intellectual life. The generation of intellectuals who came of age in the 1960s and formed the core of the New Left were hence unable to envisage a life outside the university, and indeed moved from being student agitators to academic sociologists, radical Marxists and feminists, writing for restricted professionalised audiences in an exclusionary jargon.

Jacoby's thesis follows much of what has been said about the professionalisation of criticism. In 1984 Terry Eagleton argued that 'criticism today lacks all substantive social function. It is either part of the public relations branch of the literary industry, or a matter wholly internal to the academies' (7). Gerald Graff and Reginald Gibbons wrote in 1985 that 'literary critics were once journalists and men (and too rarely women) of letters, usually outsiders to the university; . . . they wrote either for general readers or for the community of imaginative writers, rather than for a coterie of specialized professors and graduate students, and thus delivered their findings and opinions in an accessible style rather than in an esoteric jargon of methodological terms' (8). What is more important than distinguishing between contemporary schools of academic criticism, they argue, is a discussion of 'the relation between academic literary criticism and the writing and reading that go on outside the academy' (8).

That the function of criticism has become absorbed in a wider concern with the social role of the intellectual is evidenced by Edward Said's 1993 Reith Lectures, published in 1994 as *Representations of the Intellectuals*. In *The World, the Text and the Critic*, Said spoke of the 'critical consciousness' being embodied in the oppositional critic, and called for a more 'worldly' textual criticism (1983: 1–30). Ten years later he had shifted from a vision of criticism within the university to a vision of the intellectual outside the university, characterising the intellectual 'as exile and marginal, as amateur, and as the author of a language that tries to speak the truth to power' (1994: xiv).

Since the publication of Jacoby's book the idea of a public intellectual has engaged critical interest, becoming the subject of several symposia, conferences and books, and seeping into our general lexicon.[2] Debate about the figure of the public intellectual and what it represents is generally organised around the terms established by Jacoby's book: that intellectual work now takes place largely within the academy. Those who agree with Jacoby are concerned with how academics can overcome their professional myopia and engage with the general public by moving between academia and the world of journalism: either to overcome the obscurantist jargon of theory, or to disseminate the insights of theory more broadly. Those who disagree challenge his outmoded concept of the public sphere and argue that as teachers in public institutions, as researchers who publish their work, and as professional media consultants, academics already operate as public intellectuals. Or they point out that one cannot simply choose to become a public intellectual: this depends on the workings of the media.

What has given the figure of the public intellectual its current cachet, however, is the fact that jeremiads against its disappearance, attempts to revive it and defences of academic work all overlap with moves to reconfigure the humanities as an *institution* with greater public influence. One recommendation of *Knowing Ourselves and Others*, the 1998 publication of the Australian Academy of the Humanities, was that 'Universities further facilitate and provide incentives for the contributions that academics make to the public discussion of issues of importance' and 'extend the connections between Humanities scholars and the media'. These moves are a response to the external pressures of anti-Political Correctness campaigns and of diminished funding as a result of moves towards an Enterprise University: in short, they are the result of the pressures of a post-Theory academy.

Political Correctness and the Enterprise University

In *The Last Intellectuals*, Jacoby noted that there had been a growing conservative backlash against the infiltration of radical Marxist views into university curricula. He also noted that conservatives had tended to resist professionalisation because they maintained an ideal of the aristocratic man of letters ([1987] 1989: 195–209). It is from this conservative backlash that the debate concerning Political Correctness began. Concerns about a moral decline in the humanities had been voiced in such bestselling books as Allan Bloom's *The Closing of the American Mind* and E.D. Hirsch's *Cultural Literacy*, both published in the same year as Jacoby's book, and followed by Roger Kimball's *Tenured Radicals* (1990) and Dinesh D'Souza's *Illiberal Education* (1991). These concerns coalesced around the term Political Correctness and operated under the assumption that radical leftists of the 1960s had come to power in the universities and politicised the disinterested academy by challenging the occlusions of gender, race and class in the Western liberal tradition.

An anti-Political Correctness media campaign began in America at the end of 1990 when *Newsweek*, sporting the Orwellian phrase

'Thought Police' on its front cover, published an article entitled 'Taking Offense'. 'Political Correctness' became a term of abuse signifying the claims of multiculturalism (or the imposition of ethnic-minority group interests on the general public: a domain which supposedly consists of citizens with individual rights rather than one on which a *majority* group agenda is imposed), the introduction of speech codes on university campuses to prevent vilification, and the relativistic and obscurantist jargon of an exclusionary professional language known as Theory. The paradox of this attack is that the supposed relativism of humanities departments, which had attacked the notion of core values and had licensed pluralism, was seen as the imposition of an orthodoxy. 'In short,' Jeffrey Williams wrote in 1995, Political Correctness signified 'the very public backlash against what's gone on in the humanities and in critical social thought these past twenty-five years' (1). In the same year, Bob Hodge wrote that in Australia the 'values which people working in cultural studies and the New Humanities sincerely and strongly hold are labelled as political correctness' (1997: 10).

This narrative about the invasion of the traditionally disinterested academy and the undermining of the Western liberal tradition is the flip side of Jacoby's assertion that radical intellectuals have been *disempowered* by entering the academy. The argument that left-leaning intellectuals sold out after the disillusionment of the failed May 1968 uprisings by entering the academy and cutting themselves off from society is also made by Eagleton in *Literary Theory* when he draws a connection between the decline of Marxism and the rise of post-structuralism (1983: 142–3). It was due to both the conservative critique within the media of the dangers of Political Correctness, and the disillusionment with dehistoricised Theory of left-leaning intellectuals within the academy, that the idea of the public intellectual gained purchase throughout the 1990s.

These influences can be found in Michael Bérubé's *Public Access*. In this book Bérubé claims that the 'smear campaign against contemporary scholarship in the humanities has successfully set the terms for further public discussion on the subject', and it is necessary for academics to defend themselves (1994: ix). 'The decisive issue in the academic culture wars', Bérubé claims, 'is the issue of public access: public access to university education, in the first place, and public access to the academic criticism and theory in which some of the most interesting, provocative, and rewarding university education is currently taking place' (38). Hence the important goal for academic criticism today, Bérubé asserts, is to popularise academic cultural criticism rather than to generate new theoretical paradigms, to set up 'a public address system' in order to safeguard public access to the academy (38).

In the introduction to an anthology of essays entitled *After Political Correctness*, Newfield and Strickland claim that a result of the PC phenomenon was that 'the aroused media attention marked an opening for the academic intellectual' (1995: 1). There was now public debate over the role of the humanities in higher education and the broader community. After media attacks on Political Correctness were rebutted by left-leaning academics, accusation shifted to debate, which now involves 'a broad spectrum of progressive humanists moving beyond temporary self-defense toward a greatly expanded public presence' (1). The anthology is designed to develop prospects 'for a more public humanities' by 'redesigning and expanding the social and cultural role of the academic humanities' (1).

Critics such as Bérubé (1994: 20) and Paul Lauter (1995: 73) assert that the anti-Political Correctness campaign was a smokescreen for conservative government attacks on universities, through funding cuts designed to restrict access to higher education. David Bennett provides a similar argument regarding the function of Political Correctness in Australia. In a 1993 article entitled 'PC Panic, the Press and the Academy', Bennett describes the existence of Political Correctness debates in Australia as the result of an importation of syndicated articles from North America into the popular media. 'Those of us who have worked in Australian humanities departments in the 1980s', Bennett argues, 'know that in-house versions of the PC debate have been going on – in often bitterly factionalized arguments over curricula, the canon, critical methodology and academic appointments – for at least ten or fifteen years' (439). These debates entered the popular media, Bennett claims, as an intervention in public debate about academic accountability to government funding and responsibility to economic growth; a debate which had been prominent since the Dawkins reforms were proposed. 'If we are to take Australian media attacks on academic PC seriously,' Bennett argues, 'it must be in the context of the media's own broad support, not for an "apolitical" pedagogy, but for direct political intervention in the reform of the humanities' (440).

Complaints about Political Correctness gained a much broader social context in Australia with the election of a conservative federal government in 1996. The term was levelled against so-called cultural 'elites', characterised as left-wing apologists for minority interest groups. This coincided with savage funding cuts to university budgets, forcing universities to seek alternative sources of funding in order to maintain resources (see Keane 1997). So the need for humanities departments to identify ways in which they are relevant to society also arose in the face of a growing managerial culture in universities, the rise of the Enterprise University, evident in Australia in the decade or so from the Dawkins reforms to the 1999 white paper on research and research training by David Kemp, which emphasised accountability to public funds and encouraged a culture of entrepreneurialism (see Kemp 1999).

These social and institutional pressures overlap with the goals of Cultural Studies itself, an interdisciplinary enterprise concerned with producing politically engaged critiques of the everyday and of the power relationships involved in culture as a whole way of life. For instance, in 'Cultural Studies and its Theoretical Legacies', Stuart Hall has suggested that the Birmingham Centre for Contemporary Cultural Studies was originally envisaged as the institutional site for the elaboration of an 'organic intellectual' who, in Gramscian terms, would be linked to a working-class culture, and hence be committed to a greater engagement with social and political life beyond the academy. For Hall, the 'organic intellectual cannot absolve himself or herself from the responsibility of transmitting those ideas, that knowledge, through the intellectual function, to those who do not belong, professionally, in the intellectual class' (1992: 281).

The overlap of this goal with the institutional conditions of the New Humanities is most evident in the development of that section of Cultural Studies known as Cultural Policy, which, according to Tony Bennett, was both a practical response to the Dawkins reforms and a theoretical reformulation of cultural theory and critical practice along Foucauldian lines (see T. Bennett, 1992a and 1992b). Bennett's ideal figure here is not the critic or intellectual providing cultural commentary, but a cultural technician involved in policy formation. It can also be argued that Cultural Studies is being forced to redefine itself to fit the Enterprise University. In 1997 Simon During, editor of the popular anthology/textbook *A Cultural Studies Reader*, published an article entitled 'Teaching Culture', in which he claimed that Cultural Studies has overtaken English Studies largely because it is responding to the vocational demands of students. These demands are the product of a global economy, suggests During, who goes on to argue that Cultural Studies prepares students for jobs in the 'cultural sector' of advanced economies (6). The original emancipatory and politicised agenda of this movement has been so muted that the best it can do is make students 'canny and picky consumers of the products of increasingly sophisticated cultural industries' (6).

The cultural criticism espoused by public intellectuals in the New Humanities or the Post-Theory academy is designed to make Theory more applicable to contemporary cultural practice and to translate its insights to the public sphere. This shares with Lentricchia's literary intellectual a commitment to oppositional critical politics, but it differs not only in its move beyond theoretical rereadings of the literary canon, but in its recognition that the university is an institution crucially interrelated with the public sphere. This is not because the university is a training ground for future citizens (which is Jim Merod's argument in *The Political Responsibility of the Critic*), but because it is subject to public challenge in the form of government control or media criticism.

Creative Writing and public intellectuals

The public intellectual has become the exemplary figure of the New Humanities, not necessarily as a model which individual academics can aspire to and train students to take up, but as a zone of contestation, a discursive site in which debates about the institutional function of the humanities in the wider community are played out. There is no specific figure of *literary* authority in the New Humanities, no critic to proclaim upon literature as a distinct realm. Rather, there is a more free-ranging figure of the intellectual whose work is motivated by oppositional criticism in its broadest sense, that is, textual or cultural critique of received opinion, with the ultimate aim of effecting social change, or at least an alteration of public opinion, beyond the refinements of disciplinary knowledge. If Creative Writing is able to elaborate a figure of the writer as a *literary* intellectual in this sense, it will claim a stronger disciplinary position within the New Humanities than it will by perpetuating a theory/practice divide or evading it with hybrid forms of writing.

One of the main problems facing attempts by academics to operate as public intellectuals is that they are professionally rewarded for refereed journal articles, but not for articles in mass-circulation newspapers or magazines, which are not deemed to count as research. This is also the problem faced by teachers of Creative Writing. Those who teach in Creative Writing are hired not because of their academic records, but because of their publishing record outside the academy. In this case, teachers of writing wish to claim research points for their 'public' writing.

The traditional PhD is a rite of passage for young intellectuals seeking academic work, but its emphasis on what Judith Brett calls 'the endless qualification' (qtd in Dessaix 1998: 24), and the necessity for specialisation rather than overarching commentary, means that it is designed for examiners rather than a general, even a general academic readership. Creative Writing is somewhat different. Those who undertake postgraduate work in this discipline are more likely to be seeking a general audience than an academic one, because their medium is not academic prose, but fictional or poetic writing. But if writers address a public, they are not considered as intellectuals, or at least, not in the form with which they make this address.

If the forum of the public intellectual is the media, the form is non-fiction – reviews, essays, newspaper columns, public lectures, panel sessions, television and radio interviews. A writer of novels and stage or screenplays, and less commonly of poetry, can command a presence as a public intellectual, but only by stepping outside the realms of fiction and operating in the forms mentioned above. That is, writers' fictional work may get them noticed in the public sphere, but they can only operate and be acknowledged as public intellectuals if they write columns, give lectures or provide interviews.

'If there is one little window,' McKenzie Wark has claimed, 'through which younger people get into traditional zones of public life at the moment it is creative writing' (1997: 89). Here he is thinking specifically of writers of 'grunge' fiction and the possibilities of a 'young public' being formed around them. These writers were popular at writers' festivals, Wark claims, when 'grunge' was a marketable category, but 'I'm still waiting for the gatekeepers to give them a go as broadcasters on ABC Radio National, or as columnists in the newspapers, or to feature at conferences organised by bodies like the National Book Council' (89). In making this point, Wark demonstrates that it is what he calls the media 'vector' of fiction, alongside the internet and women's magazines, which he points out as unacknowledged public forums of debate, that militates against these writers as much as their youth: they cannot be acknowledged as public intellectuals unless they have access to forums for the dissemination of 'non-fiction'. The question, of course, is why should they be granted this access? In an interview with Robert Dessaix, the literary critic Don Anderson claimed: 'I don't think that literary intellectuals – or let's say literary practitioners such as poets, novelists or dramatists – ought to have more attention paid to them when they speak about larger issues of state than anybody else with an informed vote' (qtd in Dessaix 1998: 14).

At any rate, to encourage a view of literary practice as preparatory work for the role of public social commentary in more authoritative forms of discourse is not a viable option for the discipline of Creative Writing, as this neglects a consideration of the work writers do in the public sphere through their fictional writing. Some writing courses teach fiction and poetry alongside journalistic and professional writing, and many writers function as reviewers and journalists to supplement their income, but I am interested in retaining the integrity of Creative Writing as a discipline of intellectual work rather than denying that writers can perform in other modes of public discourse.

It is, of course, notoriously difficult to define exactly what litera-ture is: is it non-fiction; figurative language; writing which employs 'literary' techniques such as narrative, character, etc.; writing which evokes emotional rather than intellectual responses; writing which is creative or imaginative? It is relatively easy, however, to accept what sort of writing *operates* as literature. Literature is what fiction or poetry editors accept for publication, what gets shelved in those sections in bookshops, what is reviewed in those categories in newspapers and magazines, what wins literary prizes and grants. Literature is what people read when they want to be entertained, or to escape into a fictional world, or to appreciate the heightened uses of language. Literature is what thousands of students across Australia want to write when they enrol in Creative Writing courses. So while litera-ture may be just another form of cultural production which cannot be defended as a special type of language, it is nonetheless the assump-tion of aesthetic difference that governs its operation in society. 'The ontological groundlessness of literature', John Guillory reminds us, 'in no way diminishes its social effects as a means of marking the status of certain texts and genres' (1993: 65). In which case, to treat it simply as another type of writing, as a form of rhetoric to be mastered alongside advertising and journalistic copy, may help over-come unproductive preconceptions held by some students, such as that of untrammelled inspiration, but it nonetheless glosses over the specificity and complexity of the functions of literature.

In 'Creative Writing and its Discontents', David Fenza names several teachers of Creative Writing who are also bestselling authors with high public profiles. 'These writers are "public intellectuals",' he claims. 'Few literary scholars and fewer theorists have reached the degree of public stature enjoyed by these writers' (2000: 8). This is an important point, as it draws attention to the potential of the discipline of Creative Writing to act as a medium between the academy and the public sphere, and hence to contribute to the goals of the New Humanities. However, Fenza is content to demonstrate only that writers can command a public presence, not how they, as intellectuals, might contribute to public debate through their writing, nor how the discipline of Creative Writing might encourage this contribution. One benefit of a Creative Writing programme, Fenza claims, is that it '[a]dvances the ideals of a liberal and humane education by inspiring, exercising, and strengthening the efficacy of the human will to do good, to make a meaningful difference in art and in society' (15). For Fenza, one must assume, simply teaching students how to write is enough because literature itself is a force for social good, purely by being literature. And what makes it literature is that writing is a creative act of the individual human will.

In conceiving of a public to be addressed through the media, public intellectuals imagine a citizenry to be influenced by argument, especially about current and particular social issues. 'Creative' writers, in seeking publication, obviously seek a readership, but the audience they imagine is an abstract construct. Literature does influence the public, however, which is why some literary works are used to educate citizens and some are censored or banned for the ostensible good of the populace. The responsibility of writers lies not in whom they address or speak for, but in recognising how literature functions in society.

How might this responsibility be encouraged in the discipline of Creative Writing? As well as professional artists who pass on their knowledge to literary aspirants, university teachers of writing must be recognised as academics who practise criticism in the workshop. The question is, what sort of criticism should this be? A 'more practical institution' of practical criticism, as Robert Miles suggests (1992: 39), or a socially conscious oppositional criticism? I am interested in developing a poetics which can be applied to all student work, from confessional poems to discontinuous narratives, without establishing a heirarchy in which 'experimental' modes of writing are considered more radical or politically efficacious than 'mainstream' genres. A poetics which engages with questions of literary quality and aesthetic power while still remaining committed to the oppositional criticism of the New Humanities. And a poetics which encourages a view of literature as a public intellectual practice, rather than a means for the empowerment of individual identities and subjectivities.

Conclusion

Towards a sociological poetics

I have argued in this book that the discipline of Creative Writing is more than a formal system of literary patronage and apprenticeship which has arisen as the result of an academic absorption of literary culture. It is an element of Literary Studies that developed as a series of pedagogical responses to the perennial crisis in English, and it provides an institutional space for writers to assert their literary authority as writers. I have concluded that in order for Creative Writing to negotiate a space for this authority within the university it is necessary to reassert the academic importance of literature not only as an influential agent in the cultural life of a society which demands critical attention, but as an intellectual practice which makes an active contribution to English Studies (envisaged as a form of knowledge constituted at the dialogic junction of literature and criticism).

Since intellectuals within the post-Theory academy are concerned not only with the refinement of disciplinary knowledge, but with the deployment of this knowledge within public debate, students and teachers of Creative Writing who perform intellectual work as writers are positioned to contribute to the New Humanities by virtue of the fact that their work is geared towards an audience in the public sphere. The reconceptualisation of Creative Writing as an institutional site for literary intellectuals, however (by which I mean writers who are critically aware of how literature circulates in social power relations, and who accept responsibility for their own work), requires a pedagogical reformation. If we accept that the best way to learn how to write is to read, and that this is the focus of the workshop, any reformation must be centred on a practice of critical reading of exemplary texts and student manuscripts. The question is, how do we introduce the current theoretical and political concerns of the New Humanities into this reading?

In his preface to *Dramatic Technique* George Pierce Baker claimed that 'Complete freedom of choice in subject and complete freedom in treatment so that the individuality of the artist may have its best expression are indispensable in the development of great art', and that creative courses should provide students with 'technique based on study of successful dramatists' (1919: vi). This model for teaching Creative Writing is based on the assumption that talent can't be taught, but can be nurtured by a training in literary craft. This may seem reasonable enough, but its persistence today indicates an unwillingness to engage with contemporary critiques of aesthetic autonomy, or to extend the critical range of the workshop.

If Creative Writing is to negotiate a position within the New Humanities, perhaps the idea of complete artistic freedom for individual expression needs to be challenged – if only because this idea encourages a pedagogy restricted to commentary upon craft as an abstract technique, and an approach to writing as an individual practice removed from society. It is not viable, of course, to prescribe the content of students' writing, but it is possible to provide a critical context for its reception, beyond consideration of the quality of metaphors or the number of adjectives in a sentence or the rhythmic timing of line breaks. Is it enough for students to write stories of obviously unreconstructed sexism in the name of personal expression or artistic exploration when theoretically untenable prejudices will not be accepted in essays for other classes? Granted, problems such as these may be profitably addressed and challenged within the workshop, and most likely by peers. However, I am not talking of shifting from practical considerations of craft to general discussion where the manuscript – and, by extension, its author – is put on trial for sexism, or readers imagine themselves in the moral situations of the characters, or the work is considered to fail aesthetically because of a lack of thematic complexity. I am talking about employing oppositional criticism precisely to interrogate the assumptions about literature underpinning these responses and then to consider how the work in question differs from and interrelates with a range of non-literary (scholarly, political, journalistic, legal) discourses of gendered power relations.

The problem with eschewing any form of programmatic provision for this, in favour of the general dynamic of workshop discussion, is that a well-written and politically inoffensive piece will most likely pass through the aesthetic filter of the workshop process without a consideration of how it relates to anything beyond the writer's own personal satisfaction. This is buttressed by the fact that exemplary texts are generally studied for their formal qualities rather than their social or political resonances.

While formalist analysis of texts is the necessary first step in the workshop, it is unproductive for texts to be considered from a purely aesthetic critical perspective. If, for example, the work of Anne Sexton is to be studied as a model for students who wish to write of their own experiences, discussion could entail not just her use of free verse or her ability to distil autobiographical detail into poetic form, but the historical and critical context of confessional poetry, its relationship to feminist politics and psychoanalysis, its association with psychic stress and insanity (and hence its concept of writing as therapy), and its shift away from 'impersonal' modernist symbolism. This would provide students not just with a range of ahistorical devices and forms, but with an awareness of the political effects of aesthetic decisions.

Furthermore, it would be worthwhile for students to consider literary works from countries where social unrest or political censorship force a greater sense of responsibility upon writers to view themselves as intellectuals (especially those writers supported by International PEN via the Writers in Prison Committee and the *Index on Censorship*). How does this social responsibility impact upon aesthetic decisions? While in a country such as France there is a tradition of accepting writers as intellectuals, and in a country such as South Africa many writers feel compelled to explore their social responsibility, one problem with literary culture in countries where Creative Writing is taught is that it tends to be absorbed in its institutional function as an entertainment industry. As a result most publishers are increasingly unwilling to take the financial risk of publishing first-time authors whose work is deemed 'experimental'. How are writing programmes to position themselves in relation to these conditions?

It may also be useful to encourage students to engage in activities such as book reviewing, analysis of literary media controversies, research into the history and operations of institutions such as publishing companies and funding bodies, all of which can be justified professionally whether graduates go on to become teachers or writers, and give students a broader intellectual context for their work. In other words, the grooming of students for professional involvement in the literary establishment can be complemented with a cultural analysis of the power relations implicit in its machinations. This is the model adopted by Communication and Cultural Studies. In fact, the sort of analysis characterised by Cultural Studies would be helpful in conceiving literary texts as, to use a phrase from

Tony Bennett, 'directly active components in the organisation of social relations themselves' (1990: 35).

One strategy may be to introduce to the Creative Writing classroom critical or theoretical works from a Cultural Studies perspective which actively interrogate the category of 'literature' in relation to things such as popular cultural practices, the media and new technologies, identity politics, policy formation and public debate. This would be more helpful than getting students to read Barthes's 'The Death of the Author' and asking how it confronts their own views on authorship. Ultimately, however, intervention by teachers in the actual workshopping process will have greater effect than a more varied reading list. Any attempt at reforming Creative Writing must take place at the level of the workshop, as this is the pedagogical centre of the discipline. If each student manuscript is not only afforded a remedial technical overhauling in the workshop, but is placed within a broader cultural or political context by the critical expertise of the teacher, then student writers will be given a greater understanding of how their creative work might relate to their essays in other classes, and of how they might consider placing themselves as writers in society, as intellectuals who can potentially contribute to public debate via the medium of literature, rather than merely seeing potential publication as affirmation of their 'talent'.

In the poetics of the workshop which I outlined in Chapter 3, the main critical tools for developing professional craft skills revolve around the practice of *reading as a writer*, the advice to *show, don't tell*, and the goal of *discovering a voice*. How can these be adapted or reformed according to the reconceptualised discipline of Creative Writing which I am arguing is necessary? The problem requires shifting the pedagogical focus of the workshop from narrowly formalist conceptions of craft to the social context of literature, but without diminishing the importance of craft as an intellectual skill, and without detracting from the purpose of improving students' writing. This means paying attention to the content of a literary work, as this is what connects it to the outside world, but without isolating content from form. What is required, then, is to demonstrate how content is realised in the formal construction of a text, and this means shifting from a formalist poetics to a sociological poetics.

In order to suggest how this transition might be achieved I will draw on Mikhail Bakhtin's essay, 'Discourse in the Novel', which appears in *The Dialogic Imagination*. 'The principal idea of this essay', Bakhtin states in the opening line, 'is that the study of verbal art can and must overcome the divorce between an abstract "formal" approach and an equally abstract "ideological" approach. Form and content in discourse are one, once we understand that verbal discourse is a social phenomenon' ([1934–5] 1981: 259). Bakhtin's work is founded upon a critique of traditional linguistics and the philosophy of discourse. Language, Bakhtin argues, cannot be analysed in formal linguistic terms, as an hermetic and immutable pre-existing system of neutral words. Language only acquires meaning in specific acts of communication, in the concrete utterances of a person in a particular social context. As a result, any national language is internally stratified into a series of languages. Here the linguistic notion of dialects within languages becomes a sociological concept, whereby it is the ideological, not regional, use of language by specific groups within society which stratifies it.

This 'diversity of social speech types' is what Bakhtin calls heteroglossia. Language is fundamentally heteroglot, and each of its internally stratified elements embodies the belief system and world views of its users. Furthermore, language operates dialogically. Every word contains within it the associations of its prior use in a specific context, and a speaker must appropriate this word for his or her own expressive purposes within a concrete utterance; an utterance which is always directed towards another person and the anticipated response of this person. Hence every word and every utterance becomes laden with a whole background of contradictory resonances built up over time and shifting with every socio-historical context.

All these stratified languages and the world views which they embody 'encounter one another and co-exist in the consciousness of real people – first and foremost in the creative consciousness of people who write novels' (292). Literature is, in essence, a conscious artistic dramatisation of this dialogic clashing of living discourses in society. 'The prose writer makes use of words that are already populated with the social intentions of others and compels them to serve his own new intentions' (299–300). In which case, translating the insights of Saussurean linguistics to literature, as the Russian formalists tried to do, cannot provide an adequate sociological stylistics, for a literary work cannot be studied 'as if it were a hermetic and self-sufficient whole' (274). Nor can a poetics centred around an author's individual style or technique sufficiently apprehend the dialogic nature of literature. The author is not a craftsman who employs an ideologically neutral and formalistically pure language to express a unified personal vision or to master the objective world. Instead, writers represent within the literary work a range of extra-literary languages which organise social relations.

This means that an attention to form also requires an attention to the prior utterances, dialogised words, and world views of the heteroglot, and ideologically conflicting, social languages being artistically orchestrated within the text. This is the key to a reconceptualisation of the concept of voice. In Bakhtin's formulation voice is neither the author's pre-linguistic creative self realised in an individual style, nor the speaking position adopted by a narrator in relation to the story. In fact, the question 'who speaks?' can never be answered in the singular for it is a question of which social languages, and the belief systems they embody, are being torn from the actual world of discourse and represented within the literary text:

> The novel orchestrates all its themes, the totality of the world of objects and ideas depicted and expressed in it, by means of the social diversity of speech types [*raznorecie*] and by the differing individual voices that flourish under such conditions. Authorial speech, the speeches of narrators, inserted genres, the speech of characters are merely those fundamental compositional unities with whose help heteroglossia [*raznorecie*] can enter the novel; each of them permits a multiplicity of social voices and a wide variety of their links and interrelationships (always more or less dialogized).
>
> (263)

Literary works are polyphonic because the dialogue of characters, the written genres and professional languages which are included, the speech of the narrator, and even the direct speech of the author, are points at which diverse 'social speech types' enter the work and are embodied as concrete utterances. While all these voices are orchestrated by the author, they are still literally the voices through which social languages find articulation in the novel. Language in the novel is thus double-voiced or hybridised because every word contains simultaneously both the author's (literary) language and the language of social groups. 'Heteroglossia, once incorporated into the novel (whatever the forms for its incorporation), is *another's speech in another's language*, serving to express authorial intentions but in a refracted way. Such speech constitutes a special type of *double-voiced discourse*' (324).

Adapting this insight to the critical practice of the workshop would mean considering how these 'voices' are transformed by their inclusion and manipulation within a text. It would mean tracing the dialogic connections being made between the text and the extra-literary discourses it mobilises, and thus studying how authorial voice is positioned in relation to other social voices. The practice of *reading as a writer* involves a formalist analysis of how a literary work is constructed by paying attention to the conscious decisions an author has made regarding plot, structure, point of view, narrative voice, character, dialogue, etc. In Bakhtin's formulation, however, these elements are merely compositional devices which incorporate and organise heteroglossia. A sociological poetics would thus require a recognition that *aesthetic* or craft-based decisions of a writer are always the result (consciously or otherwise) of ideological or *political* choice: the choice to employ social languages and the ideologies they embody in certain ways, and hence the choice to position a literary work in relation to these languages, as an active intervention in the ideological work they perform.

Craft must therefore be conceived as a conscious and deliberate intervention in the social life of a discourse as well as a series of aesthetic decisions regarding the artistic quality of a work. The advice to show rather than tell, then, would be governed not by purely aesthetic considerations, founded in a desire to efface the role of the author (at both the narrative and the syntactic level), but by the political implications of this advice. What is being gained or lost, what ideological function is peformed, by an author's adoption or disregard of this technical practice of 'showing'?

As a concrete example I will briefly discuss the work of the Australian poet Coral Hull. Hull is an excellent example of a graduate of a writing programme who might be seen as a public intellectual in terms of her 'creative' writing. Hull completed a doctorate in Creative Arts at the University of Wollongong, and part of her thesis was published by Five Islands Press as *Broken Land: 5 Days in Bre, 1995*. Hull is an animal rights activist, and in this work, which won the Victorian Premier's Award, she employs an autobiographical narrative sequence of poems in which the narrator travels to an outback town, Brewarrina, in order to spend time with her father and to visit various abbatoirs and slaughterhouses. The narrator in this book is referred to as Coral, forcing us to identitfy her with the author and to read the poems as a direct representation of experience.

These elements may seem to align the work with what is called 'workshop poetry', leaving it open to be dismissed as theoretically unsophisticated by 'avant-garde' writers. However, despite being a personal and expressive description of nature and the world, the book is more practically engaged in forging a connection between poetics and politics. After visiting the slaughterhouses, Coral says in response to her father's attempts to soothe her, 'I do not want to pick the paper daisies, dad. / I want the slaughterhouses to shut down. / I want to write poetry & then be gone' (1997: 62). This is both poetry as therapy and poetry as politics. It is the political made personal.

I do not mean to suggest that Hull's work is an exemplar for Creative Writing because it deals with a 'worthy' issue, or that to be politically engaged one must write in a social realist mode. I choose this collection as an example because it highlights the political issues surrounding the 'aesthetic' question of showing and telling, and to demonstrate how Bakhtin's theory of novelistic discourse can also be applied to contemporary poetry.

Let me consider a poem from *Broken Land* as a brief example. 'Inside the Boning Factory' consists of what at first appears to be a fairly neutral description of the 'Roo Works': 'Carcasses are brought in from / kangaroo shooting boxes / throughout country sites' (31). This description is at times punctuated by italicised interpolations registering emotional responses to the process being witnessed: 'Skin is temporarily preserved / by freezing. / Storage of skins in metal cages. / *It's so cold*' (31). It could easily be argued that Hull is telling rather than showing here. Do we need to be told it is cold? Does not the description show us this? If one were to examine the political reasons for this telling, however, such advice may be counter-productive. For a start, these italicised lines place the narrator within the scene she is describing. But why doesn't the narrator 'show' the goosebumps riddling her flesh, for instance? Later she writes 'Freezer. / Chiller. / *I can't get warm*' (33). Why have another internal level of speech?

The italicised interpolations, however, begin to dictate a shift from description to commentary, a conflation of the two levels of narration: '*Where does the life go? / Is it processed into heat? / Is it brought into the factory?*' (32). Finally, they become verbalised as part of a dialogue the narrator is having with her guide: '*Any kangaroos out there? /* Hey, don't take any photos of that' (33). Once we realise that the narrator is being taken through the Roo Works by the 'manager's son' we realise that the description of the place is actually a hybrid of his language and the author's poetic language. We begin to wonder, then, can these questions and interpolated thoughts be assigned wholly to the narrator, especially considering her guide is the 'Most nervous manager's son I've ever met' (33)? The last stanza begins, 'G'day / Welcome to / Australia's Kangaroo / Harvesting Program', and finishes with 'Southern Game Meat Pty Ltd. You'd have to be game to eat it' (33). Is this a case of showing the language of the manager's son and then telling us what we should think? Or is this final comment a representation of the self-ironising Australian vernacular, linking it with the 'ocker' greeting, 'G'day'?

The question of showing and telling in this case cannot be offered as a merely technical consideration of the categories of description and narrative voice being mobilised by the author. The italicised interpolations are designed to open an ethical space for the reader to inhabit, and by being invited to ask whether they tell rather than show we cannot avoid addressing the ideological connection between the didactic heresy and political quietude. What must be considered is how Hull is positioning extra-literary discourses (the semi-official language of the manager's son) within the poem in such a way as to insert her own poetical discourse back into the ideological realm these discourses inhabit.

In a later poem, 'As I Kept Walking', the narrator deliberates over her own implication in the slaughtering of animals; she is not intervening, but politely participating in the tour so she can gather material to write poetry: ' I could even laugh lightly on the way out / & make small talk with the manager, / as he lit up a smoke' (54). We are thus forced to consider what role Hull's poetry actually plays in the verbal-ideological life of the discourses it is representing, and to what extent the act of *reading as a writer* is implicated in this role.

A series of questions arises from this consideration. Can we avoid discussing animal rights when reading Hull's poetry? Does sticking stringently to questions of craft devalue or fail to adequately comprehend the work? Is it possible to isolate authorial decisions about craft from decisions about political efficacy? Does Hull's work fail if we are not convinced to become vegetarians or animal-rights activists? If it can be appreciated simply as poetry, are the powerful descriptions of animal slaughter responsible for its aesthetic quality? In which case, why can we be moved 'aesthetically' yet remain politically unconvinced? These are all questions derived from an expanded understanding of what a writer's craft entails: they are not concerned with reading the poetry mimetically or with inviting students to offer personal responses.

I do not wish to rest my entire argument on this isolated example. It is intended only as a brief description of the considerations which must accompany any advice offered on purely aesthetic grounds. Studying plot, dialogue, structure, point of view, etc., can be more than a means of abstracting formal properties from an exemplary text as examples of craft, or a method of determining whether a student's 'voice' has been adequately expressed. It can be a critical exploration of how these compositional devices introduce heteroglossia into the work. A sociological workshop poetics will not abstract the language of the author, but rather free its socially dialogic associations by tracing their resonances outside the text. When this critical practice is applied by individual students to the act of revision and redrafting, and is hence eventually internalised as part of the creative process, student writers may come to see themselves as inescapable participants in a social dialogue through the practice of writing.

If, in the formalist poetics of the traditional workshop, craft is a neutral linguistic technique for translating an author's voice from self to text, in a sociological poetics it would be a device for populating a text with multiple speaking positions, concrete textual utterances that embody the verbal-ideological life of living discourse, and hence dialogise the text as a literary participant in 'public' discourse. The author is always engaged in a dialogue with the belief systems or ideologemes which stratify a national language and give meaning to words by employing them in concrete social utterances. As a result, the work of literature is itself a concrete utterance within those discourses, existing on the same discursive plane as a contribution to their verbal-ideological life. An oppositional criticism within the workshop would draw attention to the ways in which the privileged cultural status afforded to literature regulates the nature of this dialogic exchange.

The discipline of Creative Writing hovers today between a vocational traineeship for the publishing industry and an artistic haven from the pressures of commercialism. The university, however, cannot be seen as a neutral site where these negotiations take place. In the paradigm of the New Humanities, the university is a public institution which fosters a dialogue between academic analysis, social discourse and public policy. Creative Writing is an academic discipline which can contribute to this dialogue, but a more socially engaged and intellectually aware pedagogy needs to be articulated. It is not by reasserting authorial intention as the basis of critical evaluation that writers will claim intellectual authority within the academy, but by exploring the political and discursive effects of their literary products and accepting responsibility for them.

Within the workshop the literary work can be conceptualised as a zone of social contestation not by dismantling the desire to craft an individual work of art, or by policing the literary representation of identity in the service of social justice, but by exploring how the compositional process is a mode of social intervention at the level of discourse. By doing this writers can be seen as public intellectuals, not in the nostalgic sense of independent freelance thinkers, but as participants in the intellectual work of the New Humanities.

Notes

Introduction

1   *The Writers' Workshop Brochure.* Online. <http://www.uiowa.edu/~iww/bro-1.htm> (accessed 9 Feb. 2004).
2   The clearest illustration of this style of teaching is offered by McFarland (1993), and the best critique of it is provided by Dooley (1990).
3   See D. Hall (1983), Kuzma (1986), J. Epstein (1988), Dooley (1990).
4   See Watkins (1989: 191–6) for an account of this idea of the placeless writer and how it complemented the Arnoldian concept of critical freeplay.

Chapter 2

1   In 1922, Middlebury College advertised its Summer School of English, and one of the courses was in 'Creative Writing (verse and prose)'. This advertisement can be found in *The English Journal* 11.4 (April 1922): 264. The School had been held since 1920, but, this was the first time the phrase 'Creative Writing' was used to denote instruction in fiction and poetry writing. It is out of this Summer School that the Breadloaf Conference on Creative Writing emerged in 1926.
2   I take this phrase from Ian Hunter's *Culture and Government* (1988), a compelling account of the relationship of progressive education to modern Literary Studies in the popular school system in England. Hunter draws attention to an influential textbook by Randolph Stow which describes the role of the teacher as a supervisor in the government school playground. For Hunter, the role of the English teacher, as an ethical exemplar who encourages the play and self-expression of the student within the classroom, is an extension of this practice of moral supervision in the playground. Not only was progressive education deployed in this regard, but so was the Romantic caste practice of reading and writing as a means of ethical self-formation; both operated within the governmental apparatus of the popular school system as a means of population management. The 'unfathomable' text of literature, coupled with the role of the teacher as an ethical exemplar, encouraged students to internalise the practice of ceaseless self-scrutiny via the reading of literature. Hunter skirts around the role of Creative Writing, preferring to concentrate on the role of drama, and the way post-Romantic conceptions of literature have been

deployed in the education system. Creative Writing was crucial to the reformation of school English, however, right up to one of Hunter's important exhibits, John Dixon's *Growth Through English* (1967). In Creative Writing, the unfathomable text is the student's own personality.

3   Letter to Stephen Wilbers, 10 March 1977 (University of Iowa Archives).

4   In 'The History of the Writers' Workshop: A Discussion with Jack Legget, Jean Wylder, Bill Murray' (University of Iowa Archives).

5   Letter to Jean Wylder, 3 July 1973 (University of Iowa Archives).

6   In 'The University of Iowa Writers' Workshop: A Reminiscence', The University of Iowa in Retrospect: A Repository of Relevant Writings (University of Iowa Archives): 1.

7   Letter to Jean Wylder, 2 July 1973 (University of Iowa Archives).

8   For a contemporaneous account of the various critical trends which circulated at the time of Foerster's arrival at Iowa see Grattan (1932). The most significant critical movements besides the New Humanism included: impressionism, practised by figures such as H.L. Mencken and James Huneker (see Mencken 1921); Marxism, the most prominent proponent of which was Granville Hicks (see Glicksberg 1937); the Chicago New Aristoteleans, the major figure of which, R.S. Crane, established the first course in criticism at Chicago University (see Crane 1967); and the Southern Agrarians, such as John Crowe Ransom and Allen Tate, who would later become major figures in the New Criticism (see Davidson et al. 1962). Another important figure was J.E. Spingarn, whose book *Creative Criticism* (1917) was mistakenly seen as an endorsement of impressionist criticism deriving from Anatole France. In fact Spingarn was concerned with promulgating an aesthetic formalism, or 'expressionism' as Foerster called it, derived from the work of Benedetto Croce. Most of these movements derived their identity by distinguishing their critical aims and their theories from competing movements and from the scholarly research which prevailed in universities. Foerster (1929) and Ransom ([1937] 1984) provide helpful accounts in this regard. For historical accounts of these competing types of criticism see Graff (1987: 121–61) and Cain (1984: 89–100).

9   Bronson Howard, address to the Shakspere Club, 1886, qtd in Kinne (1968: 87).

Chapter 3

1   For example, Todorov (1981) and Genette (1980) both quote Percy Lubbock, E.M. Forster and Wayne Booth, while Genette also quotes from Brooks and Warrens's *Understanding Fiction*.

2   In the late 1960s, what John Barth (1967) called the 'literature of exhaustion' and David Lodge (1969) called the 'problematic novel' were attempts to move beyond the exhausted possibilities of the Modernist experimentation with form by ironically appropriating the conventions of realistic fiction. This development of a new literary aesthetic was explored by both critics and writers throughout the 1970s, especially in the pages of the journal *TriQuarterly*. At the same time, Robert Scholes (1979) used the term 'metafiction' (coined by William Gass) to denote the 'death' or epistemological supersession of realist fiction. In 1980, Catherine Belsey's *Critical Practice*, a text emblematic of the shift in methodologies which

signalled the 'crisis' in English Studies, outlined the possibility for a fictional 'interrogative text', accompanied by a new 'critical practice' which would dismantle the philosophical assumptions of expressive realism. Following this, books such as Linda Hutcheon's *Narcissistic Narrative* (1984), and Patricia Waugh's *Metafiction* (1984) – which prompted the widespread currency of the term in postmodern theory – assigned to metafiction this function of the interrogative text. Books by Margaret Rose (1979) and Michael Boyd (1983) had also characterised metafiction as a form of postmodern criticism. By 1995, Mark Currie, in the introduction to the anthology *Metafiction*, used the word to designate a site at which the boundaries between writing and criticism had collapsed.

Chapter 4

1   In an unpublished paper delivered at the first AAWP conference, 1996.
2   <http://www.humanities.curtin.edu.au/cgi-bin/view?area=ccs&dir=Courses&page=Creative_Writing_Major> (accessed 9 Feb. 2004).
3   In a personal interview, 24 June 1998.
4   The website address for the Writing and Cultural Studies Programme Area at UTS is: <http://www.hss.uts.edu.au//departments/dwscs.html> (accessed 9 Feb. 2004).

Chapter 5

1   The website addresses for the English Subject Centre and the NAWE, respectively, are: <http://www.english.ltsn.ac.uk/>; <http://www.nawe.co.uk/> (accessed 9 Feb. 2004).
2   See: <http://www.cascv.brown.edu/cavewriting/workshop.html> (accessed 9 Feb. 2004).
3   The website address for the Poetics Program is: <http://wings.buffalo.edu/epc/poetics/> (accessed 9 Feb. 2004).

Chapter 6

1   In 'The Author's Apology for Heroic Poetry' (1900: 179). I make this claim on the authority of George Watson in *The Literary Critics* (1973: 3). Johnson recorded definitions of both judging and censuring in his 1775 dictionary (1986: 49–51).
2   See 'Symposium: The Professionalisation of Intellectuals', in *University of Toronto Quarterly* 58 (1989): 439–512; Robbins (1990); the special issue on public intellectuals in *Meanjin* 50.4 (1991); 'Symposium: The Public Intellectual', in *Australian Book Review* 182 (1996): 19–22; Bartoloni, Lynch and Kendal (1997); Dessaix (1998); Posner (2001); Small (2002).

Bibliography

Abrams, M.H. (1953) *The Mirror and the Lamp: Romantic Theory and the Critical Tradition*, New York: Oxford University Press.

Ackerman, Diane (1985) 'Campus Writes', *Denver Quarterly*, 20.1: 72–88.

Adams, Glenda (1991) 'Calling up the Spirits', *Island* 47: 26–9.

Adams, Katherine H. (1993) *A History of Professional Writing Instruction in American Colleges: Years of Acceptance, Growth, and Doubt*, Dallas: Southern Methodist University Press.

Addison, Joseph (1982a) 'The Pleasures of the Imagination', 1712, in Angus Ross (ed.) *Selections from* The Tatler *and* The Spectator *of Steele and Addison*, Harmondsworth: Penguin.

—— (1982b) 'No. 267. Saturday, 5 January 1712', in Angus Ross (ed.) *Selections from* The Tatler *and* The Spectator *of Steele and Addison*, Harmondsworth: Penguin.

—— (1965) 'No. 160. Monday, September 3, 1711', in Donald F. Bond (ed.) *The Spectator Vol. II*, Oxford: Clarendon Press.

Akenside, Mark (1996) 'The Poet: A Rhapsody', 1737, *The Poetical Works of Mark Akenside*, Robin Dix (ed.), London: Associated University Presses.

Alden, Christian (2003) 'Imaginative Leap', *Guardian* 24 June. Online. <http://education.guardian.co.uk/egweekly/story/0,5500,983306,00.html> (accessed 1 July 2003).

Aldridge, John W. (1992) *Talents and Technicians: Literary Chic and the New Assembly-Line Fiction*, New York: Charles Scribner's Sons.

Allen, Walter (1958) *The English Novel: A Short Critical History*, Harmondsworth: Penguin.

Amato, Joe and Fleisher, Kassia (2001) 'Reforming Creative Writing Pedagogy: History as Knowledge, Knowledge as Activism', *Electronic Book Review* 12. Online. <http://www.altx.com/ebr/riposte/rip2/rip2ped/amato.htm> (accessed 9 Feb. 2004).

Aristotle (1984) 'Poetics', *The Complete Works of Aristotle*, Jonathan Barnes (ed.), rev. Oxford trans., Vol. 2, Bollingen Series LXXI, Princeton: Princeton University Press.

Arnold, Matthew (1993) 'Culture and Anarchy: An Essay in Political and Social Criticism', 1867–9, *Culture and Anarchy and Other Writings*, Stefan Collini (ed.), Cambridge: Cambridge University Press.

—— (1967) 'Literature and Science', 1885, *Matthew Arnold*, J. Gribble (ed.), London: Collier-Macmillan.

—— (1937) 'The Function of Criticism at the Present Time', 1865, *Essays in Criticism: First Series*, London: Macmillan.

—— (1935) 'The Study of Poetry', 1888, *Essays in Criticism: Second Series*, London: Macmillan.

Associated Writing Programs (1997) 'A Template for the Evaluation of Creative Writing Programs: Hallmarks of a Successful MFA Program', *AWP Chronicle* 29.5: 28.

—— (1990) 'AWP Guidelines for Creative Writing Programs and Teachers of Creative Writing', *AWP Chronicle* 22.4: 12–13.

Attebury, Brian (1998) 'Metafictions: Stories of Reading', Introduction to *Paradoxa* 10. Online. <http://paradoxa.com/excerpts/4–10intro.htm> (accessed 9 Feb. 2004).

Babbitt, Irving (1955) *Rousseau and Romanticism*, 1919, New York: Meridian.

Bacon, Francis (n.d.) *The Advancement of Learning*, 1605, G.W. Kitchin (ed.), London: Heron Books.

Baker, George Pierce (1919) *Dramatic Technique*, Boston: Houghton Mifflin Company.

Baker, J.E. (1942) 'The Philosopher and the "New Critic"', *Sewanee Review* 50: 167–71.

Bakhtin, M.M. (1981) 'Discourse in the Novel', 1934–5, *The Dialogic Imagination*, M. Holquist (ed.), trans. C. Emerson and M. Holquist, Austin: Texas University Press, 259–422.

—— and P.N. Medvedev (1985), *The Formal Method in Literary Scholarship: A Critical Introduction to Sociological Poetics*, 1928, trans. A.J. Wehrle, Cambridge, Mass.: Harvard University Press.

Baldick, Chris (1987) *The Social Mission of English Criticism 1848–1932*, 1983, Oxford: Clarendon Press.

Barker, L.J. (ed.) (1975) *Governance of the Australian Colleges of Advanced Education*, Toowoomba: Darling Downs Institute of Advanced Education Press.

Barnard, Eunice (1937) 'Scholastic Principles Applied to Themselves by 150 Teachers', *New York Times*, 1 Aug.: Society News 5.

Barnes, J. et al. (1994) 'Literary Magazine Editors on the State of the Story', *Literary Review* 37: 619–48.

Barrett, C.R. (1900) *Short Story Writing: A Practical Treatise on the Art of the Short Story*, 1898, New York: The Baker and Taylor Co.

Barron, F. and Harrington, D.M. (1988) 'Creativity', in J. Kuper (ed.), *A Lexicon of Psychology, Psychiatry and Psychoanalysis*, London: Routledge, 102–7.

Barth, John (1995) 'Can It Be Taught?', *Further Fridays: Essays, Lectures, and Other Nonfiction, 1984–94*, Boston: Little, Brown and Company, 22–34.

—— (1968) 'Lost in the Funhouse', *Lost in the Funhouse: Fiction for Print, Tape, Live Voice*, New York: Doubleday, 72–97.

—— (1967) 'The Literature of Exhaustion', *Atlantic* 220.2: 29–34.

Barthes, Roland (1977) 'From Work to Text', 1971, *Image Music Text*, trans. S. Heath (ed.), London: Fontana Press, 155–64.

—— (1977) 'The Death of the Author', *Image Music Text*, trans. S. Heath (ed.), London: Fontana Press, 142–8.

—— (1968) 'Style as Craftsmanship', *Writing Degree Zero*, 1953, trans. Annette Lavers and Colin Smith, New York: Hill and Wang, 62–6.

Bartoloni, Paolo, Lynch, Karen and Kendal, Shane (eds) (1997) *Intellectuals and Publics: Essays on Cultural Theory and Practice*, Melbourne: School of English, La Trobe University.

Beach, Christopher (1999) *Poetic Culture: Contemporary American Poetry Between Community and Institution*, Evanston, Ill.: Northwestern University Press.

Beach, Stewart (1929) *Short-Story Technique*, Boston: Houghton Mifflin.

Beilharz, Peter (1998) 'Public Intellectuals: A Room of Their Own?', *Meridian* 17.1: 31–5.

Bell, Sharon (1998) 'The Doctor of Creative Arts: Mature Cheese or Bad Wine?', in T.W. Maxwell and P.J Shanahan (eds) *Professional Doctorates: Innovations in Teaching and Research*, Armidale, NSW: University of New England, 109–13.

Belsey, Catherine (1980) *Critical Practice*, New Accents, London: Methuen.

Bennett, David (1993) 'PC Panic, the Press and the Academy', *Meanjin* 52: 435–46.

Bennett, Tony (1992a) 'Useful Culture', *Cultural Studies* 6: 395–408.

—— (1992b) 'Coming Out of English: A Policy Calculus for Cultural Studies', in K.K. Ruthven (ed.) *Beyond the Disciplines: The New Humanities*, Occasional Paper 13, Canberra: Australian Academy of the Humanities, 33–44.

—— (1990) *Outside Literature*, London: Routledge.

Berlin, James A. (1984) *Writing Instruction in Nineteenth-Century American Colleges*, Carbondale: Southern Illinois University Press.

Bernstein, Charles (1999) 'Revenge of the Poet-Critic, or The Parts are Greater than the Sum of the Whole', *My Way: Speeches and Poems*, Chicago: Chicago University Press, 3–17.

—— (1992) 'State of the Art', *A Poetics*, Cambridge, Mass.: Harvard University Press, 1–8.

Bersani, Leo (1981), Introduction to Leo Bersani (ed.) *Madame Bovary by Gustave Flaubert*, trans. Lowell Blair, Toronto: Bantam, ix–xxii.

Bérubé, Michael (1994) *Public Access: Literary Theory and American Cultural Politics*, London: Verso.

—— and Nelson, Carey (1995) *Higher Education Under Fire: Politics, Economics, and the Crisis of the Humanities*, New York: Routledge.

Besant, Walter (1899) *The Pen and the Book*, London: Thomas Burleigh.

—— (1884) *The Art of Fiction: A Lecture Delivered at the Royal Institution on Friday Evening, April 25, 1884 (with Notes and Additions)*, London: Chatto and Windus.

Bishop, Wendy (1990) *Released into Language: Options for Teaching Creative Writing*, Urbana, Ill.: National Council of Teachers of English.

—— and Ostrom, Hans (eds) (1994) *Colors of a Different Horse: Rethinking Creative Writing Theory and Pedagogy*, Urbana, Ill.: National Council of Teachers of English.

Blackmur, R.P. (1958) 'A Feather-Bed for Critics: Notes on the Profession of Writing', 1940, *The Expense of Greatness*, Gloucester, Mass.: Peter Smith, 277–305.

—— (1941) 'The Undergraduate Writer as Writer', *College English* 3: 251–64.

Blake, William (1972) 'Annotations to "Poems" by William Wordsworth', 1826, in Geoffrey Keynes (ed.) *Blake: Complete Writings*, Oxford: Oxford University Press, 782–3.

—— 'Annotations to Berkeley's "Siris"', circa 1820, in Geoffrey Keynes (ed.) *Blake: Complete Writings*, Oxford: Oxford University Press, 773–5.

Bloom, Allan (1987) *The Closing of the American Mind: How Higher Education has Failed Democracy and Impoverished the Souls of Today's Students*, New York: Simon and Schuster.

Bloom, Harold (1996) *The Western Canon: The Books and School of the Ages*, 1994, London: Papermac.

Booth, Wayne C. (1983) *The Rhetoric of Fiction*, 1961, 2nd edn, Chicago: Chicago University Press.

Borthwick, John (1977) 'The Professional Writing Course at Canberra's CAE', *Australian Author* 9.3: 17–19.

Bove, Paul (1986) *Intellectuals in Power: A Genealogy of Critical Humanism*, New York: Columbia University Press.

Boyd, Michael (1983) *The Reflexive Novel: Fiction as Critique*, London: Associated University Presses.

Bradbury, Malcolm (1992) 'The Bridgeable Gap: Bringing Together the Creative Writer and the Critical Theorist in an Authorless World', *Times Literary Supplement* 17 Jan.: 7–9.

—— (1968) *Stepping Westward*, 1965, Harmondsworth: Penguin.

Brande, Dorothea (1983) *Becoming a Writer*, 1934, London: Papermac.

Braun-Bau, Susanne (1996) 'A Conversation with Gerald Murnane', *Antipodes* 10.1: 43–8.

Bredin, Hugh (1986) 'I.A. Richards and the Philosophy of Practical Criticism', *Philosophy and Literature* 10.1: 26–37.

Brereton, John C. (ed.) (1995) *The Origins of Composition Studies in the American College, 1875–1925: A Documentary History*, Pittsburgh: Pittsburgh University Press.

Breton, André (1978) *What is Surrealism? Selected Writings*, trans. Franklin Rosemont (ed.), London: Pluto Press.

—— (1972) *Manifestoes of Surrealism*, trans. Richard Seaver and Helen R. Lane, Ann Arbor: Michigan University Press.

Brett, Judith (1991) 'The Bureacratization of Writing: Why so Few Academics are Public Intellectuals', *Meanjin* 50: 513–22.

Brewster, Anne (1996) 'Fictocriticism: Undisciplined Writing', in *Teaching Writing*, Proceedings of the First Annual Conference of the Association of University Writing Programmes, October 1996, UTS, 29–32.

Britton, James, et al. (1975) *The Development of Writing Abilities (11–18)*, Schools Council Research Studies, London: Macmillan.

Brook, Scott (2002) '"Does Anybody Know What Happened to Fictocriticism?": Toward a Fractal Genealogy of Australian Fictocriticism', *Cultural Studies Review* 8.2: 104–18.

Brooks, Cleanth (1981) 'I.A. Richards and *Practical Criticism*', *Sewanee Review* 89: 586–95.

——— (1968) *The Well Wrought Urn: Studies in the Structure of Poetry*, 1947, London: Methuen.

——— (1940) 'Literary History vs. Criticism', *Kenyon Review* 2: 403–12.

——— and Warren, Robert Penn (1960) *Understanding Poetry*, 1938, 3rd edn, New York: Holt, Rinehart and Winston.

——— (1943) *Understanding Fiction*, New York: Appleton-Century-Crofts.

Brophy, Kevin (1998) *Creativity: Psychoanalysis, Surrealism and Creative Writing*, Parkville: Melbourne University Press.

Brown, Thomas (1715) 'The Preface [from *The Works* (1715)]', *Literature Online*. <http://lion.chadwyck.com> (accessed 1 Feb. 2001).

Buckley, Vincent (1967) 'Towards an Australian Literature', 1959, in Clement Semmler (ed.) *Twentieth Century Australian Literary Criticism*, Melbourne: Oxford University Press, 75–85.

Buford, Bill (1983) Editorial, *Granta* 8: 4–5.

Burt, C.L. (1970) 'Critical Notice', 1962, in P.E. Vernon (ed.) *Creativity: Selected Readings*, Harmondsworth: Penguin, 203–16.

Butler, Judith, Guillory, John and Thomas, Kendall (eds) (2000) *What's Left of Theory? New Work on the Politics of Literary Theory*, New York: Routledge.

Byrom, John (1894–5) 'The Poetaster [from *The Poems* (1894–1895)]', *Literature Online*. <http://lion.chadwyck.com> (accessed 1 Feb. 2001).

Cain, William E. (1984) *The Crisis in Criticism: Theory, Literature, and Reform in English Studies*, Baltimore: Johns Hopkins University Press.

Campbell, Walter S. (1938) *Professional Writing*, New York: The Macmillan Company.

Carter, Alex S. (ed.) (1969) *The Rhythm of Our Footsteps: A Collection of Modern Verse by Australian Children*, Kilmore: Lowden Publishing.

Cassill, R.V. (1962) *Writing Fiction*, New York: Pocket Books.

Chapple, A. (1977) *Creative Writing in the Primary School*, Perth: Education Department of Western Australia.

Charvat, William (1992) *The Profession of Authorship in America, 1800–1870*, Matthew J. Bruccoli (ed.), New York: Columbia University Press.

Clark, Glenn (1922) *A Manual of the Short Story Art*, New York: The Macmillan Company.

Clarke, Joan (1969) 'Can Writing Be Taught?', *Australian Author* 1.3: 38–9.

Cocking, J.M. (1991) *Imagination: A Study in the History of Ideas*, Penelope Murray (ed.), London: Routledge.

Coleridge, Samuel Taylor (1956) *Biographia Literaria: Or, Biographical Sketches of My Literary Life and Opinions*, 1817, George Watson (ed.), Everyman's Library 11, London: J.M. Dent and Sons.

Conference on Teaching Creative Writing, Library of Congress, 1973 (1974) *Teaching Creative Writing*, Washington: Gertrude Clarke Whittal Poetry and Literature Fund.

Conrad, Lawrence H. (1937) *Teaching Creative Writing*, New York: D. Appleton-Century Company.

Cook, H. Caldwell (1917) *The Play Way: An Essay in Educational Method*, London: William Heinemann.

Cook, Luella B. (1931) 'Creative Writing in the Classroom: It's How, When, What, and What Not', *English Journal* 20: 195–202.

Cooley, Nicole (2000) 'Untitled', *PMLA* 115: 1998.

Cowley, Malcolm (1958) *The Literary Situation*, 1947, New York: Viking Press.

Crane, R.S. (1967) 'History versus Criticism in the Study of Literature', 1935, *The Idea of the Humanities and Other Essays Critical and Historical*, vol. 2, Chicago: Chicago University Press, 3–24.

—— (ed.) (1952) *Critics and Criticism*, Chicago: Chicago University Press.

Cross, Ethan Allen (1914) *The Short Story: A Technical and Literary Study*, Chicago: A.C. McClurg and Co.

Cross, Gustav (1965) 'Australian Poetry in the 'Sixties', *Poetry Australia* 5: 33–8.

Culler, Jonathan (1997) *Literary Theory: A Very Short Introduction*, Oxford: Oxford University Press.

—— (1988) *Framing the Sign: Criticism and its Institutions*, Oxford: Basil Blackwell.

—— (1975) *Structuralist Poetics: Structuralism, Linguistics, and the Study of Literature*, Ithaca: Cornell University Press.

Currie, Mark (1995) Introduction to *Metafiction*, Mark Currie (ed.), London: Longman, 1–18.

Dale, Leigh (1997) *The English Men: Professing Literature in Australian Universities*, Toowoomba: Association for the Study of Australian Literature.

Dana, Robert (ed.) (1999) *A Community of Writers: Paul Engle and the Iowa Writers' Workshop*, Iowa City: Iowa University Press.

Davidson, Donald, et al. (1962) *I'll Take My Stand: The South and the Agrarian Tradition by Twelve Southerners*, 1930, New York: Harper and Brothers.

Dawkins, J.S. (1988) *Higher Education: A Policy Statement*, Canberra: Australian Government Publishing Service.

—— (1987) *Higher Education: A Policy Discussion Paper*, Canberra: Australian Government Publishing Service.

Dawson, Paul (1997) 'Grunge Lit: Marketing Generation X', *Meanjin* 56: 119–25.

Deakin University (1978–93) *Calendar*, Melbourne: Deakin University.

De Bono, Edward (1990) *The Use of Lateral Thinking*, 1967, London: Penguin.

De Certeau (1984) *The Practice of Everyday Life*, trans. Steven Rendall, Berkeley: California University Press.

De Man, Paul (1983) 'Criticism and Crisis', *Blindness and Insight: Essays in the Rhetoric of Contemporary Criticism*, 1971, 2nd edn, Theory and History of Literature 7, Minneapolis: Minnesota University Press, 3–19.

Derrida, Jacques (1992) '"This Strange Institution Called Literature": an Interview with Jacques Derrida', *Acts of Literature*, Derek Attridge (ed.), New York: Routledge, 33–74.

Dessaix, Robert (ed.) (1998) *Speaking Their Minds: Intellectuals and the Public Culture in Australia*, Sydney: ABC Books.

Devitt, Marian (1998) 'Going with the Territory', *Overland* 152: 33.

Dewey, John (1966) *Democracy and Education: An Introduction to the Philosophy of Education*, 1916, New York: Free Press.

—— (1963) *Experience and Education: The Kappa Delta Pi Lecture Series*, 1938, London: Collier Books.

—— (1959) *Dewey on Education: Selections*, Martin S. Dworkin (ed.), Classics in Education 3, New York: Teachers College Press.

Dibble, Brian (1997) 'Caring for and Feeding a Creative Writing Department', *TEXT: The Journal of the Australian Association of Writing Programmes* 1.1. Online. <http://www.gu.edu.au/school/art/text/april97/dibble.htm> (accessed 10 Feb. 2004).

Dick, William (1974) 'The Novelist and Creative Writing Schools', *Australian Author* 6.2: 31–4.

Dickinson, Emily (1970) 'Untitled (Publication is the Auction)', *The Complete Poems*, Thomas H. Johnson (ed.), London: Faber and Faber, 348–9.

Disch, Thomas M. (1995) 'The Castle of Indolence', *Hudson Review* 48: 521–31.

Dixon, John (1969) *Growth Through English: A Report Based on the Dartmouth Seminar 1966*, 1967, 2nd edn, Huddersfield: National Assocation for the Teaching of English.

Docker, John (1984) *In a Critical Condition: Reading Australian Literature*, Ringwood: Penguin.

Doecke, Brenton (1997) 'Disjunctions: Australian Literature and the Secondary English Curriculum', in Delys Bird, Robert Dixon and Susan Lever (eds) *Canonozities: The Making of Literary Reputations in Australia*, spec. issue of *Southerly* 57.3: 67–77.

Donaldson, Ian (1990) 'Defining and Defending the Humanities', in A.M. Gibbs (ed.) *The Relevance of the Humanities*, occasional paper 8, Canberra: Australian Academy of the Humanities, 18–36.

Dooley, David (1990) 'The Contemporary Workshop Aesthetic', *Hudson Review* 43: 259–80.

D'Orsay, Laurence (1942) *Stories You Can Sell: A Volume of Collected Stories of Various Acceptable Types, with Explanatory Analyses by the Author, Showing How Plots May Be Obtained and Stories Written and Sold by the Reader*, 1932, 4th edn, Parker and Baird Company.

Dramatist, A. (1888) *Playwriting: A Handbook for Would-Be Dramatic Authors*, London: Stage Office.

Drennan, Marie (1940) 'Workshop Methods in Freshman English,' *College English* 1: 532–6.

Dryden, John (1900) *Essays of John Dryden*, 2 vols, W.P. Ker (ed.) Oxford: Clarendon Press.

D'Souza, Dinesh (1991) *Illiberal Education: The Politics of Race and Sex on Campus*, New York: Free Press.

Duff, William (1995) *An Essay on Original Genius*, 1767, London: Routledge/ Thoemmes Press.

Dugan, Michael (1973) 'Writing Schools', *Australian Author* 5.3: 22–3.

During, Simon (1997) 'Teaching Culture', *Australian Humanities Review* 7. Online. <http://www.lib.latrobe.edu.au/AHR/archive/Issue-August-1997/ during.html> (accessed 9 Feb. 2004).

―― (ed.) (1999) *A Cultural Studies Reader*, 1993, 2nd edn, London: Routledge.

Eagleton, Terry (2003) *After Theory*, London: Allen Lane.

―― (1984) *The Function of Criticism: From* The Spectator *to Post-Structuralism*, London: Verso.

―― (1983) *Literary Theory: An Introduction*, Oxford: Blackwell.

―― (1976) *Marxism and Literary Criticism*, London: Methuen.

Egerton, Sarah Fyge (1987) 'An Ode on the Death of Mr. Dryden', *Poems on Several Occasions*, 1703, Delmar, New York: Scholars' Facsimiles and Reprints, 74–80.

Ehrenreich, Barbara and Ehrenreich, John (1979) 'The Professional-Managerial Class', in Pat Walker (ed.) *Between Labor and Capital*, Boston: South End Press, 5–45.

Eliot, T.S. (1964) 'The Function of Criticism', 1923, *Selected Essays*, New York: Harcourt, Brace and World Inc., 12–22.

―― (1962) 'Experiment in Criticism,' 1929, in Morton Dauwen Zabel (ed.) *Literary Opinion in America: Essays Illustrating the Status, Methods and Problems of Criticism in the United States in the Twentieth Century*, vol. 2, 3rd edn, New York: Harper Torchbooks, 607–17.

―― (1960) *The Sacred Wood: Essays on Poetry and Criticism*, 1920, London: Methuen.

―― (1958) Introduction to Jackson Matthews (ed.) *The Collected Works of Paul Valéry Vol. 7: The Art of Poetry*, trans. Denise Folliot, Bollingen Series XLV, New York: Pantheon Books, vii–xxiv.

―― (1957) 'The Frontiers of Criticism', 1956, *On Poetry and Poets*, London: Faber and Faber, 103–18.

―― (1954) Introduction to T.S. Eliot (ed.) *Literary Essays of Ezra Pound*, London: Faber and Faber, ix–xv.

Emerson, Ralph Waldo (1907) 'The American Scholar', 1837, *Works of Ralph Waldo Emerson*, A.C. Hearn (ed.), Edinburgh: W.P. Nimmo, Hay, and Mitchell, 847–61.

Engell, James (1981) *The Creative Imagination: Enlightenment to Romanticism*, Cambridge, Mass.: Harvard University Press.

Engle, Paul (1964) 'The Writer on Writing', in Paul Engle (ed.) *On Creative Writing*, New York: E.P. Dutton and Co., 3–17.

―― (1961) 'The Writer and the Place', Introduction to Paul Engle (ed.) *Midland: Twenty-five Years of Fiction and Poetry Selected from the Writing Workshops of the State University of Iowa*, New York: Random House, xxi–xxxvii.

Epstein, Andrew (2000) 'Verse vs. Verse', *Lingua Franca* 10.6: 46–54.

Epstein, Joseph (1988) 'Who Killed Poetry?', *Commentary* 86.2: 13–20.

Esenwein, J. Berg (1918) *Writing the Short-Story: A Practical Handbook on the Rise, Structure, Writing, and Sale of the Modern Short-Story*, 1909, rev. edn, New York: Hinds, Hayden and Eldredge.

Ewers, John K. (1962) *Creative Writing in Australia: A Selective Survey*, 1945, 3rd edn, Melbourne: Georgian House.

Farred, Grant (2000) 'Endgame Identity?: Mapping the New Left Roots of Identity Politics', *New Literary History* 31: 627–48.

Feirstein, Frederick (ed.) (1989) *Expansive Poetry: Essays on the New Narrative and the New Formalism*, Santa Cruz: Story Line Press.

Fenza, David (2000) 'Creative Writing and its Discontents', *Writer's Chronicle* 32.5. Online. <http://awpwriter.org/magazine/writers/fenza1.htm> (accessed 12 Feb. 2003).

—— (n.d.) 'A Brief History of AWP', *AWP Online.* <http://awpwriter.org/aboutawp/index.htm> (accessed 10 Feb. 2004).

Fielding, Henry (1992) *The History of Tom Jones, a Foundling*, 1749, Hertfordshire: Wordsworth Classics.

—— (1948) *Joseph Andrews*, 1742, San Francisco: Rinehart Press.

Fish, Stanley (1995) 'Public Justification and Public Intellectuals', *Professional Correctness: Literary Studies and Political Change*, Oxford: Clarendon Press, 115–26.

Flaubert, Gustave (1981) 'Letter to Louise Colet December 9, 1852', *Madame Bovary*, Leo Bersani (ed.), trans. Lowell Blair, Toronto: Bantam Books, 319.

Flavell, Helen (1999a) 'Situation Occupied in the *Space Between*', review of *The Space Between*, Heather Kerr and Amanda Nettelbeck (eds), *The UTS Review* 5.1: 235–8.

—— (1999b) 'The Investigation: Australian and Canadian Fictocriticism', *Antithesis* 10: 104–16.

—— (1998) 'Fictocriticism: The End of Criticism as We Write It?', *Paradoxa* 4.10: 197–204.

Florida, Richard (2003) *The Rise of the Creative Class*, 2002, Melbourne: Pluto Press.

Foerster, Norman (1966) 'The Esthetic Judgment and the Ethical Judgment', in Donald A. Stauffer (ed.) *The Intent of the Critic*, 1941, New York: Bantam Books, 52–72.

—— (1962) *American Criticism: A Study in Literary Theory from Poe to the Present*, 1928, New York: Russel and Russel.

—— (1941) 'The Study of Letters', in Norman Foerster (ed.) *Literary Scholarship: Its Aims and Methods*, Chapel Hill: North Carolina University Press, 3–32.

—— (1936) 'Literary Scholarship and Criticism', *English Journal* coll. edn 25: 224–32.

—— (1930) *Towards Standards: A Study of the Present Critical Movement in American Letters*, New York: Farrar and Rhinehart.

—— (1929) *The American Scholar: A Study in Litterae Inhumaniores*, Chapel Hill: North Carolina University Press.

—— (1922) 'Matthew Arnold and American Letters Today', *Sewanee Review* 30: 298–306.

Foucault, Michel (1990) 'The Functions of Literature', *Politics, Philosophy, Culture: Interviews and Other Writings 1977–1984*, Lawrence D. Kritzman (ed.), trans. Alan Sheridan et al., New York: Routledge, 307–13.

—— (1980) 'Truth and Power', *Power Knowledge: Selected Interviews and Other Writings 1972–1977*, C. Gordon (ed.), trans. C. Gordon et al., New York: Pantheon, 109–33.

—— (1977) 'Intellectuals and Power: A Conversation Between Michel Foucault and Gilles Deleuze', *Language, Counter-Memory, Practice: Selected Essays and Interviews*, Donald F. Bouchard (ed.), trans. Bouchard and Sherry Simon, Ithaca: Cornell University Press, 205–17.

Fowles, John (1992) *The French Lieutenant's Woman*, 1969, London: Picador.

Fraser, Russell (1981) 'R.P. Blackmur at Princeton', *Sewanee Review* 89: 540–59.

Freadman, Richard (ed.) (1983) *Literature, Criticism and the Universities: Interviews with Leonie Kramer, S.L. Goldberg, and Howard Felperin*, Nedlands: Centre for Studies in Australian Literature.

Frederick, John T. (1933) 'The Place of Creative Writing in American Schools', *English Journal* 22: 8–16.

—— (1924) *A Handbook of Short Story Writing*, New York: Alfred A. Knopf.

Freiman, Marcelle (2001) 'Crossing the Boundaries of the Discipline: A Post-colonial Approach to Teaching Creative Writing in the University', *TEXT* 5.2. Online. <http://www.gu.edu.au/school/art/text/oct01/freiman.htm> (accessed 10 Feb. 2004).

Freud, Sigmund (1972) 'Creative Writers and Day-Dreaming', 1908, in David Lodge (ed.) 2*0th Century Literary Criticism: A Reader*, London: Longman, 36–42.

Frow, John (1995) *Cultural Studies and Cultural Value*, Oxford: Clarendon Press.

—— (1990) *The Social Production of Knowledge and the Discipline of English*, St. Lucia: Queensland University Press.

Frye, Northrop (1971) *Anatomy of Criticism: Four Essays*, 1957, Princeton: Princeton University Press.

Galef, David (2000) 'Words, Words, Words', in Peter C. Herman (ed.) *Day Late, Dollar Short: The Next Generation and the New Academy*, Albany: State University of New York Press, 161–74.

Gandhi, Leela (1998) *Postcolonial Theory: A Critical Introduction*, Sydney: Allen and Unwin.

Gardner, John (1983) *On Becoming a Novelist*, New York: Harper and Row.

Garrett, George (1992) 'Creative Writing and American Publishing Now', *Sewanee Review* 100: 669–75.

—— (1989) 'The Future of Creative Writing Programs', in Joseph M. Moxley (ed.) *Creative Writing in America: Theory and Pedagogy*, Urbana, Ill.: National Council of Teachers of English, 47–61.

Gelder, Ken and Salzman, Paul (1989) *The New Diversity: Australian Fiction 1970–88*, Melbourne: McPhee Gribble.

Genette, Gérard (1980) *Narrative Discourse: An Essay in Method*, 1972, trans. Jane E. Lewin, Ithaca: Cornell University Press.

Gibbons, F.P. and Gibbons, T.H. (1963–64) 'The Teaching of English Literature in Universities: Some Australian Notes on Problems and Possible Solutions', *College English* 25: 365–70.

Gibbons, Reginald (1985) 'Academic Criticism and Contemporary Literature', in Gerald Graff and Reginald Gibbons (eds) *Criticism in the University*, *TriQuarterly* Series on Criticism and Culture 1, Evanston, Ill.: Northwestern University Press, 15–34.

Gibbs, Anna (1997) 'Bodies of Words: Feminism and Fictocriticism – Explanation and Demonstration,' *TEXT* 1.2. Online. <http://www.gu.edu.au/school/art/text/oct97/gibbs.htm> (accessed 10 Feb. 2004).

Gilbert, Pam (1984) 'Creative Writing in the Senior English Classroom: Re-Reading the Texts', *English in Australia* 70: 4–13.

Gioia, Dana (1992) *Can Poetry Matter?: Essays on Poetry and American Culture*, Saint Paul: Graywolf Press.

Giroux, Henry A. (1995) 'Academics as Public Intellectuals: Rethinking Classroom Politics', in Jeffrey Williams (ed.) *PC Wars: Politics and Theory in the Academy*, New York: Routledge, 294–307.

Glicksberg, Charles I. (1937) 'Granville Hicks and Marxist Criticism', *Sewanee Review* 45: 129–40.

Golding, Alan (1995) *From Outlaw to Classic: Canons in American Poetry*, Madison: Wisconsin University Press.

Goldsworthy, Kerryn (ed.) (1983) *Australian Short Stories*, Melbourne: J.M. Dent.

Good, Graham (1989) 'Cultural Criticism or Textual Theory?', *University of Toronto Quarterly* 58: 463–9.

Gordimer, Nadine (1985) 'The Essential Gesture: Writers and Responsibility', *Granta* 15: 137–50.

Gouldner, Alvin (1979) *The Future of Intellectuals and the Rise of the New Class: A Frame of Reference, Theses, Conjectures, Arguments, and an Historical Perspective on the Role of Intellectuals and Intelligentsia in the International Class Contest of the Modern Era*, New York: Seabury Press.

Graff, Gerald (1992) *Beyond the Culture Wars: How Teaching the Conflicts Can Revitalize American Education*, New York: Norton.

—— (1987) *Professing Literature: An Institutional History*, Chicago: Chicago University Press.

—— (1979) 'What Was New Criticism?', *Literature Against Itself: Literary Ideas in Modern Society*, Chicago: Chicago University Press, 129–49.

—— and Gibbons, Reginald (1985) Preface to Gerald Graff and Reginald Gibbons (eds) *Criticism in the University*, *TriQuarterly* Series on Criticism and Culture 1, Evanston, Ill.: Northwestern University Press, 7–12.

Grattan, C. Hartley (1932) 'The Present Situation in American Literary Criticism', *Sewanee Review* 40: 11–23.

Graves, Donald (1983) *Writing: Teachers and Children at Work*, Exeter: Heinemann.

Gray, Robert and Lehmann, Geoffrey (eds) (1983) *The Younger Australian Poets*, Sydney: Hale and Iremonger.

Green, Chris (2001) 'Materializing the Sublime Reader: Cultural Studies, Reader Response, and Community Service in the Creative Writing Workshop', *College English* 64.2: 153–74.

Green, Dorothy (1991) *Writer-Reader-Critic*, Sydney: Primavera Press.

Greenblatt, Stephen (1989) 'Towards a Poetics of Culture', in H. Aram Veeser (ed.) *The New Historicism*, New York: Routledge, 1–14.

Greenfield, Cathy (1999) 'A Change, a Theme', Editorial, *Southern Review* 32: 118.

Grenville, Kate (1990) *The Writing Book: A Workbook for Fiction Writers*, Sydney: Allen and Unwin.

Gross, John (1973) *The Rise and Fall of the Man of Letters: Aspects of English Literary Life Since 1800*, 1965, Harmondsworth: Penguin.

Gudding, Gabriel (1999) 'From Petit to Langpo: A History of Solipsism and Experience in Mainstream American Poetics Since the Rise of Creative Writing', *Flashpoint* Web Issue 3. Online. <http://www.flashpointmag.com/guddin~1.htm> (accessed 22 Mar. 2001).

Guffin, Jan A. (1974) 'Writing', in R. Baird Shuman (ed.) *Creative Approaches to the Teaching of English: Secondary*, Itasca, Ill.: F.E. Peacock Publishers, 133–85.

Guilford, J.P. (1968) *Intelligence, Creativity and their Educational Implications*, San Diego: Robert R. Knapp.

Guillory, John (1993) *Cultural Capital: The Problem of Literary Canon Formation*, Chicago: Chicago University Press.

Haig, Anna F. (1933) 'The Teaching of Creative Writing', *English Journal* 22: 719–27.

Hale Jr., Edward Everett and Dawson, Fredrick T. (1915) *The Elements of the Short Story*, New York: Henry Holt and Company.

Hall, Donald (1983) 'Poetry and Ambition', *Kenyon Review* ns 5.4: 90–104.

Hall, Rodney and Shapcott, Thomas W. (eds) (1968) *New Impulses in Australian Poetry*, Brisbane: Queensland University Press.

Hall, Stuart (1992) 'Cultural Studies and its Theoretical Legacies', in Lawrence Grossberg, Cary Nelson and Paula Treichler (eds) *Cultural Studies*, New York: Routledge, 277–94.

Halligan, Marion (1997) 'The Comfort of Words', *Australian Book Review* 189: 36–9.

Harding, D.W. (1982) 'The Character of Literature from Blake to Byron', in Boris Ford (ed.) *From Blake to Byron*, New Pelican Guide to English Literature 5, Harmondsworth: Penguin, 1982, 35–66.

Harper, Graeme (2003) 'A State of Grace?: Creative Writing in UK Higher Education, 1993–2003', *TEXT* 7.2. Online. <http://www.gu.edu.au/school/art/text/oct03/harper.htm> (accessed 10 Feb. 2004).

Harre, Rom and Lamb, Roger (eds) (1986) *The Dictionary of Developmental and Educational Psychology*, Oxford: Basil Blackwell.

Harrison-Ford, Carl (1977) 'Fiction', *Australian Literary Studies* 8: 172–8.

—— (1975) 'How Good is the Boom in Australian Fiction?', *Australian Author* 7.2: 4–10.

—— (1970) 'Poetics Before Politics: A Note on Kris Hemensley's "New Australian Poetry"', *Meanjin Quarterly* 29: 226–31.

Hartman, Geoffrey H. (1980) 'Literary Commentary as Literature', *Criticism in the Wilderness: The Study of Literature Today*, New Haven: Yale University Press, 189–213.

Hatfield, W. Wilbur (1925) 'The Creative Spirit', review of *The Creative Spirit* by Rollo Walter Brown, *Foundations of Method* by William Heard Kilpatrick and *Creative Youth* by Hughes Mearns, *English Journal* 14: 573–5.

Hawthorne, Nathaniel (1957) 'Preface to *The House of the Seven Gables*', in Albert D. Van Nostrand (ed.) *Literary Criticism in America*, Forum Books 15, New York: The Liberal Arts Press, 90–2.

Hay, John (1974) 'Professional Writing', *Australian Author* 6.2: 34–8.

Hazlitt, William (1910) *Lectures on English Poets and the Spirit of the Age*, 1818, London: J.M. Dent and Sons.

Hemensley, Kris (1976) '"A Vague All-Exaggerating Twilight of Wonder": Australia's New Poetry', *Meanjin Quarterly* 35: 56–70.

—— (1970) 'First Look at "The New Australian Poetry"', *Meanjin Quarterly* 29: 118–21.

Herman, Peter C. (2000) ''60s Theory/'90s Practice', Introduction to Peter C. Herman (ed.) *Day Late, Dollar Short: The Next Generation and the New Academy*, Albany: State University of New York Press, 1–23.

Heseltine, Harry (ed.) (1972) *The Penguin Book of Australian Verse*, Ringwood: Penguin.

Hewett, Dorothy (1971) 'Creative Writing and Education', *English in Australia* 18: 23–4, 41–5.

Hirsch, E.D. (1987) *Cultural Literacy: What Every American Needs to Know*, Boston: Houghton Mifflin.

Hobbes, Thomas (1968) *Leviathan*, 1651, C.B. Macpherson (ed.), Harmondsworth: Penguin.

—— (1908) 'The Answer of Mr. Hobbes to Sir Will. D'Avenant's Preface Before Gondibert', 1650, in J.E. Spingarn (ed.) *Critical Essays of the Seventeenth Century, Vol. 2: 1650–1685*, Oxford: Clarendon Press, 54–76.

Hodge, Bob (1997) 'What is the New Humanities (and Why are They Saying Such Horrible Things About it)?', Preface to Andrew Johnson, Murray Lee, Katrina Schlunke, Felicity Sheaves (eds) *Off the Sheep's Back: New Humanities*, Sydney: University of Western Sydney, Hawkesbury, 7–14.

Hogrefe, Pearl (1940) 'Self-exploration in Creative Writing', *College English* 2: 156–60.

Holbrook, David (1968) 'Creativity in the English Programme', in Geoffrey Summerfield (ed.) *Creativity in English: Papers Relating to the Anglo-American Seminar on the Teaching of English at Dartmouth College, New Hampshire, 1966*, Urbana, Ill.: National Council of Teachers of English, 1–20.

—— (1965) *English for the Rejected: Training Literacy in the Lower Streams of the Secondary School*, Cambridge: Cambridge University Press.

—— (1964) *The Secret Places: Essays on Imaginative Work in English Teaching and on the Culture of the Child*, London: Methuen.

Hope, A.D. (1965) 'Literature versus the Universities', *The Cave and the Spring: Essays on Poetry*, Adelaide: Rigby, 164–73.

—— (1962) 'Creative Writing', *Drylight*: 3–6.

Horace (1965) 'On the Art of Poetry', *Classical Literary Criticism*, trans. T.S. Dorsch, Harmondsworth: Penguin, 79–95.

Hough, Graham (1964) 'Crisis in Literary Education', in J.H. Plumb (ed.) *Crisis in the Humanities*, Harmondsworth: Penguin, 96–109.

Housh, Snow Longley (1931) 'Report on Creative Writing in Colleges', *English Journal* coll. edn 20: 672–6.

Howe, M.A. DeWolfe (1924) *Barrett Wendell and his Letters*, Boston: Atlantic Monthly Press.

Hugo, Richard (1979) 'In Defense of Creative-Writing Classes', *The Triggering Town: Lectures and Essays on Poetry and Writing*, New York: W.W. Norton and Company, 53–66.

Hull, Coral (1997) *Broken Land: Five Days in Bre, 1995*, Wollongong: Five Islands Press.

Hunter, Ian (1988) *Culture and Government: The Emergence of Literary Education*, London: Macmillan.

Hutcheon, Linda (1984) *Narcissistic Narrative: The Metafictional Paradox*, New York: Methuen.

Indyk, Ivor (1997) 'Literary Authority', *Australian Book Review* 196: 36–40.

Iowa University (1939) *Creative Writing in the University of Iowa: Announcements for the Summer Session June 12–August 4, 1939*, University of Iowa Publication 5 April, 1939, ns No. 1047, Iowa City: University of Iowa.

—— (1895–1942) *University of Iowa Catalogue 1895–1942*, Iowa City: University of Iowa.

Jach, Antoni (2002) 'The Narrator and Narrative Modes in the Novel', in Brenda Walker (ed.) *The Writer's Reader: A Guide to Writing Fiction and Poetry*, Sydney: Halstead Press, 58–66.

Jacoby, Russell (1989) *The Last Intellectuals: American Culture in the Age of Academe*, 1987, New York: Noonday Press.

James, Henry (1972) 'The Art of Fiction', 1884, *Theory of Fiction: Henry James*, James E. Miller, Jr. (ed.), Lincoln: Nebraska University Press, 28–44.

Jauss, David (1989) 'Articles of Faith', in Joseph M. Moxley (ed.) *Creative Writing in America: Theory and Pedagogy*, Urbana, Ill.: National Council of Teachers of English, 63–75.

Johnson, Samuel (1986) *Dr. Johnson's Critical Vocabulary: A Selection from his Dictionary*, Richard L. Harp (ed.), Lanham, MD: University Press of America.

—— (1971) 'The Rambler No. 117. Tuesday, April 30, 1751', *Rasselas, Poems, and Selected Prose*, Bertrand H. Bronson (ed.), 3rd edn, New York: Holt, Rinehart and Winston, 102–7.

—— (1906) *Lives of the English Poets*, 2 vols, 1779, 1781, London: Oxford University Press.

Jones, Evan (1969) 'The Poet in the University', *Australian Author* 1.4: 21–5.

Jones, Peter (ed.) (1972) *Imagist Poetry*, Harmondsworth: Penguin.

Jonson, Ben (1908) 'Timber, or Discoveries', 1620–35, in J. E. Spingarn (ed.) *Critical Essays of the Seventeenth Century, Vol. 1: 1605–1650*, Oxford: Clarendon Press, 17–64.

Jurman, Elizabeth (1990) 'Writers' Bloc', *Sydney Morning Herald* 20 Jan.: 72.

Kant, Immanuel (1952) *The Critique of Judgement*, 1790, trans. James Creed Meredith, Oxford: Clarendon Press.

Keane, Colleen (1997) 'PIs and PC: The Context of Current Debates on "Public Intellectuals and Political Correctness"', in Paolo Bartoloni, Karen Lynch and Shane Kendal (eds) *Intellectuals and Publics: Essays on Cultural Theory and Practice*, Melbourne: School of English, LaTrobe University, 11–18.

Keats, John (1963) 'Letter to John Taylor, 27 February, 1818', in Daniel G. Hoffman and Samuel Hynes (eds) *English Literary Criticism: Romantic and Victorian*, New York: Appleton-Century-Crofts, 117–18.

Kemp, The Hon. Dr D.A. (1999) *Knowledge and Innovation: A Policy Statement on Research and Research Training*, Canberra: Dept. of Education, Training and Youth Affairs.

Kenny, Robert and Talbot, Colin (eds) (1974) *Applestealers: A Collection of the New Poetry in Australia, Including Notes, Statements, Histories on La Mama*, Melbourne: Outback Press.

Ker, W.P. (1900) Introduction to W.P. Ker (ed.) *Essays of John Dryden Vol. 1*, Oxford: Clarendon Press, xiii–lxxi.

Kermode, Frank (1957) *Romantic Image*, London: Routledge and Kegan Paul.

Kerr, Heather (1996) 'Fictocriticism, the "Doubtful Category" and "The Space Between"', in Caroline Geurin, Philip Butterss and Amanda Nettelbeck (eds) *Crossing Lines: Formations of Australian Culture, Proceedings of the Association for the Study of Australian Literature Conference, Adelaide 1995*, Adelaide: ASAL, 93–6.

Kerr, Heather and Nettelbeck, Amanda (eds) (1998) *The Space Between: Australian Women Writing Fictocriticism*, Nedlands: UWA Press.

Kiernan, Brian (1975) 'Short Story Chronicle, 1974', *Meanjin Quarterly* 34: 34–9.

—— (ed.) (1977) *The Most Beautiful Lies: A Collection of Stories by Five Major Contemporary Fiction Writers: Bail, Carey, Lurie, Moorhouse and Wilding*, Sydney: Angus and Robertson.

Kiley, Dean (1988) 'So then I said to Helen', *Meanjin* 4: 799–808.

Kimball, Roger (1990) *Tenured Radicals: How Politics has Corrupted our Higher Education*, New York: Harper and Row.

King, Noel (1994) 'My Life Without Steve: Postmodernism, Ficto-Criticism and the Paraliterary', *Southern Review* 27: 261–75.

—— (1993) 'Occasional Doubts: Ian Hunter's Genealogy of Interpretative Depth', *Southern Review* 26: 5–27.

—— (1991) 'Reading *White Noise*: Floating Remarks on Postmodernism', *Meridian* 10.1: 52–63.

Kinne, Wisner Payne (1968) *George Pierce Baker and the American Theatre*, New York: Greenwood Press.

Kinsella, John (ed.) (1999) *Landbridge: Contemporary Australian Poetry*, Fremantle: Fremantle Arts Centre Press.

Knickerbocker, William S. (1941) 'Wam for Maw: Dogma versus Discursiveness in Criticism', review of *The New Criticism* by John Crowe Ransom, and *The Philosophy of Literary Form* by Kenneth Burke, *Sewanee Review* 49: 520–36.

Koestler, Arthur (1967) *The Act of Creation*, New York: Dell Publishing Co.

Koethe, John (1991) 'Contrary Impulses: The Tension Between Poetry and Theory', *Critical Inquiry* 18: 64–75.

Krauss, Rosalind (1985) 'Poststructuralism and the Paraliterary', 1981, *The Originality of the Avant-Garde and Other Modernist Myths*, Cambridge, Mass.: MIT Press, 291–5.

Krauth, Nigel (2000) 'Where is Writing Now?: Australian University Creative Writing Programmes at the End of the Millenium', *TEXT* 4.1. Online. <http://www.gu.edu.au/school/art/text/april00/krauth.htm> (accessed 10 Feb. 2004).

——— (1999) 'Literary Awards and Creative Writing Schools', *TEXT* 3.1. Online. <http://www.gu.edu.au/school/art/text/april99/mousekrauth.html> (accessed 10 Feb. 2004).

——— and Brady, Tess (1997) 'Writing Beyond the Reading List', *Australian Book Review* 191: 47.

Kuzma, Greg (1986) 'The Catastrophe of Creative Writing', review of *The Catastrophe of Rainbows* by Martha Collins, *Poetry* 148: 342–54.

Labrant, Lou L. (1936) 'The Psychological Basis for Creative Writing', *English Journal* 25: 292–301.

Landow, George P. (1992) *Hypertext: The Convergence of Contemporary Critical Theory and Technology*, Baltimore: Johns Hopkins University Press.

Laurenson, Diana and Swingewood, Alan (1971) *The Sociology of Literature*, London: Paladin.

Lauter, Paul (1995) ' "Political Correctness" and the Attack on American Colleges', in Michael Bérubé and Cary Nelson (eds) *Higher Education Under Fire: Politics, Economics, and the Crisis of the Humanities*, New York: Routledge, 73–90.

Leavis, F.R. (1979) *English Literature in Our Time and the University: The Clark Lectures 1967*, Cambridge: Cambridge University Press.

——— (1972) *The Great Tradition*, 1948, Harmondsworth: Penguin.

——— (1964) *D.H. Lawrence: Novelist*, 1955, Harmondsworth: Penguin.

——— (1948) *Education and the University: A Sketch for an 'English School'*, 1943, 2nd edn, London: Chatto and Windus.

——— and Thompson, Denys (1962) *Culture and Environment: The Training of Critical Awareness*, 1933, London: Chatto and Windus.

Lee, S.E. (1960) 'The Universities and Creative Writing', *Drylight*: 33–6.

Lentricchia, Frank (1983) *Criticism and Social Change*, Chicago: Chicago University Press.

—— (1980) *After the New Criticism*, Chicago: Chicago University Press.

Lever, Susan (1993) 'The Cult of the Author', *Australian Literary Studies* 16: 229–33.

Levy, Andrew (1993) *The Culture and Commerce of the American Short Story*, Cambridge: Cambridge University Press.

Lewis, B. Roland (1918) *The Technique of the One-Act Play: A Study in Dramatic Construction*, Boston: John W. Luce and Company.

Livingston, Myra Cohn (1984) *The Child as Poet: Myth or Reality?*, Boston: The Horn Book, Inc.

Locke, John (1964) *An Essay Concerning Human Understanding*, 1690, A.D. Woozley (ed.), London: Collins.

Lodge, David (1996) 'Creative Writing: Can it/Should it be Taught?', *The Practice of Writing: Essays, Lectures, Reviews and a Diary*, London: Secker & Warburg, 171–8.

—— (1971) *The Novelist at the Crossroads and Other Essays on Fiction and Criticism*, London: Routledge and Kegan Paul.

—— (1969) 'The Novelist at the Crossroads', *Critical Quarterly* 11.2: 105–32.

Lubbock, Percy (1954) *The Craft of Fiction*, 1921, London: Jonathan Cape.

MacCabe, Colin (1986) 'Broken English', *Critical Quarterly* 28.1&2: 3–14.

MacDonald, John D. (1989) 'Guidelines and Exercises for Teaching Creative Writing,' in Joseph M. Moxley (ed.) *Creative Writing in America: Theory and Pedagogy*, Urbana, Ill.: National Council of Teachers of English, 83–7.

McFarland, Ron (1993) 'An Apologia for Creative Writing', *College English* 55: 28–45.

McKemmish, Jan (1996) 'Degrees of Writing – How to Learn the Tango', in *Teaching Writing*, Proceedings of the First Annual Conference of the Association of University Writing Programs, Oct. 1996, UTS: 69–71.

Macksey, Richard and Donato, Eugenio (eds) (1972) *The Structuralist Controversy: The Languages of Criticism and the Sciences of Man*, 1970, Baltimore: Johns Hopkins University Press.

MacLeish, Archibald (1960) 'On the Teaching of Creative Writing', in John Fischer and Robert B. Silvers (eds) *Writing in America*, New Brunswick: Rutgers University Press, 88–94.

Macquarie University (1997) *Handbook for Postgraduate Research Candidates*, Sydney: Macquarie University.

—— (1970–84) *Calendar of Macquarie University, 1970–1984*, Sydney: Macquarie University.

McQuillan, Martin, et al. (eds) (1999) *Post-theory: New Directions in Criticism*, Edinburgh: Edinburgh University Press.

Madden, David (1989) 'The "Real Life" Fallacy', in Ben Siegel (ed.) *The American Writer and the University*, Newark: Delaware University Press, 179–89.

Mann, James W. (1926) 'Creative Verse Writing – A Class Experiment', *English Journal* 15: 468–9.

Marginson, Simon and Considine, Mark (2000) *The Enterprise University: Power, Governance and Reinvention in Australia*, Cambridge: Cambridge University Press.

Martin, L.H. (Committee on the Future of Tertiary Education in Australia) (1964) *Tertiary Education in Australia: Report of the Committee on the Future of Tertiary Education in Australia to the Australian Universities Commission*, vol. 1, Canberra: Government of the Commonwealth of Australia.

Maslen, Geoffrey and Slattery, Luke (1994) *Why Our Universities are Failing: Crisis in the Clever Country*, Melbourne: Wilkinson Books.

Mathieson, Margaret (1975) *The Preachers of Culture: A Study of English and its Teachers*, London: George Allen and Unwin.

Matthews, Brander (1957) 'An Apology for Technic', 1905, in Albert D. Van Nostrand (ed.) *Literary Criticism in America*, New York: Liberal Arts Press, 214–27.

—— (1901) *The Philosophy of the Short Story*, New York: Longmans, Green, and Co.

Mead, Philip (1993) 'Creative Writing: Undergraduate and Postgraduate Studies', Discussion Paper, English Department, University of Melbourne, September 1993.

Mearns, Hughes (1958) *Creative Power: The Education of Youth in the Creative Arts*, 1929, 2nd edn, New York: Dover Publications.

—— (1925) *Creative Youth: How a School Environment Set Free the Creative Spirit*, Garden City: Doubleday, Page and Company.

Melbourne University (1981–93) *Calendar, 1981–1993*, Parkville: University of Melbourne.

Mencken, H.L. (1991) 'Short Story Courses', 1925, *The Impossible H.L. Mencken: A Selection of his Best Newspaper Stories*, Marion Elizabeth Rodgers (ed.), New York: Doubleday, 537–40.

—— (1957) 'The Critical Process', 1949, in Albert D. Van Nostrand (ed.) *Literary Criticism in America*, New York: The Liberal Arts Press, 239–52.

—— (1921) 'The Motive of the Critic', *New Republic* 26 Oct.: 249–50.

Merod, Jim (1987) *The Political Responsibility of the Critic*, Ithaca: Cornell University Press.

Messud, Claire (1991) 'Creative Writing Program Guns Go Off', *Times Literary Supplement* 31 May: 14.

Miles, Robert (1992) 'Creative Writing, Contemporary Theory and the English Curriculum', in Moira Monteith and Robert Miles (eds) *Teaching Creative Writing: Theory and Practice*, Buckingham: Open University Press, 34–44.

Minot, Stephen (1989) 'How a Writer Reads', in Joseph M. Moxley (ed.) *Creative Writing in America: Theory and Pedagogy*, Urbana, Ill.: National Council of Teachers of English, 89–95.

Mirrielees, Edith (1929) *Writing the Short Story*, Garden City: Doubleday, Doran and Company.

Mitcalfe, Barry (1971) 'Creative Writing: A Workshop Approach to the Teaching of English', *English in Australia* 17: 25–33.

Miyoshi, Masao (2000) 'Ivory Tower in Escrow', *Boundary 2* 27.1: 7–50.

Modjeska, Drusilla (1981) *Exiles at Home: Australian Women Writers 1925–1945*, Sydney: Sirius Books.

Moorhouse, Frank (1984) '*State of the Art* Contributors – A Survey', *Australian Literary Studies* 11: 493–5.

—— (1977) 'What Happened to the Short Story?', *Australian Literary Studies* 8: 179–82.

—— (ed.) (1983) *The State of the Art: The Mood of Contemporary Australia in Short Stories*, Ringwood: Penguin.

—— (ed.) (1973) *Coast to Coast: Australian Stories, 1973*, Sydney: Angus and Robertson.

Morris, Meaghan (1992) 'Cultural Studies', in K.K. Ruthven (ed.) *Beyond the Disciplines: The New Humanities*, Occasional Paper 13, Canberra: Australian Academy of the Humanities, 1–21.

—— and McCalman, Iain (1998) 'Public Culture', in *Knowing Ourselves and Others: The Humanities in Australia into the 21st Century*, 3 vols, Prepared by a Reference Group for the Australian Academy of the Humanities, Canberra: Department of Employment, Education, Training and Youth Affairs, vol. 3: 1–20.

—— and Muecke, Stephen (1996) Editorial, *UTS Review* 2.1: 1.

Morris, Pam (ed.) (1994) *The Bakhtin Reader: Selected Writings of Bakhtin, Medvedev, Voloshinov*, London: Edward Arnold.

Morris, R.L. (1939) 'Can Poetry be Taught?', review of *The Study of Literature* by Louise Dudley, and *Understanding Poetry* by Cleanth Brooks Jr. and Robert Penn Warren, *Sewanee Review* 47: 89–94.

Morton, Donald and Zavarzadeh, Mas'ud (1988–9) 'The Cultural Politics of the Fiction Workshop', *Cultural Critique* 11: 155–73.

Moss, Peter (1981) *Writing Matters*, Sydney: St. Clair Press.

Moss, Tara (1999) *Fetish*, Sydney: HarperCollins.

Moxley, Joseph M. (ed.) (1989) *Creative Writing in America: Theory and Pedagogy*, Urbana, IU.: National Council of Teachers of English.

Muecke, Stephen (1997) *No Road: Bitumen all the Way*, Fremantle: Fremantle Arts Centre Press.

—— (1992) 'Marginality, Writing, Education', *Cultural Studies* 6.2: 261–70.

—— and King, Noel (1991) 'On Ficto-Criticism', *Australian Book Review* 135: 13–14.

Muller, H.J. (1940–41) 'The New Criticism in Poetry', *Southern Review* 6: 811–39.

Munro, Craig (ed.) (1999) *UQP: The Writer's Press, 1948–1998*, Brisbane: Queensland University Press.

—— (1980) *The First UQP Story Book*, Brisbane: Queensland University Press.

Myers, D.G. (1996) *The Elephants Teach: Creative Writing since 1880*, Prentice Hall Studies in Writing and Culture, Englewood Cliffs, NJ: Prentice Hall.

—— (1994) 'The Lesson of Creative Writing's History', *AWP Chronicle* 26.4: 11–14.

Nettelbeck, Amanda (1998) 'Notes Towards an Introduction', in Heather Kerr and Amanda Nettelbeck (eds) *The Space Between: Australian Women Writing Fictocriticism*, Nedlands: UWA Press, 1–17.

New Literary History (1999) Editorial, *New Literary History* 30.1: 1–3.

New South Wales Institute of Technology (1972–78) *Calendar, 1972–1978*, Sydney: NSWIT.

Newbolt, Henry (Great Britain. Committee on English in the Education System of England) (1921) *The Teaching of English in England: Being the Report of the Departmental Committee Appointed by the President of the Board of Education to Inquire into the Position of English in the Educational System of England*, London: His Majesty's Stationery Office.

Newfield, Christopher and Strickland, Ronald (eds) (1995) *After Political Correctness: The Humanities and Society in the 1990s*, Politics and Culture 2, Boulder, Colo.: Westview Press.

Newlyn, Lucy and Lewis, Jenny (eds) (2003) *Synergies: Creative Writing in Academic Practice*, St Edmund Hall: Chough Publications.

Oakley, Barry (1995) 'Chapter and Verse of Ozlit', *Weekend Australian* 1 July: Review 4.

Ommundsen, Wenche (1993) *Metafictions?: Reflexivity in Contemporary Texts*, Interpretations, Melbourne: Melbourne University Press.

Ozick, Cynthia (1995) 'Public and Private Intellectuals', *American Scholar* 64: 353–8.

Page, Geoff (1995) *A Reader's Guide to Contemporary Australian Poetry*, Brisbane: Queensland University Press.

Palmer, D.J. (1965) *The Rise of English Studies: An Account of the Study of English Language and Literature from its Origins to the Making of the Oxford English School*, London: Oxford University Press.

Parini, Jay (1997) 'Literary Theory and the Culture of Creative Writing', *Some Necessary Angels: Essays on Writing and Politics*, New York: Columbia University Press, 231–9.

Parrinder, Patrick (1991) *Authors and Authority: English and American Criticism 1750–1990*, London: Macmillan.

Parry, Albert (1960) *Garrets and Pretenders: A History of Bohemianism in America*, 1933, rev. edn, New York: Dover Publications.

Partridge, P.H. (1972) 'The Future of Higher Education: Problems and Perspectives', in G.S. Harman and C. Selby Smith (eds) *Australian Higher Education: Problems of a Developing System*, Modern Education Series, Sydney: Angus and Robertson, 169–85.

Pattee, Fred Lewis (1975) *The Development of the American Short Story: An Historical Survey*, 1923, New York: Biblo and Tannen.

—— (1923) 'The Present Stage of the Short Story', *English Journal* 12: 439–47.

Perelman, Bob (1996) *The Marginalization of Poetry: Language Writing and Literary History*, Princeton: Princeton University Press.

Perloff, Marjorie (2002) 'Amato/Fleisher Too Pessimistic', *Electronic Book Review*, posted 17 Aug. 2002. Online. <http://www.altx.com/ebr/riposte/rip2/rip2ped/perlo.htm> (accessed 9 Feb. 2004).

—— (1986) '"Homeward Ho!": Silicon Valley Pushkin', *American Poetry Review* 15: 37–46.

Perry, Bliss (1902) *A Study of Prose Fiction*, Boston: Houghton, Mifflin and Company.

Phillips, Glen (1966) 'Approaches to Poetry Writing', *English in Australia* 3: 41–5.

Piaget, Jean (1971) *Science of Education and the Psychology of the Child*, trans. Derek Coltman, London: Longman.

PiO (ed.) (1985) *Off the Record*, Ringwood: Penguin.

Plato (1961) *The Collected Dialogues of Plato, Including the Letters*, Edith Hamilton and Huntington Cairns (eds), trans. Lane Cooper, et al., Bollingen Series LXXI, Princeton: Princeton University Press.

Poe, Edgar Allen (1984) 'The Philosophy of Composition', 1846, *Essays and Reviews*, New York: Library of America, 13–25.

—— (1968) 'The Poetic Principle', *Complete Poetry and Selected Criticism*, Allen Tate (ed.) New York: New American Library, 153–77.

—— (1957) 'Review of New Books', 1842, in Albert D. Van Nostrand (ed.) *Literary Criticism in America*, Forum Books 15, New York: Liberal Arts Press, 32–8.

Pope, Alexander (1965) *Literary Criticism of Alexander Pope*, Bertrand A. Goldgar (ed.) Lincoln: Nebraska University Press.

Posner, Richard A. (2001) *Public Intellectuals: A Study of Decline*, Cambridge, Mass.: Harvard University Press.

Potter, Stephen (1937) *The Muse in Chains: A Study in Education*, London: Jonathan Cape.

Pound, Ezra (1972) 'A Few Don'ts by an Imagiste', 1913, in Peter Jones (ed.) *Imagist Poetry*, Harmondsworth: Penguin, 130–4.

Preminger, Alex and Brogan, T.V.F. (eds) (1993) *The New Princeton Encyclopedia of Poetry and Poetics*, Princeton: Princeton University Press.

Pretty, Ron (1987) *Creating Poetry*, Melbourne: Edward Arnold.

Price, W.T. (1909) *The Technique of the Drama: A Statement of the Principles Involved in the Value of Dramatic Material, in the Construction of Plays, and in Dramatic Criticism*, 1892, New York: Brentano's.

Puttenham, George (1869) *The Arte of English Poesie*, 1589, Edward Arber (ed.) London: n.p., 1869.

Quarles, Francis (1632) 'Sions Sonets. Sung By Solomon the King; And Periphras'd: Bridegroome. Sonet XX [from *Divine Poems* (1632)]', *Literature Online*. <http://lion.chadwyck.com> (accessed 1 Feb. 2001).

Quiller-Couch, Sir Arthur (1946) *On the Art of Writing*, 1916, Guild Books 426, Cambridge: British Publishers Guild Ltd.

Ragan, James (1989) 'The Academy and the "You Know?" Generation', in Ben Siegel (ed.) *The American Writer and the University*, Newark: Delaware University Press, 161–76.

Ransom, John Crowe (1984) 'Criticism, Inc.', 1937, *Selected Essays of John Crowe Ransom*, Thomas Daniel Young and John Hindle (eds), Baton Rouge: Louisiana State University Press, 93–106.

—— (1944) 'The Bases of Criticism', *Sewanee Review* 52: 556–71.

—— (1940–1) 'Strategy for English Studies', *Southern Review* 6: 226–35.

—— (1940) 'Mr. Tate and the Professors', *Kenyon Review* 2: 348–50.

—— (1939) 'The Teaching of Poetry', *Kenyon Review* 1: 81–3.

Rasula, Jed (1996) *The American Poetry Wax Museum: Reality Effects, 1940–1990*, Urbana, Ill.: National Council of Teachers of English.

Readings, Bill (1996) *The University in Ruins*, Cambridge, Mass.: Harvard University Press.

Reid, Ian (1984) *The Making of Literature: Texts, Contexts and Classroom Practices*, Norwood: Australian Association for the Teaching of English.

—— (1982) 'The Crisis in English Studies', *English in Australia* 60: 8–18.

Reiner, Vivienne (2000) 'Write of Passage', *Weekend Australian* 13–14 May: Orbit 1–2.

Richards, I.A. (1964) *Practical Criticism: A Study of Literary Judgment*, 1929, London: Routledge and Kegan Paul.

—— (1960) *Coleridge on Imagination*, 1934, Bloomington: Indiana University Press.

Richards, Max (1970) 'A Poetry which Matters: Notes from Above Ground', *Meanjin Quarterly* 29: 122–4.

Ringler, William (1941) '*Poeta Nascitur Non Fit*: Some Notes on the History of an Aphorism', *Journal of the History of Ideas* 2: 497–504.

Roberts, H.D. (1929a) Editorial, *English Journal* 18: 345–6.

—— (1929b) Editorial, *English Journal* 18: 55–6.

Robbins, Bruce (ed.) (1990) *Intellectuals: Aesthetics, Politics, Academics*, Minneapolis: University of Minnesota Press.

Rose, Margaret A. (1979) *Parody/Metafiction: An Analysis of Parody as a Critical Mirror to the Writing and Reception of Fiction*, London: Croom Helm.

Rosemont, Franklin (1978) *André Breton and the First Principles of Surrealism*, London: Pluto Press.

Ross, Bruce Clunies (1981) 'Some Developments in Short Fiction, 1969–1980', *Australian Literary Studies* 10: 165–80.

Rothenberg, Albert and Hausman, Carl R. (eds) (1976) *The Creativity Question*, Durham, NC: Duke University Press.

Rousseau, Jean Jacques (1974) *Emile*, trans. Barbara Foxley. London: Dent.

—— (1953) *The Confessions*, 1781, trans. J.M. Cohen, Harmondsworth: Penguin.

Rowlands, Graham (1978) 'The New Writing: Rallying or Going Under', *Meanjin* 37: 370–4.

Rugg, Harold and Shumaker, Ann (1928) *The Child-Centered School: An Appraisal of the New Education*, London: George G. Harrup and Co. Ltd.

Russell, David R. (1991) *Writing in the Academic Disciplines, 1870–1990: A Curricular History*, Carbondale: Southern Illinois University Press.

Ruthven, K.K. (1979) *Critical Assumptions*, Cambridge: Cambridge University Press.

—— (ed.) (1992) *Beyond the Disciplines: The New Humanities*, Occasional Paper 13, Canberra: Australian Academy of the Humanities.

Rymer, Thomas (1908) 'The Tragedies of the Last Age Consider'd and Examin'd by the Practice of the Ancients and by the Common Sense of

All Ages', 1678, in J.E. Spingarn (ed.) *Critical Essays of the Seventeenth Century*, *Vol. 2: 1650–1685*, Oxford: Clarendon Press, 181–208.

Said, Edward (1994) *Representations of the Intellectual: The 1993 Reith Lectures*, London: Vintage.

—— (1983) *The World, the Text, and the Critic*, Cambridge, Massachusetts: Harvard University Press.

Saintsbury, George (1907) *A Short History of English Literature*, 1898, London: Macmillan.

Sandys, George (1641) 'A Paraphrase Upon the Song of Solomon (1641)', *Literature Online*. Online. <http://lion.chadwyck.com> (accessed 1 Feb. 2001).

Scholes, Robert (1985) *Textual Power: Literary Theory and the Teaching of English*, New Haven: Yale University Press.

—— (1979) *Fabulation and Metafiction*, Urbana: Illinois University Press.

Schramm, Wilbur (1941) 'Imaginative Writing', in Norman Foerster (ed.) *Literary Scholarship: Its Aims and Methods*, Chapel Hill: North Carolina University Press, 177–213.

—— (1938) *The Story Workshop*, Boston: Little, Brown and Company.

Sexton, Anne (1985) *No Evil Star: Selected Essays, Interviews, and Prose*, Steven E. Colburn (ed.), Ann Arbor: Michigan University Press.

Shapcott, Thomas (1988) *The Literature Board: A Brief History*, Brisbane: Queensland University Press.

—— (ed.) (1970) *Australian Poetry Now*, Melbourne: Sun Books.

Shapiro, Alan (1993) 'Horace and the Reformation of Creative Writing', *In Praise of the Impure: Poetry and the Ethical Imagination, Essays, 1980–1991*, Evanston, Ill.: Northwestern University Press, 164–81.

Sheffield, John (1908) 'An Essay Upon Poetry', 1682, in J.E. Spingarn (ed.) *Critical Essays of the Seventeenth Century, Vol. 2: 1650–1685*, Oxford: Clarendon Press, 286–96.

Shelley, Percy Bysshe (1963) *A Defence of Poetry*, 1821, in Daniel G. Hoffman and Samuel Hynes (eds) *English Literary Criticism: Romantic and Victorian*, New York: Appleton Century Crofts, 159–90.

Shelnutt, Eve (1989) 'Notes from a Cell: Creative Writing Programs in Isolation', in Joseph M. Moxley (ed.) *Creative Writing in America: Theory and Pedagogy*, Urbana, Ill.: National Council of Teachers of English, 3–24.

Shetley, Vernon (1993) *After the Death of Poetry: Poet and Audience in Contemporary America*, Durham, NC: Duke University Press.

Showalter, Elaine (1986) 'The Feminist Critical Revolution', Introduction to Elaine Showalter (ed.) *The New Feminist Criticism: Essays on Women, Literature and Theory*, London: Virago Press, 3–17.

Sidney, Philip (1922) 'An Apology for Poetry', 1595, in Edmund D. Jones (ed.) *English Critical Essays (Sixteenth, Seventeenth and Eighteenth Centuries)*, The World's Classics 240, London: Oxford University Press, 1–54.

Slattery, Luke (1996) 'Booked for Stardom', *Weekend Australian* 16–17 Mar.: Review 1–2.

Slaughter, Sheila and Leslie, Larry (1997) *Academic Capitalism: Politics, Policies and the Entrepeneurial University*, Baltimore: Johns Hopkins University Press.

Small, Helen (ed.) (2002) *The Public Intellectual*, Oxford: Blackwell.

Smith, Dave (1985) *Local Assays: On Contemporary American Poetry*, Urbana: Illinois University Press.

Smith, James (1968) 'Wordsworth: A Preliminary Survey', 1938, in F.R. Leavis (ed.) *A Selection from Scrutiny*, 2 vols, Cambridge: Cambridge University Press, vol. 2: 137–56.

Smith, L.E.W. (1972) *Towards a New English Curriculum*, London: Dent.

—— (1970) 'Creative Writing and Language Awareness', *English in Education* 4.1: 4–9.

Smith, Logan Pearsall (1925) 'Four Romantic Words', *Words and Idioms: Studies in the English Language*, 2nd edn, London: Constable and Company, 66–134.

Smith, Vivian (1965) 'Writer and Reader', review of *The Cave and the Spring* by A.D. Hope, *Southerly* 4: 282–4.

Soliman, I.K. (1988) 'Creative Writing and Literature Study', *English in Australia* 85: 49–58.

Solotaroff, Ted (1985) 'Writing in the Cold', *Granta* 18: 264–79.

Souba, Jane (1925) 'Creative Writing in High School', *English Journal* 14: 591–602.

Spingarn. J.E. (1917) *Creative Criticism: Essays on the Unity of Genius and Taste*, New York: Henry Holt and Company.

Stegner, Wallace (1997) *On the Teaching of Creative Writing: Responses to a Series of Questions*, 1988, Edward Connery Lathem (ed.), Hanover: Montgomery Endowment, Dartmouth College.

Storr, Anthony (1972) *The Dynamics of Creation*, London: Secker and Warburg.

Summerfield, Geoffrey (1968) 'A Short Dialogue on Some Aspects of That Which We Call Creative English', in Geoffrey Summerfield (ed.) *Creativity in English: Papers Relating to the Anglo-American Seminar on the Teaching of English at Dartmouth College, New Hampshire, 1966*, Urbana, Ill.: National Council of Teachers of English, 21–47.

Sussex, Lucy (1997) 'Weeding the Garden of Literature', *Australian Book Review* 191: 66.

Swain, David (1970) 'So You Want to be a Writer?', *Bulletin* 5 Dec.: 49–50.

Tate, Allen (1964) 'What is Creative Writing?', *Wisconsin Studies in Contemporary Literature* 5.3: 181–4.

—— (1955) 'Techniques of Fiction', *The Man of Letters in the Modern World: Selected Essays, 1928–1955*, New York: Meridian Books, 78–92.

—— (1940) '"We Read as Writers": The Creative Arts Program and How it is Helping Freshman Would-Be Authors', *Princeton Alumni Weekly* 40: 505–6.

Tatum, Stephen (1993) '"The Thing Not Named"; or, the End of Creative Writing in the English Department', *ADE Bulletin* 106: 30–4.

Taylor, Calvin W. (ed.) (1964) *Creativity: Progress and Potential*, New York: McGraw-Hill.

Theiner, George (ed.) (1984) *They Shoot Writers, Don't They?*, London: Faber and Faber.

Thompson, Brian (ed.) (1966) *Once Around the Sun: An Anthology of Poetry by Australian Children*, Melbourne: Oxford University Press.

Todorov, Tzvetan (1981) *Introduction to Poetics*, trans. Richard Howard, Sussex: Harvester Press.

Tomkinson, W.S. (1921) *The Teaching of English: A New Approach*, Oxford: Clarendon Press.

Tranter, John (1978) 'Growing Old Gracefully: The Generation of '68', *Meanjin* 37: 76–86.

—— (1977) 'Four Notes on the Practice of Revolution', *Australian Literary Studies* 8: 127–35.

—— (1974) 'Notes on Some Recent Australian Poetry', *New Poetry* 22.1: 43–61.

—— (ed.) (1979) *The New Australian Poetry*, Brisbane: Makar Press.

Valéry, Paul (1985) 'On Literary Technique', 1889, *The Art of Poetry*, trans. Denise Folliot, Bollingen Series XLV, Princeton: Princeton University Press, 315–23.

Veeser, H. Aram (ed.) (1996) *Confessions of the Critics*, New York: Routledge, 3–16.

Vernon, P.E. (ed.) (1970) *Creativity: Selected Readings*, Harmondsworth: Penguin.

Walker, Nancy A. (1993) 'The Student Writer as Reader', *ADE Bulletin* 106: 35–7.

Wallace, David Foster (1997) 'Westward the Course of Empire Takes its Way', 1989, *Girl With Curious Hair*, London: Abacus, 231–373.

Wallace-Crabbe, Chris (1966) 'A.D. Hope as Essayist', review of *The Cave and the Spring* by A.D. Hope, *Meanjin Quarterly* 25: 115–19.

—— (ed.) (1963) *Six Voices: Contemporary Australian Poets*, Sydney: Angus and Robertson.

Wallas, Graham (1926) *The Art of Thought*, London: Jonathan Cape.

Walshe, R.D. (1982) 'The Writing Revolution', *English in Australia* 62: 3–15.

—— (1971) 'Creative Writing in the English Programme', *English in Australia* 15: 7–14.

Ward, Adolphus William (1875) *A History of English Dramatic Literature to the Death of Queen Anne, Vol. 1*, London: Macmillan.

Ward, Thomas B., Finke, Ronald A. and Smith, Steven M. (eds) (1995) *Creativity and the Mind: Discovering the Genius Within*, New York: Plenum Press.

Wark, McKenzie (1997) 'On Public Intellectuals: Ruminations from Back Paddock', in Paolo Bartoloni, Karen Lynch and Shane Kendal (eds) *Intellectuals and Publics: Essays on Cultural Theory and Practice*, Melbourne: School of English, LaTrobe University, 85–99.

Warren, Austin (1941) 'Literary Criticism', in Norman Foerster (ed.) *Literary Scholarship: Its Aims and Methods*, Chapel Hill: North Carolina University Press, 133–74.

Waten, Judah and Murray-Smith, Stephen (eds) (1974) *Classic Australian Short Stories*, Melbourne: Wren Publishing.

Watkins, Evan (1989) *Work Time: English Departments and the Circulation of Cultural Value*, Stanford: Stanford University Press.

Watson, George (1973) *The Literary Critics: A Study of English Descriptive Criticism*, 1962, 2nd edn, Harmondsworth: Penguin.

Watt, Ian (1972) *The Rise of the Novel: Studies in Defoe, Richardson and Fielding*, 1957, Harmondsworth: Penguin.

Waugh, Patricia (1984) *Metafiction: The Theory and Practice of Self-Conscious Fiction*, New Accents, London: Methuen.

Webb, Jen (2000) 'Individual Enunciations and Social Frames', *TEXT* 4.2. Online. <http://www.gu.edu.au/school/art/text/oct00/webb.htm> (accessed 9 Feb. 2004).

Weisberg, Robert W. (1993) *Creativity: Beyond the Myth of Genius*, New York: W.H. Freeman and Company.

Weiss, Theodore (1989) 'Poetry, Pedagogy, Per-versities', in Ben Siegel (ed.) *The American Writer and the University*, Newark: Delaware University Press, 149–58.

Wellek, Rene (1982) *The Attack on Literature and Other Essays*, Chapel Hill: North Carolina University Press.

—— and Warren, Austin (1963) *Theory of Literature*, 1949, Harmondsworth: Penguin.

Wendell, Barrett (1896) *English Composition: Eight Lectures Given at the Lowell Institute*, 1891, New York: Charles Scribner's Sons.

Westbury, Deborah (2002) 'Metaphor in Poetry', in Brenda Walker (ed.) *The Writer's Reader: A Guide to Writing Fiction and Poetry*, Sydney: Halstead Press, 148–51.

Western Australian Institute of Technology (1974) *School of Social Sciences Handbook, 1974*, Perth: WAIT.

—— (1972–3) *Division of Commerce and Social Sciences Handbook, 1972–1973*, Perth: WAIT.

White, Helen C. (1964) 'Creative Writing in the University', *Wisconsin Studies in Contemporary Literature* 5.1: 37–47.

White, Michael (1996) *WAIT to Curtin: A History of the Western Australian Institute of Technology*, Bentley: Paradigm Books.

White, Robert (1998) 'The State of English Studies in the 1990s', in *Knowing Ourselves and Others: The Humanities in Australia into the 21st Century*, 3 vols, prepared by a Reference Group for the Australian Academy of the Humanities, Canberra: Department of Employment, Education, Training and Youth Affairs, vol. 2: 95–105.

White, Terri-Ann, Gibbs, Anna, Jenkins, Wendy and King, Noel (eds) (1990) *No Substitute: Prose, Poems, Images*, Fremantle: Fremantle Arts Centre Press.

Widdowson, Peter (1999) *Literature, The New Critical Idiom*, London: Routledge.

Wilbers, Stephen (1980) *The Iowa Writers' Workshop: Origins, Emergence, and Growth*, Iowa City: Iowa University Press.

Wilding, Michael (1977) 'A Survey', *Australian Literary Studies* 8: 115–26.

—— (1975) 'A Random House: The Parlous State of Australian Publishing', *Meanjin Quarterly* 34: 106–11.

—— (1972) 'Little Magazines in Australia', *Australian Author* 4.2: 29–33.

—— (ed.) (1978) *The Tabloid Story Pocket Book*, Sydney: Wild and Woolley.

Williams, Jeffrey (2000) 'The Posttheory Generation', 1995, in Peter C. Herman (ed.) *Day Late, Dollar Short: The Next Generation and the New Academy*, Albany: State University of New York Press, 25–43.

—— (ed.) (1995) *PC Wars: Politics and Theory in the Academy*, New York: Routledge.

Williams, Raymond (1988) *Keywords: A Vocabulary of Culture and Society*, 1976, London: Fontana Press.

—— (1977) *Marxism and Literature*, Oxford: Oxford University Press.

—— (1965) *The Long Revolution*, 1961, Harmondsworth: Penguin.

Williamson, Dugald (1989) *Authorship and Criticism*, Critical Categories Series 1, Sydney: Local Consumption Publications.

Wilson, Helen (1989) 'Bill Bonney and the Contributors', Afterword to Helen Wilson (ed.) *Australian Communications and the Public Sphere: Essays in Memory of Bill Bonney*, Melbourne: Macmillan, 277–86.

Wimsatt Jr., W.K. and Beardsley, Monroe C. (1967) 'The Intentional Fallacy', 1946, *The Verbal Icon: Studies in the Meaning of Poetry*, 1954, Lexington: University of Kentucky Press, 3–18.

—— and Brooks, Cleanth (1964) *Literary Criticism: A Short History*, 4 vols, New York: Alfred A. Knopf.

Winchester, C.T. (1924) *Some Principles of Literary Criticism*, 1899, New York: The Macmillan Company.

Wollongong University (1986) *Calendar: Volume III, Postgraduate Handbook, 1986*, Wollongong: Wollongong University.

—— (1985) *Calendar: Volume II, Undergraduate Handbook, 1985*, Wollongong: Wollongong University.

Woodberry, Joan (1968) 'Children Writing Poetry', *English in Australia* 8: 29–41.

Wordsworth, William (1974a) 'Essay, Supplementary to the Preface 1815', *Wordsworth's Literary Criticism*, W.J.B. Owen (ed.) London: Routledge and Kegan Paul, 192–218.

—— (1974b) 'Preface and Appendix to *Lyrical Ballads* (1800, 1802),' *Wordsworth's Literary Criticism*, W.J.B. Owen (ed.) London: Routledge & Kegan Paul, 68–95.

—— (1950) *The Poetical Works of Wordsworth*, 1904, Thomas Hutchinson (ed.), new edn, rev. Ernest de Selincourt, London: Oxford University Press.

Young, Edward (1947) 'Conjectures on Original Composition', 1759, in Edmund D. Jones (ed.) *English Critical Essays: XVI–XVIII Centuries*, The World's Classics 240, Oxford: Oxford University Press, 270–311.

Zavarzadeh, Mas'ud (1976) *The Mythopoeic Reality: The Postwar American Nonfiction Novel*, Urbana: Illinois University Press.

Index

Page numbers followed by (n) represent endnotes.

Adams, Glenda 107
Adams, Katherine 56–7
Adamson, Robert 136
Addison, Joseph 26, 27, 36
Adelaide Writers' Festival 141
Akenside, Mark 15, 19
Aldridge, John W. 13
Allen, Walter 101
Amato, Joe: and Fleisher, Kassia 106, 172
American Declaration of Independence 33
Anderson, Don 139, 202
anti-didacticism 104
anti-industrialism 39–40
anti-political correctness: attacks on universities 197–9
Aristotle 25, 28, 34, 88, 101
Arnold, Matthew 38, 39, 40, 69, 77, 118, 187, 189; creative power 37, 41; criticism 186; disinterestedness 17, 19, 186
Associated Writing Programs 5, 93, 121, 123, 125, 157, 188, 194
Attebury, Brian 170
Australia: colleges of advanced education (CAE) 126 139, 141, 143–4, 149–50, 156; English Studies 127–31; history of Creative Writing 126–57; metaphysical ascendancy in universities 128, 155; new Australian writing 135–43; new fiction 137–8; new humanities 182–4; new poetry 136–7; political correctness 199–200; professionalisation of Creative Writing 155–7; universities and Creative Writing 150–5; vocational education 143–50
Australian Academy of the Humanities 158, 182–3, 197
Australian Association for the Teaching of English 133
Australian Association of Writing Programs 125, 158, 159, 168, 188; foundation of 157
Australian Literary Studies 127, 135, 143, 156
author: craft-based choices 94, 95, 211; death of 149, 156, 163–4, 208
authorship: in writing workshop 112–20; modernist craftsman 64–6, 82, 117; professionalised 65, 194
autobiographical criticism 167
automatic writing 42
avant-garde 12, 124, 165–6, 184, 211; and Creative Writing 165–71, 194

Babbitt, Irving 18, 34, 68, 69
Bacon, Francis 23, 24, 35, 37
Baker, George Pierce: Dramatic Technique 36, 206; '47 Workshop' 81
Bakhtin, Mikhail (The Dialogic Imagination) 208–12

Barrett, Charles, R. 62, 64
Barth, John 165
Barthelme, Frederick 12
Barthes, Roland 104, 149, 165, 167;
    'The Death of the Author' 149,
    163–4, 208; 'Flaubertization' of
    writing 66; 'From Work to Text'
    123
Beach, Christopher 2, 12
Beach, Stewart 10–11
Bell, Sharon 153–4
Belsey, Catherine 216n
Bennett, David 199
Bennett, Tony 182–3, 189, 200, 208
Berlin, James, A. 57, 59–60
Bernstein, Charles 166, 175, 177
Bersani, Leo 114
Berube, Michael 198–9
Besant, Walter: *The Art of Fiction*
    8–10, 35–6, 61, 79, 91; *The Pen
    and the Book* 10, 91–2
Birmingham Centre for
    Contemporary Cultural Studies
    192, 200
Black Mountain poets 108, 136, 166
Blackmur, R.P. 76
Blake, William 30, 39
Bloom, Allan 197
Bloom, Harold 164
bohemianism: American 19
Bonney, Bill 147
Booth, Wayne, C. (*Rhetoric of Fiction*)
    102
Borthwick, John 145
Bourdieu, Pierre 192
Bove, Paul 189
Bradbury, Malcolm 19
Brande, Dorothea (*Becoming a Writer*)
    96, 97; reading as a writer 92,
    119; unconscious as source of
    genius 43, 107
Bredin, Hugh 76
Breton, André 42
Brett, Judith 202
Brewster, Anne 168–9
Briggs, Le Baron Russell 57, 58
Broken Land (Hull) 211–3
Brooks, Cleanth 76, 78, 104, 188;
    and Warren, Robert Penn
    78–80

Brophy, Kevin 21, 134, 140
Brown, Rollo Walter 40, 58
Brown, Thomas 15
Buckley, Vincent 135, 154
Buford, Bill 12
Burt, C.L. 43
Byrom, John 15

Canberra College of Advanced
    Education: professional writing
    course 144–5, 146
canon debate 3, 124, 174, 175
Carver, Raymond 12–13, 112,
    142
Cassill, R.V. (*Writing Fiction*):
    Associated Writing Programs 121;
    influence of New Criticism 80;
    reading as a writer 85, 93–4, 95,
    96, 97, 102–3; show, don't tell
    98–9, 102–3; voice 107–8
Cave Writing Workshop (Brown
    University) 165–6
Chapple, A. 21
child-centred education 55, 132–3
Clarke, Joan 138
Code, Trevor 151
Coleridge, Samuel Taylor (*Biographia
    Literaria*) 7, 50, 187, 188;
    imagination 30–2; *Lyrical Ballads*
    31–2, 51; and Wordsworth 31–2,
    51, 107
composition, English 50, 52, 53,
    132; history of 56–60
confessional criticism 167–8, 184
Conrad, Joseph (*Heart of Darkness*)
    104–5
constructivism 49, 59
Cook, H. Caldwell 40
Cooley, Nicole 160–1
Coover, Robert 165
Copeland, Charles Townsend 57
Cowie, Edward 153–4
Craig, Alexander 151
creation, poetic 25–6, 31
creative: first appearance of word
    26–7
Creative Class 45–6, 162
Creative English: new educational
    paradigm 132–4
creative imagination 29–32

creative power 26–9, 41
Creative Power (Mearns) 53–4
creative reading: Emerson 33;
  Mearns 53; Lubbock 96–7
creative self-expression 49, 50–6,
  132–4
creative thinking 44–5
creative writing (phrase) 21–2, 29,
  46, 95, 127, 215n; opposed to
  criticism 38; origins of phrase
  32–41
Creative Writing (academic
  discipline) 1–6, 178–9, 184–5,
  203–4, 205, 214; in Australia
  121–57; and Cultural Studies
  172–4, 207–8; disciplinary origins
  48–86; emergence of workshop
  80–6; growth in United Kingdom
  158–9; higher degree status 67;
  impact of University teaching
  11–14; negotiating a relationship
  with Theory 158–79; and the New
  Humanities 5, 183–5, 194, 195,
  201, 204, 205–6, 214;
  postgraduate study 116, 156–7,
  194–5, 202; and public
  intellectuals 201–4; scholarly
  interest 158–60; towards a
  sociological poetics 205–14;
  undergraduate versus postgraduate
  116–17, 178–9
Creative Writing and Theory: avant-
  garde model 165–71; historical
  relationship to 4–5, 13, 122–6,
  155–6, 158–61, 180, 194;
  integrated pedagogy model 161–5;
  political model 171–9
Creative Youth (Mearns) 41, 52–3, 54,
  55
creativity 22; and anti-
  industrialisation 39–40; and
  democracy 40–1; democratisation
  of 45, 132; as a faculty 41–3; from
  imagination 21–47; science of
  43–7
Creeley, Robert 166
crisis in English Studies 2–6, 122,
  126–7, 152, 176, 205
critics: vs writers 2, 84–5, 122–5,
  185, 203

criticism 53, 96, 130; as part of
  creative process 117–19; history of
  word 185–6; opposed to reading
  as a writer 92–4; oppositional
  189–92, 201, 204, 206, 214;
  practical 3, 76, 122, 128, 185–8,
  204; professionalisation 83–4, 122,
  185, 196; and reviewing 185–6; vs
  scholarship 2–3, 4, 68–70, 216n
Cross, Ethan Allen 63
Cudworth, Ralph 27
Culler, Jonathan 3, 75, 89, 124, 165,
  183
cultural capital 116, 124, 192–3
Cultural Capital (Guillory) 124, 175
Cultural Studies 3, 5, 90, 125, 147,
  152, 155, 156, 159, 160, 168;
  cultural policy 200; and the
  Enterprise University 200;
  intellectuals 192, 200; and the
  New Humanities 183, 200–1;
  political correctness 198; the
  posttheory generation 180–1; and
  the writing workshop 172–4,
  207–8
culture wars 3, 184, 198
Currie, Mark 217n
Curtin University (Western
  Australian Institute of Technology)
  145–6, 149, 156

Dartmouth Seminar 133
Davies, John 26
Dawkins reforms 149–50, 156, 199,
  200
de Bono, Edward 44–5
de Certeau, Michel 170
de Man, Paul 122
de Maupassant, Guy 66
Deakin University 135; professional
  writing course 150, 151–2
Derrida, Jacques 108–9, 124, 165,
  167, 171
Dessaix, Robert 202
Devitt, Marian 38
Dewey, John 55, 132
Dibble, Brian 146
Dick, William 131
Dickinson, Emily 15–16, 17, 19
Dixon, John 133, 216n

Docker, John 128, 155
Doecke, Brenton 128
Donaldson, Ian 156, 182
D'Orsay, Laurence 81
Drennan, Marie 82
Dryden, John 27, 81; criticism 185,
    189; the imagination 23–5, 26;
    writer-critic 64, 195
D'Souza, Dinesh 197
Duff, William 29
Dugan, Michael 139
During, Simon 200–1

Eagleton, Terry 148, 189, 196
Egerton, Sarah Fye 27
Ehrenreich, Barbara: and
    Ehrenreich, John 36, 192
Eliot, T.S. 38, 65, 75, 82, 99, 104,
    185, 187; criticism and the
    creative process 117–19, 177,
    194–5
Emerson, Ralph Waldo 32–3, 49
Engle, Paul 119; director of Iowa
    Writers' Workshop 66, 67, 68, 74,
    83
English Studies 2–6, 20, 22, 37,
    39–40, 48, 50, 68, 77, 85, 86,
    121–2, 124, 155–6, 159, 160, 176,
    177, 179, 189, 205; in Australia
    127–31, 155–6; and creativity 22,
    39–40, crisis in 2–6, 122, 126–7,
    152, 176, 205; and criticism
    185–8; in England 37, 39–40,
    122, 127–8, 159, 187, 189; in the
    US 48, 68, 77, 85, 122–3
Enterprise University, the 3–4, 179,
    197, 200
Ewers, John K. 127, 135
exegesis 194–5

Fenza, David 50, 123, 125, 188,
    203–4
fiction: as an art 9–10; as creative
    writing 38; criticism of 96–8;
    development of novel 101–4; new
    Australian 137; and New
    Criticism 78–80; magazine 60–3,
    79; minimalist 12–13, 103; poetics
    of 89, 98
fictocriticism 166–71, 184, 195

Fielding, Henry (*Tom Jones*) 27, 35
Flaubert, Gustave (*Madame Bovary*)
    66, 82, 101, 102, 103, 114
Flavell, Helen 169–70
Florida, Richard 45–6
Foerster, Norman 50, 67–71, 73, 74,
    76, 83, 84, 85, 152, 164
Foucault, Michel 171, 189, 190
Fowles, John (*French Lieutenant's
    Woman*) 103, 114
Freadman, Richard 128
free association 42
Freiman, Marcelle 176, 177
Freud, Sigmund 42
Frow, John 155–6, 182, 192
Frye, Northrop (*Anatomy of Criticism*)
    85

Galef, David 2, 174, 182
Galton, Alexander 43
Gandhi, Leela 189
garret: and the ivory tower 14–20
Garrett, George 123
Gelder, Ken: and Salzman, Paul 138
Genette, Gerard (*Narrative Discourse*)
    89, 109–10
Gibbons, F.P.: and Gibbons, T.H.
    128
Gibbons, Reginald 122–3; and
    Graff, Gerald 196
Gibbs, Anna 168, 170
Gilbert, Pam 134
Golding, Alan 84, 180
Goldman, Arnie 148
Goldsworth, Kerryn 154, 155
Gordimer, Nadine 148–9
Gouldner, Alvin 192
Graff, Gerald 3, 68, 74, 76, 216n;
    and Gibbons, Reginald 196
Green, Chris 172–3
Green, Dorothy 131
Greenfield, Cathy 183
Greenwich Village 17, 19
Grenville, Kate (*The Writing Book*) 91,
    100, 110–11
Gross, John 145, 185
Grub Street 15, 16, 19
grunge-lit 142, 202
Guilford, J.P. 43, 44
Guillory, John 124, 175, 203

handbooks: on writing 10–11, 79,
91, 98, 102, 158; history of 60–4
Hall, Rodney: and Shapcott,
Thomas 136, 140
Hall, Stuart 200
Halligon, Marion 142
Harper, Graeme 158–9
Harrison-Ford, Carl 138
Hartman, Geoffrey 124
Harvard University: English
Composition 56–9
Hatfield, W. Wilbur 40
Hawthorne, Nathaniel 35, 61
Hay, John 145
Hemensley, Kris 136, 139
Hemingway, Ernest 112
Herman, Peter C. 181–2
heteroglossia: diversity of social
speech types 209–11, 213
Hill, Adam Sherman 57
Hobbes, Thomas 23, 30
Hodge, Bob 198
Homer 101
Hope, A.D. 129–31, 132, 133, 135,
140
Hopkins, John 27
Horace 7, 104
Hough, Graham 122
Hourd, Marjorie 132
Housh, Snow Longley 56, 66
Howells, William Dean 63
Hugo, Richard 11
Hull, Coral (*Broken Land*) 211–13
Hunter, Ian 215–16n
Hutcheon, Linda 217n
Hutchinson, Jan 157
hybridisation: and fictocriticism
170–1

identity politics 174–5, 177
imagination: Bacon 23–4; Blake 30;
Coleridge 30–2, 187, 188;
compound 23, 24, 26; creative
29–32; and creativity 22, 41–2,
43; Hobbes 23–4, 30; and reason
24; reproductive 23–4; simple 23
Imagist poetry 99–100
Indyk, Ivor 141
inspiration 25; internalised 28, 29,
42

intellectual: Gramscian 190, 200; as
member of knowledge class
192–3; literary (Lentricchia)
190–2, 202; and oppositional
criticism 189–92; organic 200;
Marxist 189, 190; public 195–7;
specific (Foucauldian) 189–90;
writer as 179, 195, 201–4; writer-
critic as 195
Iowa Writers' Workshop 11, 13, 66,
67, 84, 94, 121, 164;
establishment of 68, 74, 81, 83, 84
ivory tower: and garret 14–20;
origins of concept 16–18

Jach, Antoni 103
Jacoby, Russell (*The Last Intellectuals*)
195–6, 197, 198
James, Henry: 'The Art of Fiction',
9, 10, 61, 79; and Percy Lubbock
96, 102
Jauss, David 94–5
Johnson, Louis 134
Johnson, Samuel 18–19, 35, 36,
217n

Kant, Immanuel 8, 10
Keats, John 65
Kemp, David 200
Ker, W.P. 81
Kermode, Frank 75
Kiernan, Brian 138, 139
Kiley, Dean 103
Kimball, Roger 197
King, Noel 170
Kinross-Smith, Graeme 151
Koethe, John 108
Krauss, Rosalind 167
Krauth, Nigel 142, 176; and Brady,
Tess 128, 150, 155

Landow, George P. 165
Language poets 12, 165, 166
Lawrence, D.H. 39
Lawson, Henry 135
Leavis, F.R. 101; anti-industrialism
39–40; on Conrad 104–5; on
Creative Writing 127–8; cultural
heritage 133, 189; and English
Studies 39–40, 128, 133, 187;

practical criticism 40, 187; and Thompson, Denys 187
Lee, S.E. 129
Lentricchia, Frank 85, 189–91, 201
Lever, Susan 141
Levy, Andrew 59, 60, 61, 62, 64
Lincoln School (Teachers' College, Columbia University) 52–4
literary and critical writing: as complementary practices 178–9
literary establishment 184
literary intellectual 5, 179, 185, 195, 201, 202, 205; as public intellectual 201–4; as specific intellectual (Lentricchia) 190–2, 201; writer as 201, 202, 205, 208
Literary Studies 3, 38, 85, 89, 123; and identity politics 174; knowledge in 178–9; professionalisation of 122; relation to Creative Writing 2, 6, 13, 20, 60, 64, 76, 83, 87–8, 94, 95, 116, 123, 125, 160, 164, 176, 177, 194, 205
literature: as an art form 7, 37–8; can it be taught 6–7; creative writing as synonym for 21; definition 203; history of word 34–8; as knowledge 178–9; as public discourse 204
Literature Board of the Australian Council 138, 141
Locke, John 29, 30, 32, 39
Lodge, David 9, 89, 112, 216n
Lubbock, Percy (*The Craft of Fiction*) 96–8, 102, 103, 110, 120
Lyrical Ballads (Wordsworth and Coleridge) 31–2, 51, 106

McAuley, James 135
MacCabe, Colin 176
MacDonald, John D. 99
McFarland, Ron 95, 99
McKemmish, Jan 164
Macleish, Archibald 11
Macquarie University 150, 151, 157
Madame Bovary (Flaubert) 66, 102–3, 114
Madden, David 18
Mallet, David 27

Malouf, David 141
Marginson, Simon: and Considine, Mark 3–4
Martin, Sir Leslie (Martin Report) 143, 144, 150
Mathieson, Margaret 40
Matthews, Brander: *Philosophy of the Short Story* 61–2; technic 64, 66, 67, 72
Mead, Philip 154, 155
Mearns, Hughes 52–4, 56, 66, 79, 82, 163
Mencken, H.L. 38, 63
Merod, Jim 188, 189, 201
Messud, Claire 19
metafiction 103, 113–14, 165, 216n
Miles, Robert 163–4, 204
minimalism (dirty realism) 12–13, 103, 112, 142
Minot, Stephen 110
Miyoshi, Masao 16, 17
Modernist craftsman: origins 64–6; Creative Writing as institutionalisation of 82, 88, 117
Modernist literature 135–6; and New Criticism 3, 75, 76, 165
Modjeska, Drusilla 148
Moorhouse, Frank 137, 138, 139
Morris, Meaghan 182; and McCalman, Iain 16, 20; and Muecke, Stephen 183
Morton, Donald: and Zavarzadeh, Mas'ud 13, 108–9, 110, 111, 112, 113, 123
Moss, Peter 133
Moss, Tara 22
Moxley, Joseph 91, 94
Muecke, Stephen 167, 170; and Morris, Meaghan 183
multiculturalism 198
Murnane, Gerald 135
Myers, D.G. (*The Elephants Teach*) 4, 33–4, 49–50, 52, 58–9, 66–7, 76, 85, 93, 121, 157

narratology 90, 96, 109–10, 111, 120
narrator: in *Broken Land* 211–13; as implied author 103, 114; tradition of impersonality 100–3; and voice 109–10

New Australian Writing 135–43
New Criticism 3, 4, 74–80, 84–5, 89, 94, 117, 128, 155, 165, 177, 187, 188, 191; and Creative Writing 4, 75–80, 188; rise of 74–5
New Formalists 12
New Historicism 90, 122, 164
New Humanism 68, 69, 74, 75
New Humanities 5, 179, 188, 189, 194, 201, 214; and Creative Writing 184–5, 194, 201, 204, 205, 206; and Cultural Studies 183, 198, 200–1; origins of term 182–4; public intellectual as exemplary figure of 195, 201
New Left 174, 196
New South Wales Institute of Technology: writing course 146–9
Newbolt Report (*Teaching of English in England*) 37, 40
Newfield, Christopher: and Strickland, Ronald 199
Newlyn, Lucy: and Lewis, Jenny 162–3
Newton, Isaac 8, 29, 32, 39
novel: as an art form 35–6; modern development 101–4

Oakley, Barry 138
Old Testament: Song of Songs 17
Ommundsen, Wenche 114
oppositional criticism 5, 189–92, 201, 204, 206, 214; origins of term 189
original genius 8, 18, 32, 33, 119; democratised 33, 42–4, 45, 51; emergence of concept 27–9
originality 8, 13, 26, 27, 28, 32, 33, 43
Oxford University: St Edmund Hall Poetry Workshop (*Synergies: Creative Writing in Academic Practice*) 161–3

Parry, Albert 19
Partridge, P.H. 150
Pattee, Fred Lewis 61, 62–3
Perelman, Bob 165
Perloff, Marjorie 123, 125
Perry, Bliss 10, 63
personal growth 40, 50, 52, 132–3

Phillips, Glen 134
Piaget, Jean 132
Piper, Edwin Ford 67, 68, 74, 81
Plato 8, 25, 35, 100, 101
Poe, Edgar Allan: criticism 185; handbooks 64, 82, 98; heresy of the didactic 104; and modernist craftsmanship 64–5; 'Philosophy of Composition', 64–5; and the short story 61–2, 105
poetic creation 25–6, 31
poetics: defined 88–90; formalist to sociological 208–14; workshop 87–120
Poetics Program (SUNY Buffalo) 125, 166
poetry: avant-garde 165–6; death of 12; and the garret 15–16; history of word 34–6; and imagination 23–4; Imagist 99–100; new Australian 136–7; and personal growth 52–4; Romantic 29–32, 50–1; showing and telling in 99–100, 100–1, 212–13; and sociological poetics 211–13; teaching 72, 99, 108, 173; teaching sonnets 161–2;
political correctness: and the Enterprise university 197–201
Pope, Alexander 101
postmodern: critical theory 13, 108, 113, 122; fiction 113–14, 136, 165; hybridisation 171; poetry 136; university 158, 164; writer-critic 195
postmodernism: literary products of 167; relativisation of literary value 184
postmodernity 5, 171
post-structuralism 14, 123–4, 165, 171, 175, 180; and Creative Writing 161–2, 163–4; and fictocriticism 167–9
post-Theory academy 3–4, 5, 197, 201, 205
posttheory generation 180–2
Pound, Ezra 99–100
Powers, John 150
practical criticism 3, 5, 76, 122, 128, 204; origins of 185–8

Pretty, Ron 152
Princeton University: Creative Arts Program 76–7
process writing 134
professional-managerial class 36, 46, 193
Progressive Education Movement 40, 54–6, 80, 82, 133, 215–16n; and the workshop 82
public intellectuals 5, 20, 181, 195–7, 198, 201; and Creative Writing 201–4, 211, 214
Puttenham, George 106

Quarles, Francis 17
Quiller-Couch, Sir Arthur 6

Ragan, James 121
Ransom, John Crowe 7, 68, 73, 74, 75, 76, 78, 185, 216n
Rasula, Jed 121
reading from the inside: writing to develop literary appreciation 71, 74, 152, 164
reading as a writer 77–8, 80, 85, 103, 114, 115, 119, 120, 208, 212, 213; early concepts of 72, 73; origins 90–8
reason: and imagination 24
Reid, Ian 142, 152
Renaissance 106; art schools 73; and creativity 25, 31, 38; scholar 70
Richards, I.A. 76, 187, 188
Ringler, William, 7
Roberts, H.D. 56
Romanticism: anti-didacticism 104, 107; anti-industrialism 39; child as poet 50–1; creative imagination 22, 29–32, 41–2; literary authority of poet 187–8; relation to New Criticism 75; style 106–7
Rose, Margaret 217n
Rothenberg, Albert: and Hausman, Carl 45
Rousseau, Jean-Jacques 55, 132
Royal Society of Authors 9
Rugg, Harold: and Shumaker, Anne 52, 54, 55
Ruthven, Ken 42, 104, 182
Rymer, Thomas 24

Said, Edward 171, 190, 191, 196
Saint-Beuve, Charles 17
Saintsbury, George 37
Scholes, Robert 21, 216n
Schramm, Wilbur 13, 67, 72–4, 76, 78, 81, 82, 83, 119–20
self-expression 40, 41, 50, 52, 53, 55, 132, 133
Sexton, Anne 43, 207
Shakespeare, William 26, 29, 101, 107, 187
Shapcott, Thomas 136–7, 141; and Hall, Rodney 136, 140
Sheffield, John 24
Shelley, Percy Bysshe 32, 35, 41, 42, 187–8
Shelnutt, Eve 13–14
Shetley, Vernon 12
short story: American genre 61; emergence of critical tradition 61–3; handbooks 10, 60–4, 74, 79; revival in Australia 137, 139, 142–3
showing and telling 114, 208, 211, 212–13; origins of 98–106
Showalter, Elaine 167
Sidney, Philip 25, 35
Smith, Dave 87, 109
Smith, L.E.W. 132, 133
Smith, Logan Pearsall 26, 27
Smith, Vivian 131
Solotaroff, Ted 109
Spingarn, J.E. 45, 216n
Spivak, Gayatri Chakravorty 174
State University of New York (Buffalo): Poetics Program 125, 166
structuralism 89–90, 123
students: as apprentice writers 73–4; and creative self-expression 50–6; discovering the self 107–9; empowerment of 177, 178; as graduates 179, 207; as intellectuals 208; and personal growth 40, 132–4
Summerfield, Geoffrey 132
Sussex, Lucy 142
Swain, David 145
Sydney Teachers' College 129, 132

Tasso, Torquato 25
Tate, Allen 75, 76, 77–8, 177, 216n
TEXT (journal of the Australian Association of Writing Programs) 158
Theory: critique of workshop 108–9, 123; negotiating relationship with Creative Writing 158–79, 194; rise of 3, 4, 5, 122–5, 126, 127, 148, 152, 155–6
Theory of Literature (Wellek and Warren) 38, 84
thinking: convergent 44; divergent 44, 46, 47; lateral 44–5
Todorov, Tzvetan 89, 178
transactional writing 134
Tranter, John 136, 137

unconscious: and creativity 42–3, 44, 51, 92, 119
Understanding Fiction (Brooks and Warren) 78–80
Understanding Poetry (Brooks and Warren) 74, 75, 79, 84, 187
United Kingdom (UK): growth of Creative Writing 127–8, 158–9, 161–2
university: as a public institution 3–4, 181, 197, 198–9, 201, 214
University of Adelaide 141
University of Canberra (Canberra CAE) 144–5, 146
University of Chicago: Laboratory School 55
University of East Anglia 19
University of Iowa: School of Letters 50, 83, 85, 129; establishment of 67–74; Writers' Workshop *see* Iowa Writers' Workshop
University of Melbourne 154–5
University of Technology, Sydney (New South Wales Institute of Technology) 146–9, 156, 157
University of Wollongong: School of Creative Arts 152–4, 156

Valéry, Paul 65
Vanderbilt University: *Fugitive* group 73, 74, 75, 76, 78
Vogel awards: establishment of 142

voice 177, 194, 213, 214; Bakhtin 210–11; conflation of expressivist and narratological concepts 110–11; critique of 106, 108–9, 174–5; discovering 106–12; and identity politics 174–5; as narratological concept 109–10; relation to style 106–7, 109, 111

Walker, Nancy 95
Wallace, David Foster 165
Wallace-Crabbe, Chris 131, 154
Wallas, Graham 44, 72
Walshe, R.D. 132
Ward, A.W. 36, 42
Ward, Thomas B. et al. 45
Wark, McKenzie 202
Warren, Austin 71–2, 74, 78, 84, 187
Warren, Robert Penn 76; and Brooks, Cleanth 78–9
Waten, Judah: and Murray-Smith, Stephen 142–3
Watkins, Evan 215n
Watson, George 195, 217n
Watt, Ian 101
Waugh, Patricia 217n
Webb, Jennifer 173–4
Weiss, Theodore 13
Wellek, Renee 84–5, 128; and Warren, Austin 38, 75, 84
Wendell, Barrett 57, 58, 59, 60, 66, 67
Westbury, Deborah 105
Western Australian Institute of Technology 142, 144, 145–6, 149
White, Robert 150, 156
Widdowson, Peter 34–5
Wilbers, Stephen 67, 81, 83, 121
Wilding, Michael 137, 138, 139
Williams, Graham 146, 147, 148
Williams, Jeffrey 198; posttheory generation 180–1
Williams, Raymond 22–3, 25, 27, 36, 38, 39
Williamson, David 184
Wilson, Helen 147
Wimsatt, W.K.: and Beardsley, Monroe, C. 84
Winton, Tim 142

Woodberry, Joan 133
Wordsworth, William 14, 31, 32, 34,
    41, 42, 50, 51, 64, 104, 106–7
workshop: and authorship 112–17;
    creative writing 87–8; critique of
    11, 108–9, 112, 172–4; emergence
    80–6; exemplary texts 112–13,
    115; and identity politics 174–5;
    internalisation of critical principles
    117, 119; and notion of
    publishable quality 116–17;
    student manuscripts 97–8,
    115–16, 119, 206–8
workshop poetics 87–120; authorship
    112–20; discovering a voice
    106–12; reading as a writer 90–8;

show don't tell 98–106;
    sociological 208–14
writer-critic: tradition of 64, 195
writers vs critics 2, 6, 84–5, 94,
    123–5, 160, 185, 192
writing: can it be taught 6–11;
    should it be taught 11–14
writing programmes 11–12, 13, 14,
    19

Yale School (of deconstruction) 171
Young, Edward 18, 28

Zavarzadeh, Mas'ud 113–14; and
    Morton, Donald 13, 108–9, 110,
    111, 112, 113, 123